IMAGES
of America

WASECA COUNTY
MINNESOTA

IMAGES
of America

WASECA COUNTY
MINNESOTA

Waseca County Historical Society

ARCADIA
PUBLISHING

ISBN 978-0-7385-2047-6

Published by Arcadia Publishing
Charleston, South Carolina

Printed in the United States of America

Library of Congress Catalog Card Number: 2002112985

For all general information contact Arcadia Publishing at:
Telephone 843-853-2070
Fax 843-853-0044
E-mail sales@arcadiapublishing.com
For customer service and orders:
Toll-Free 1-888-313-2665

Visit us on the Internet at www.arcadiapublishing.com

IMAGES of America

WASECA COUNTY MINNESOTA

IMAGES
of America

WASECA COUNTY
MINNESOTA

Waseca County Historical Society

ARCADIA
PUBLISHING

ISBN 978-0-7385-2047-6

Published by Arcadia Publishing
Charleston, South Carolina

Printed in the United States of America

Library of Congress Catalog Card Number: 2002112985

For all general information contact Arcadia Publishing at:
Telephone 843-853-2070
Fax 843-853-0044
E-mail sales@arcadiapublishing.com
For customer service and orders:
Toll-Free 1-888-313-2665

Visit us on the Internet at www.arcadiapublishing.com

Contents

ACKNOWLEDGMENTS

The Waseca County Historical Society is proud to present *Images of America: Waseca County, Minnesota.*

We wish to acknowledge Margaret Sinn, WCHS Executive Director, for writing the text and laying out the book and Sheila Morris for working with the photographs and the assembly of the finished product. Joan Mooney, WCHS Program Director, for her input on Maplewood Park and for the hours she put into researching subjects laid out before her. Pauline Fenelon, WCHS Artifact Cataloguer, for her advice and research. We also wish to thank these volunteers: Donna Fostveit, Barbara Noble, Jeannette Krause, and Kandi Bertolino for their many hours of researching and editing the text. When they are needed, they always step forward.

The society also wishes to thank the Waseca County Historical Society Board of Directors: Don Wynnemer, Marj Britton, Charles Espe, John Hanson, Henry Lewer, Allan Rose, Jerry Rutledge, Rod Searle, Jerry Splett, Dan Swenson, Jim Tippy, and Don Zwach for sharing the vision and their willingness to try new ideas. Equally as appreciated are the following: Bruce Boyce, Waseca County Co-ordinator, and the Waseca County Commissioners: Wendell Armstrong, Jim Goettl, Jim Peterson, Jerry Splett, and Roy Srp. Without their support and the support of past commissioners nothing would be possible.

INTRODUCTION

The history of Waseca County, Minnesota, is like weaving a large coverlet that touches us all. The *warp* is the past that was given to us as a gift. The *woof* is what we weave into the fabric to leave our mark on history. Now we can each take our turn to weave that one small piece of woof that could make the fabric of our history weaker or stronger.

Waseca County was named from the Native American word for *Fertile Soil*. The county boundaries were formed in 1857; Minnesota became a state in 1858.

The History of Steele and Waseca Counties, Minnesota, Union Publishing Company, 1887, told of the strength of the warp that was laid out for us. Says Hon. William Brisbane, in speaking of hard times in early days: "Speaking of graham bread, I can assure you that twenty-eight years ago a loaf of graham bread or a corn dodger, with a very thin sprinkling of molasses, would have been thankfully received and no questions asked. Those were the days that tried men's stomachs as well as their souls, but we lived and hoped for better days, for we had faith in the resources of Waseca County. Thanks to the industrious energy of the people, our expectations have been fully realized; as the Good Book says: 'The rain is over and gone, and the time of the singing of birds has come'; yet I never knew or saw a tragedy acted but there was always some comical or ludicrous scenes interlarded with it ..."

This county was populated by many nationalities. It started with the Native Americans and the French traders. It is known that one small group of Alexander Faribault's men were in the area for a year trading with the Native Americans. The Europeans arrived later by covered wagon and by foot. The main nationalities appear to have been Norwegian, Swedish, German, Irish, and English, and they came for the land. It was cheap, fertile, and promised a better life for themselves and their families. The main migration was through Wisconsin but certainly not limited to that direction. With the coming of the railroads, the population shifted and some communities flourished and others became memories. All of the men, women, and children who came to Waseca County and called it home, "for a day or a lifetime," had a place in its history.

The religions of Waseca County pioneers and later residents were as diverse as their nationalities, which makes it impossible to publish each of the church histories in this edition. So, we have chosen to include whatever space allows and extend an open invitation to everyone to use our facilities to research the rest of them.

We have tried to select photographs for this book that have not been seen in print before. Our brief captions try to show the flavor of the county, the diversity, and the similarities. All of the photographs have come from the files of the Waseca County Historical Society. Dates, locations, and names are occasionally missing from photo identification. We wrote only what we knew about these photographs and felt that you would enjoy them as much as we do. We used information given to us at the time of the photograph donation and we did research in the P. C. Bailey Research Library, locally known as the "Lewer House." Some of the resources used were newspaper files, indexes from our Internet site, family files, census records, and atlases.

Thank you to all the people of Waseca County for giving us the opportunity to learn and try to interpret your history. To say it has been interesting is an understatement. We at the Historical Society learn something new every day and know we will continue to learn from you as time goes on.

We hope you will enjoy *Images of America: Waseca County, Minnesota* as much as we have enjoyed putting it together.

One

AGRICULTURE

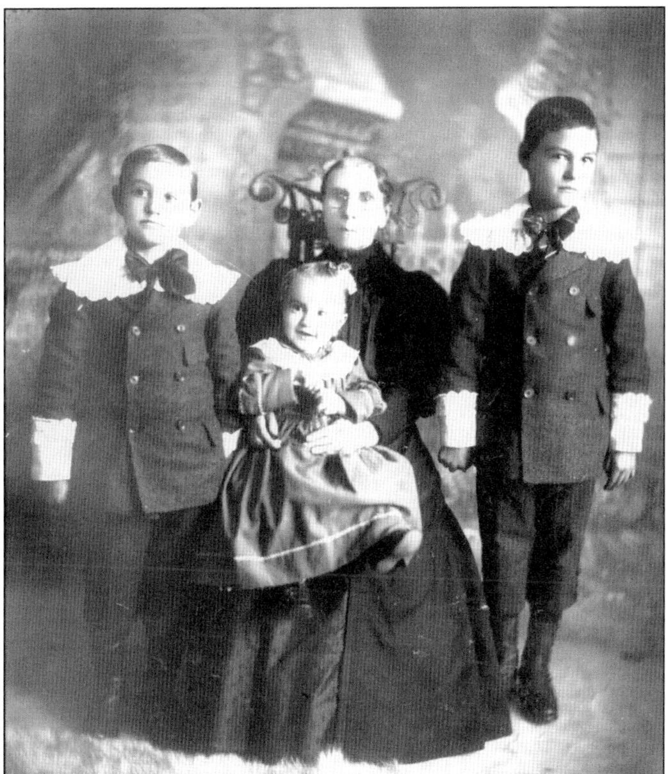

Eliza Hollingsworth Sutlief, together with her husband, Asa, and their children, Delancey and Rhoda, were the first white family to erect a cabin and take up permanent residence in what is now Waseca County. Eliza is pictured here, from left to right, with her grandchildren Arthur, Agnes (on her knee), and Thomas Sutlief.

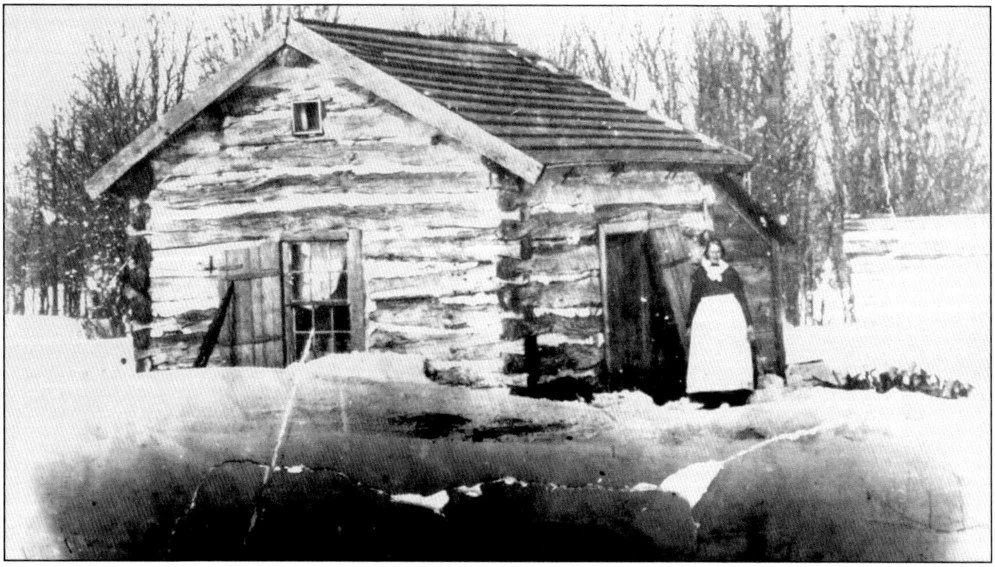

Martha Sorenson stands in front of her prairie home in 1859 in her starched collar and best "Sunday go to meeting" dress. Martha immigrated to America with her father in 1856, her son Ole Halvorson having come the year before. They resided in Wisconsin until they removed to Waseca County, arriving here May 16, 1857. She along with her son settled in section 2 of New Richland Township where they built this cabin and she spent the rest of her life.

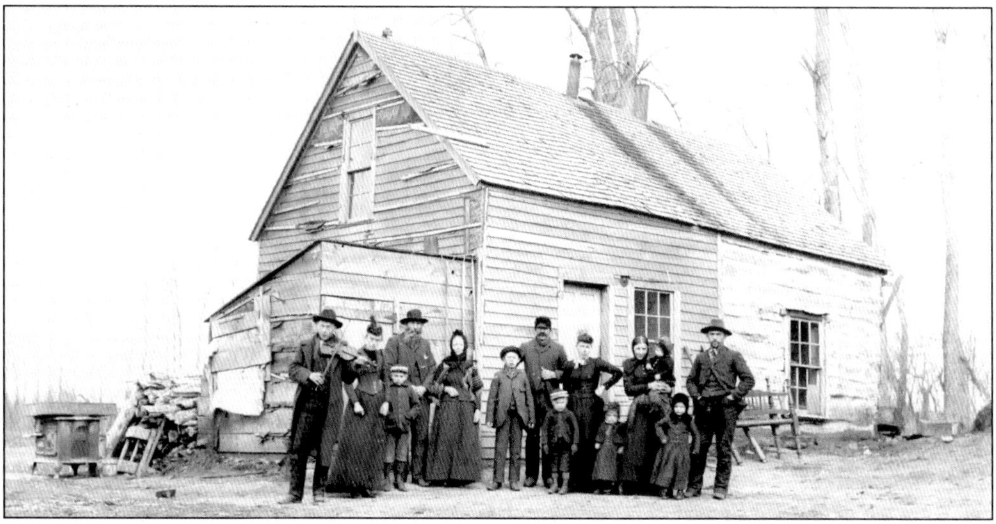

Torkild Timandsen (son of Timand) was born in 1824 on the "Lund" farm at Eftelot, Sandsvaer, Norway. He settled in 1858 on section 22 of New Richland Township. Before leaving Norway, he married Grette Kirstine Andersdatter Berg (daughter of Anders). Like many Norwegian immigrants, they took the name of the farm they came from in Norway and became the Lund Family. This photograph is of the Timandsen (Lund) family farm. As they needed more space they added a frame home with wood siding to their original log structure. Paint was not readily available and would have been a luxury. In the back yard beside the woodpile stands a wood burning stove, more than likely used for heating water to do the laundry. Everyone is dressed in their Sunday best to have their photograph taken. The first young man on the left has a violin to his chin. This violin would have been a prized possession.

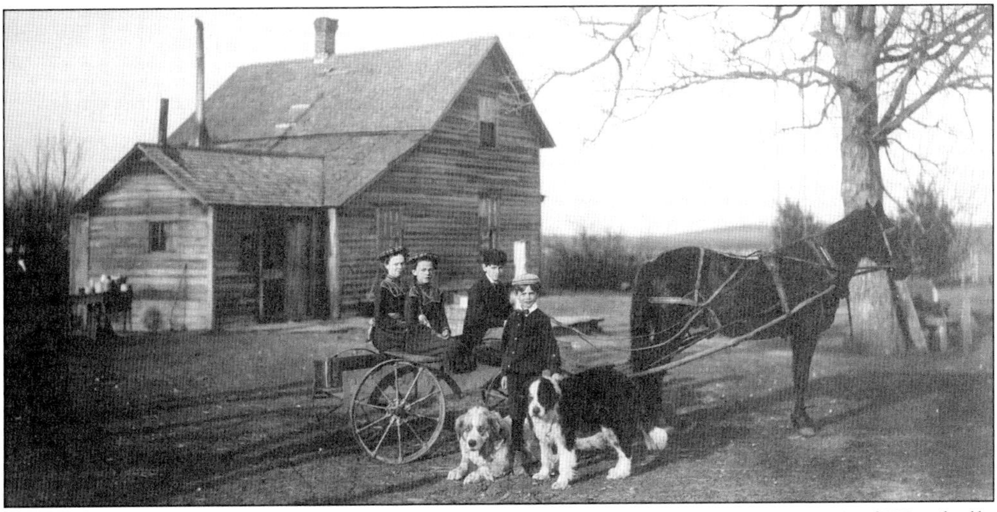

George and Anna (Buscho) Resler built this hand-hewn log home in section 20 of Woodville Township. Pictured from left to right are four of their eight children: Anna (H.Werden), Lilly (A. Grapp), Edward, and Chester. The two Newfoundland dogs were used on a treadmill to pump water. Charles was to become the father of Minnesota artist George E. Resler. Another daughter of George and Anna's was Lydia Helena who was the mother of Bernard Bierman, University of Minnesota football coach. This photograph was taken in approximately 1866.

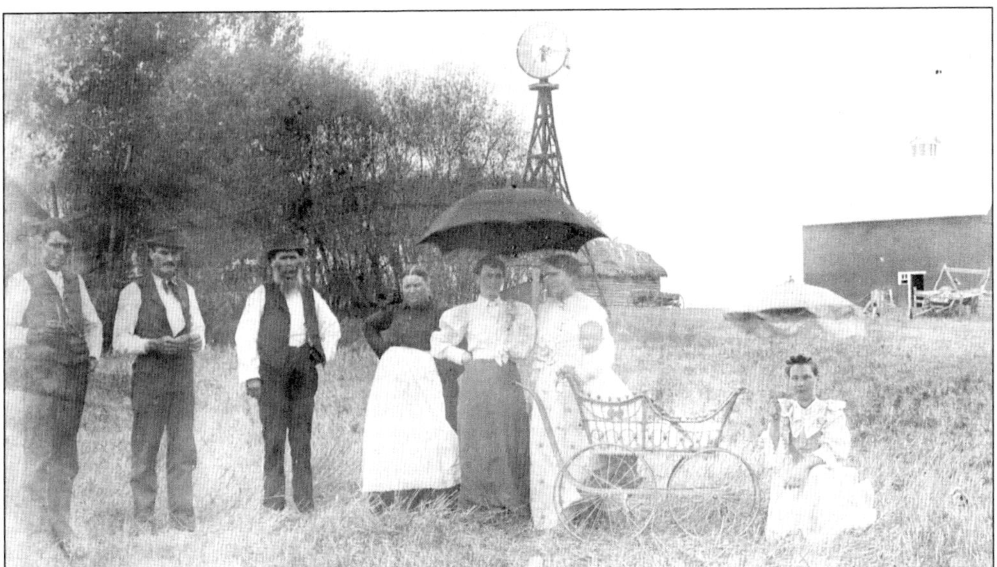

The Christian Fischer Family lived in St. Mary Township in section 5. When the photographer arrived at the farm, the family dressed in their best clothing and had their picture taken with the things they prized the most. This family prized their barn, windmill, and their farming equipment. One might wonder on what streets or sidewalks they walked the baby in the wonderful baby buggy they are so rightly proud of. The windmill in the background has wooden fans. The haystack is shaped similar to a mushroom as the stock has eaten around the base and can not reach higher. The barn is a prized possession and photo worthy. The barn was much more important than the dwelling of the family. Without the livestock and machinery, there was no living. The house and its comforts were secondary.

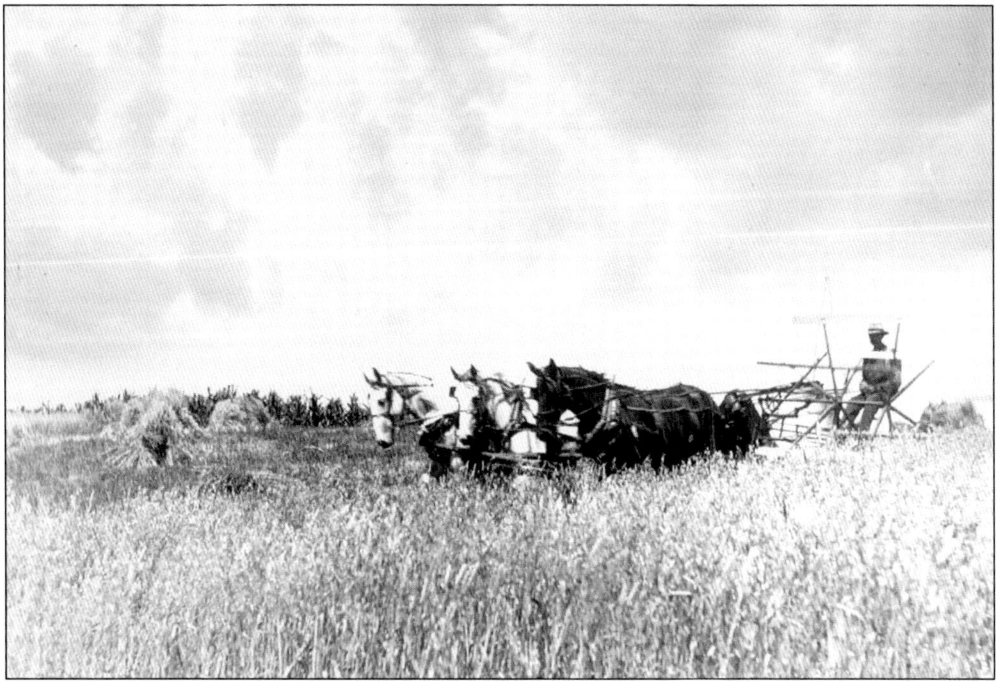

By 1890 farmers were using more and more laborsaving devices. The new machinery would not perform well with oxen, so the farmers switched to horses, which could speed the process. The number of work oxen in Minnesota in 1870 was 43,176; the oxen's number had decreased to 36,344 by 1880; and by the year 1900 they had disappeared. This early farmer in St. Mary Township is using a binder powered by the horses to cut grain.

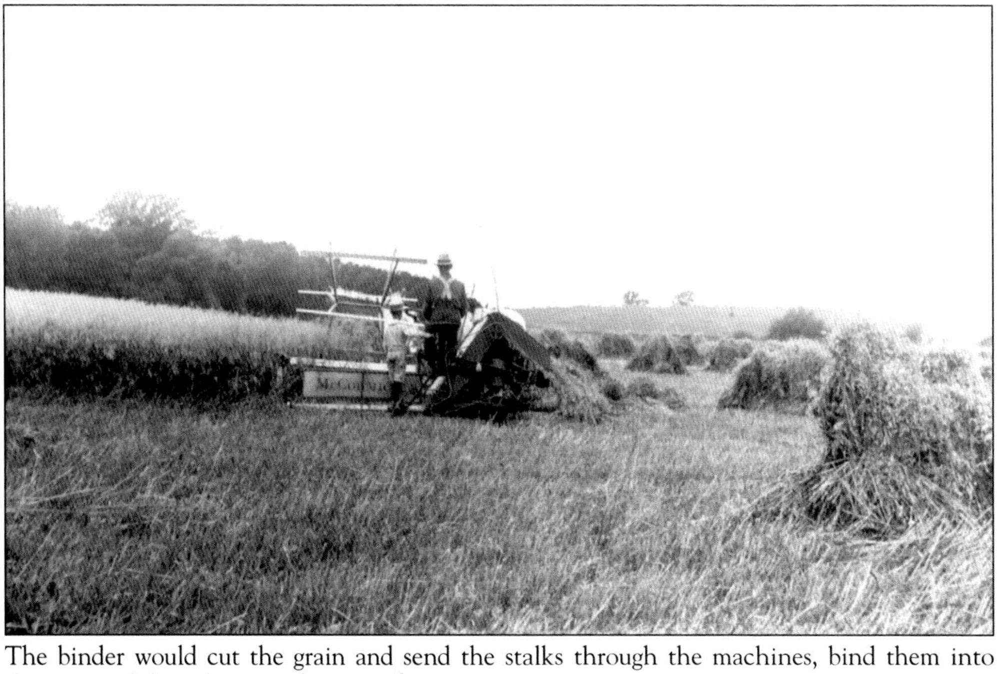

The binder would cut the grain and send the stalks through the machines, bind them into sheaves, and drop them on the grounds.

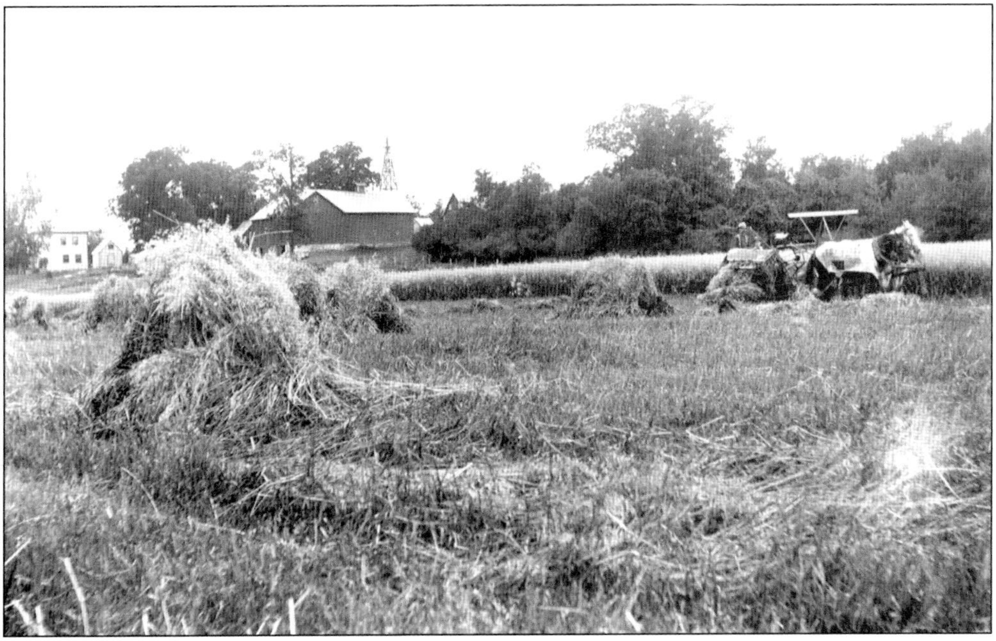

The sheaves were hand-stacked into shocks for drying upright in the field.

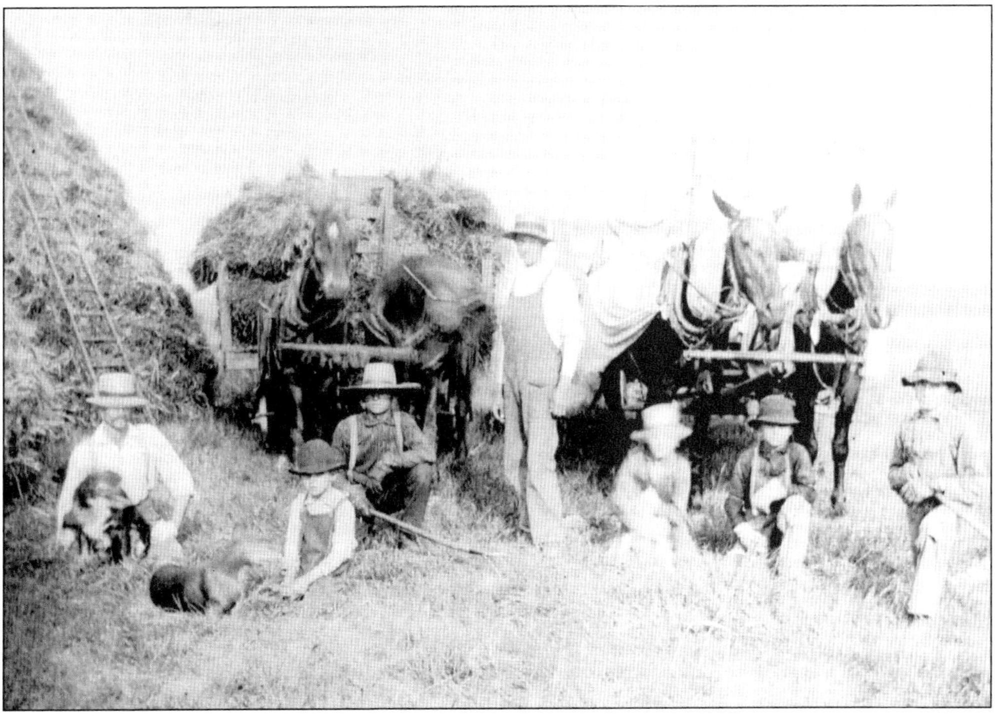

The first threshing machines were powered by horses on treadmills or by sweeps. A sweep was a device consisting of a gearbox that turned a shaft that ran along the ground to the machine it was operating. A pole or poles were attached to the gearbox radially, and the gearbox was staked to the ground. Horses were hitched to the poles and walked around in a circle providing power to the gearbox, which was geared to the drive shaft.

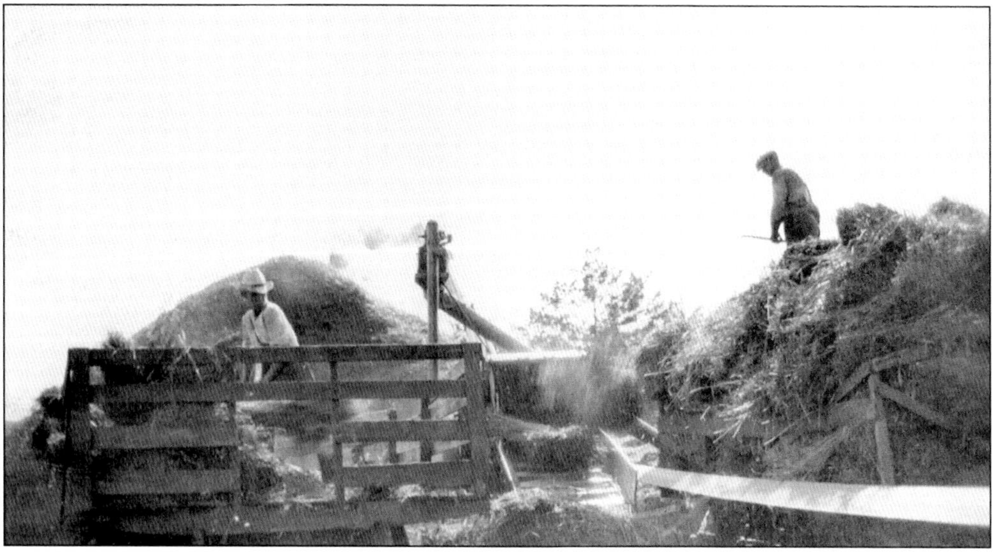

Most of the early threshing machines were small machines powered by horses. The machine separated the grain from the straw, but threw it out together.

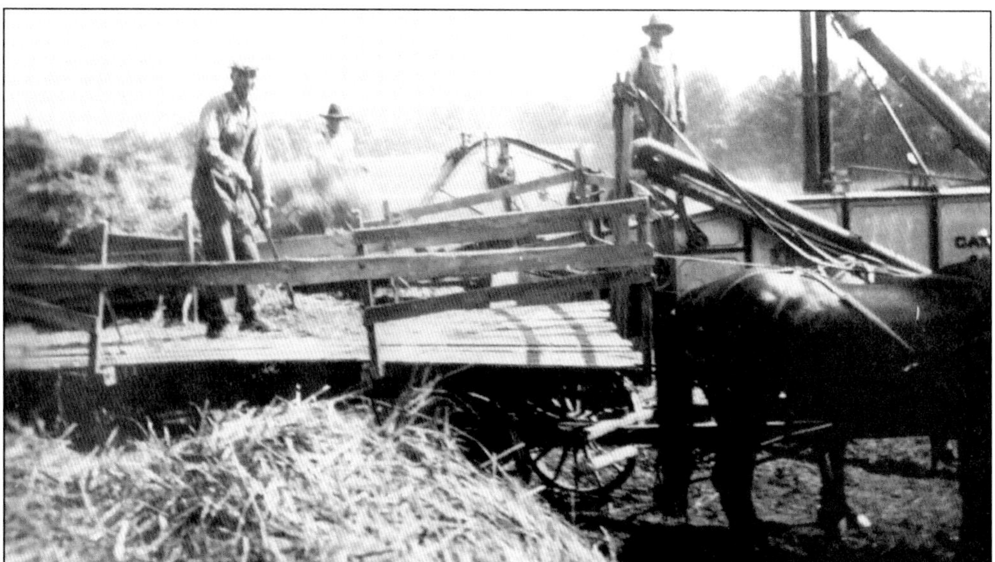

The straw was pitched onto a stack and the grain cleaned with a fanning mill. Archie Kanne, Ferdinand Kanne, and Reuben Kanne are seen threshing oats in Blooming Grove Township in 1919.

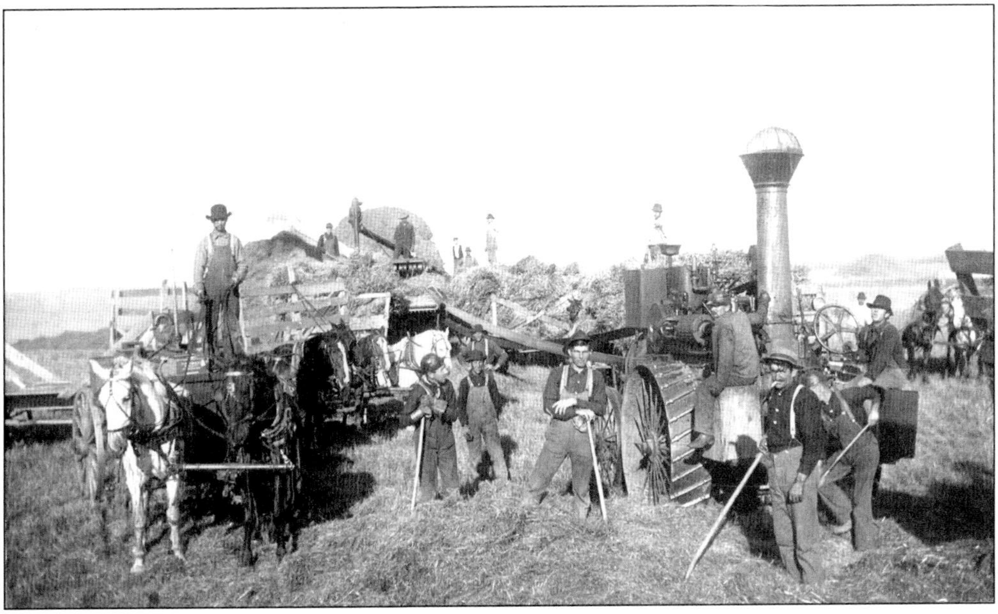

By 1870 steam powered machinery had been introduced.

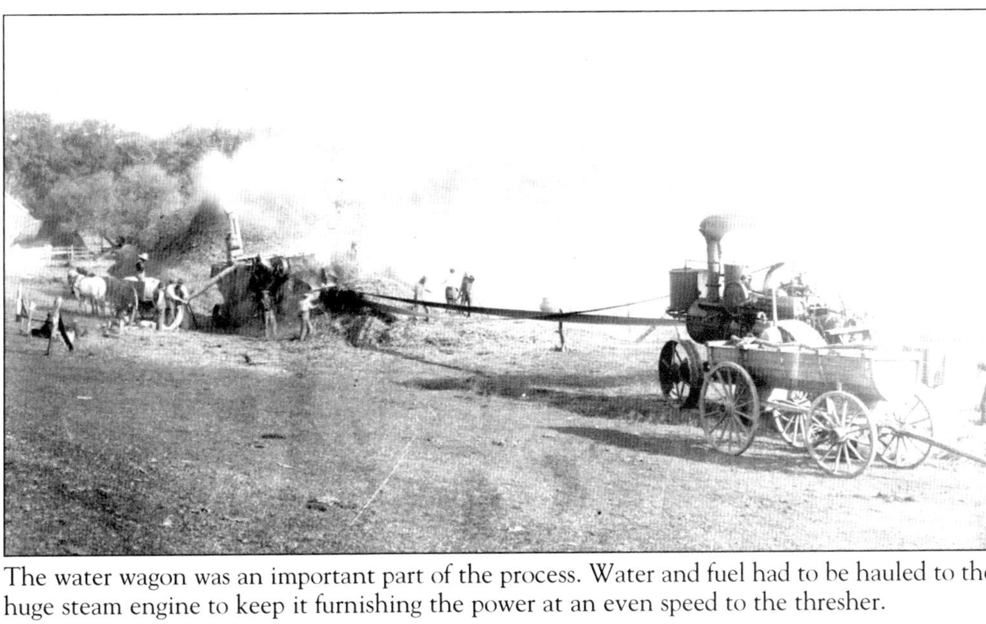

The water wagon was an important part of the process. Water and fuel had to be hauled to the huge steam engine to keep it furnishing the power at an even speed to the thresher.

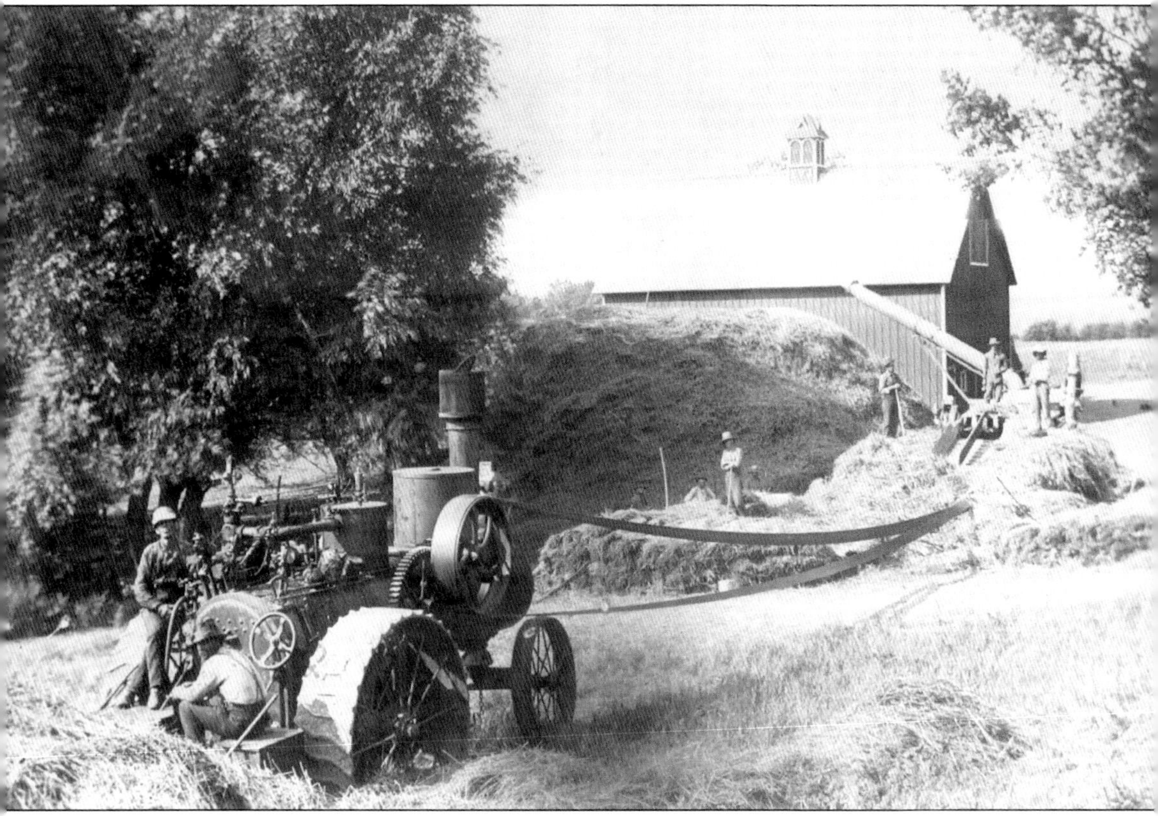

Steam tractor engines were belted to the threshing machine to operate the grain separator and also the wind stacker. These machines would sometimes throw sparks that started grass fires. The stacker would blow the straw into a pile while the clean grain is being sacked by hand. Pictured is Ben P. Bishman's second threshing machine.

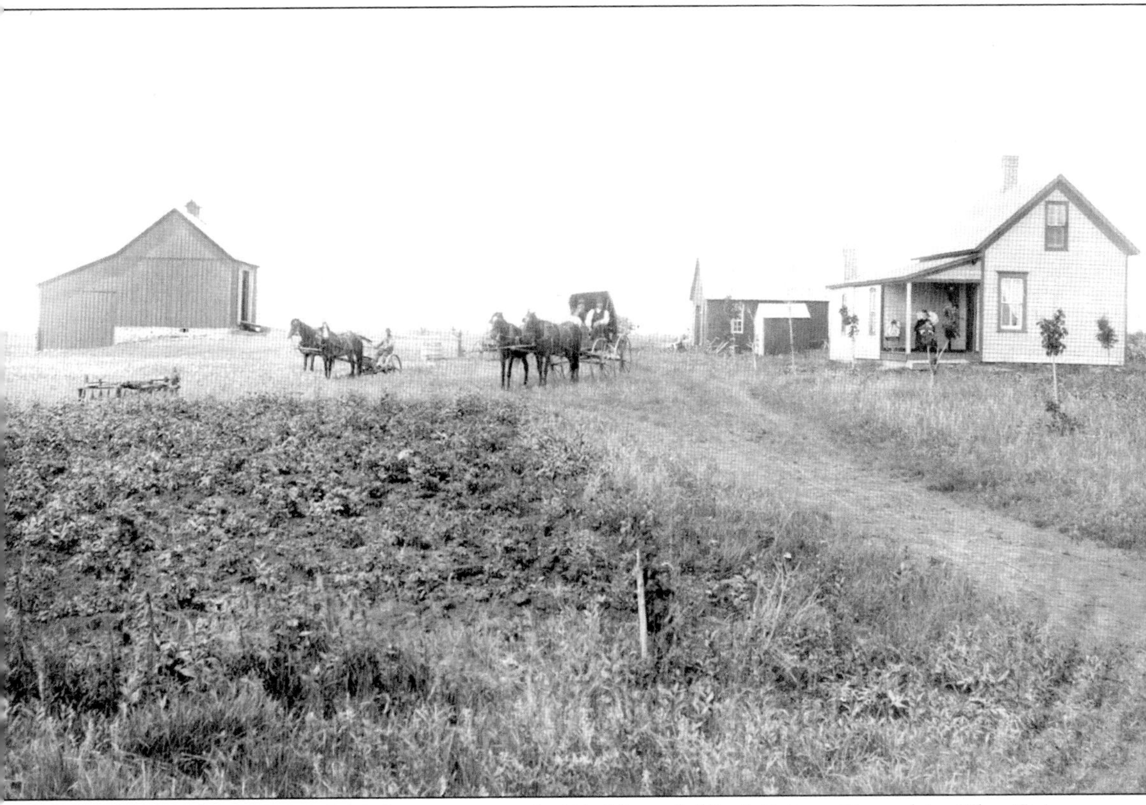

Adam Bishman owned land in sections 8, 17, 18, and 19 of Otisco Township. The Otisco Post Office was located at the Bishman farm shortly after the formation of the county. This photograph of the Adam Bishman farm shows a new home complete with trees, paint, and three new outbuildings along with two matched teams, a plow, and buggy.

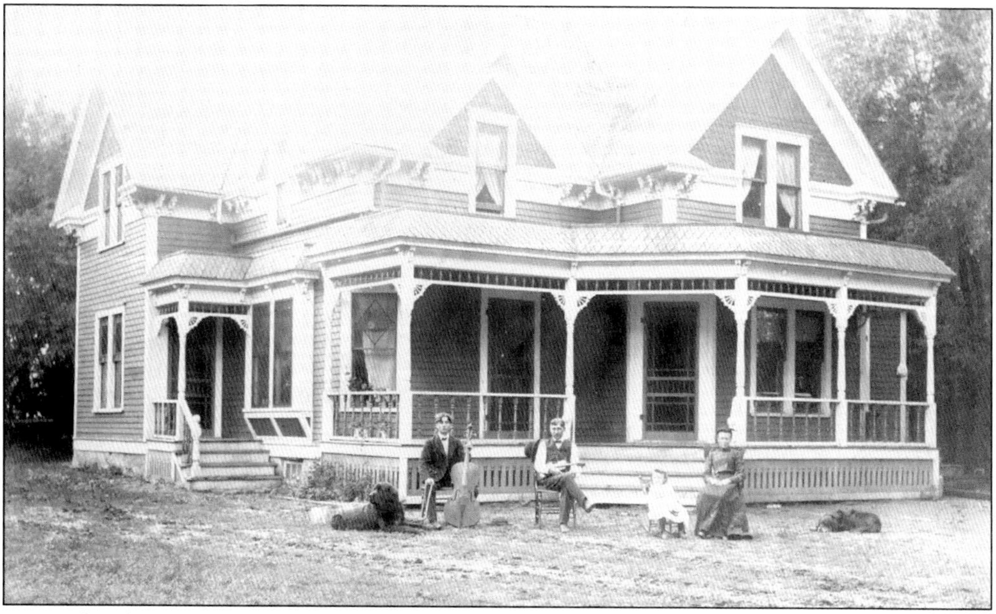

Pictured is the Patrick McDonough Jr. home near Waldorf. Seen here is believed to be Charles McDonough (son of Sheriff Michael and Rose Ann (Lynch) McDonough) and nephew of Patrick Jr. (holding the cello). Charles lived with his Uncle Patrick in 1900. He was a barber and died early of Bright's disease. Patrick McDonough Jr. played the violin in a band. He also started McDonough Hall in Waldorf. The little girl is his daughter Marcella (McDonough) Rhode and the woman Patrick's wife, Mary (McGuiness) McDonough. This photo was taken in 1902 or 1903.

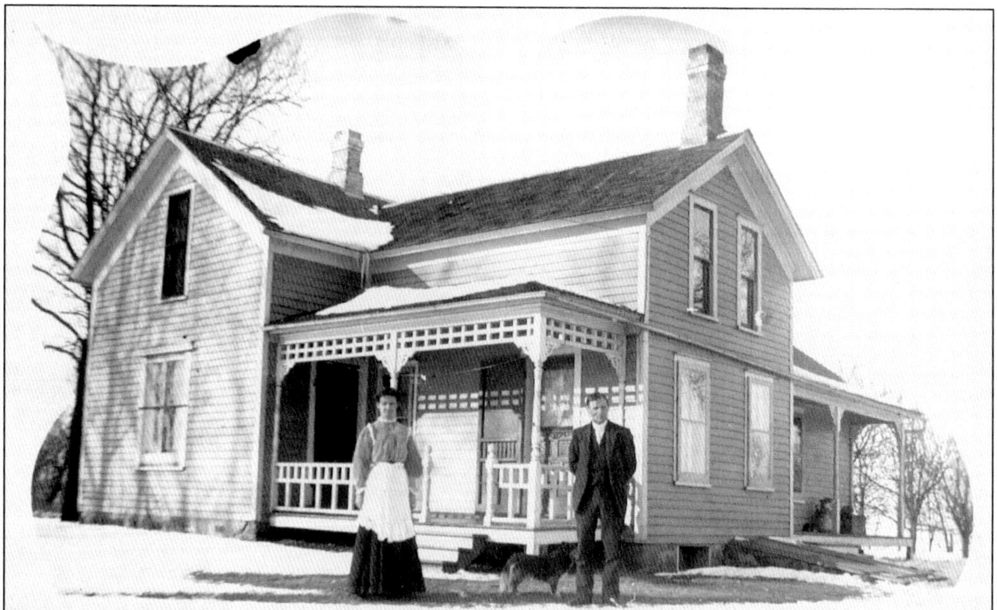

Mary (Koplean) Grawunder and Herman Grawunder's farm was located on the northwest quarter of section 16 of Freedom Township. Their home is a fairly typical rural home of the late 1800s. The home has a front porch and two front entries. One likely goes to the drawing room and one to the dining room of the house. The back entrance would typically go into the kitchen.

Two

RAILROADS

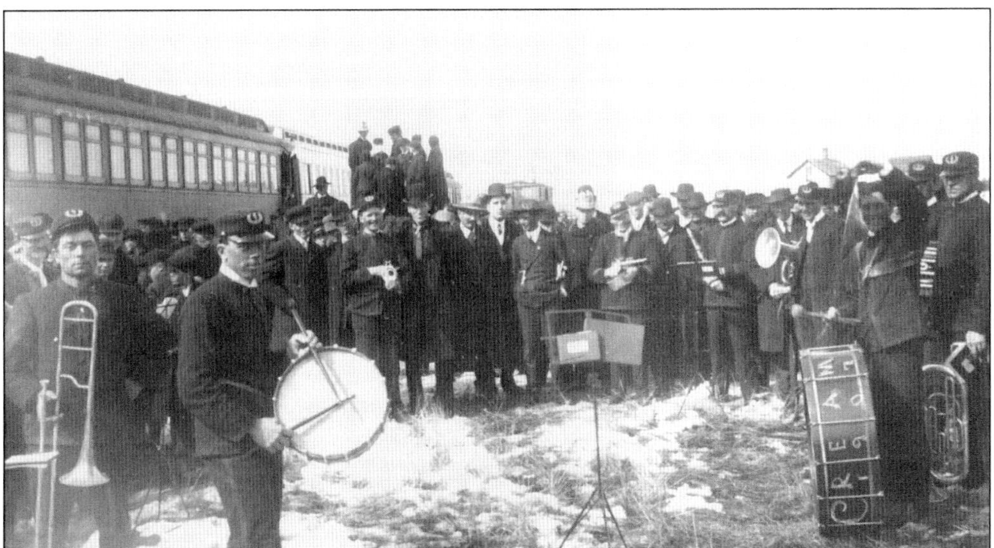

The Cream band is playing for the arrival of the first passenger train to Cream, Minnesota, on March 10, 1907. Cream welcomed its first train on January 9, 1907. A railroad boxcar served as a depot. The first agent was Byron Graham.

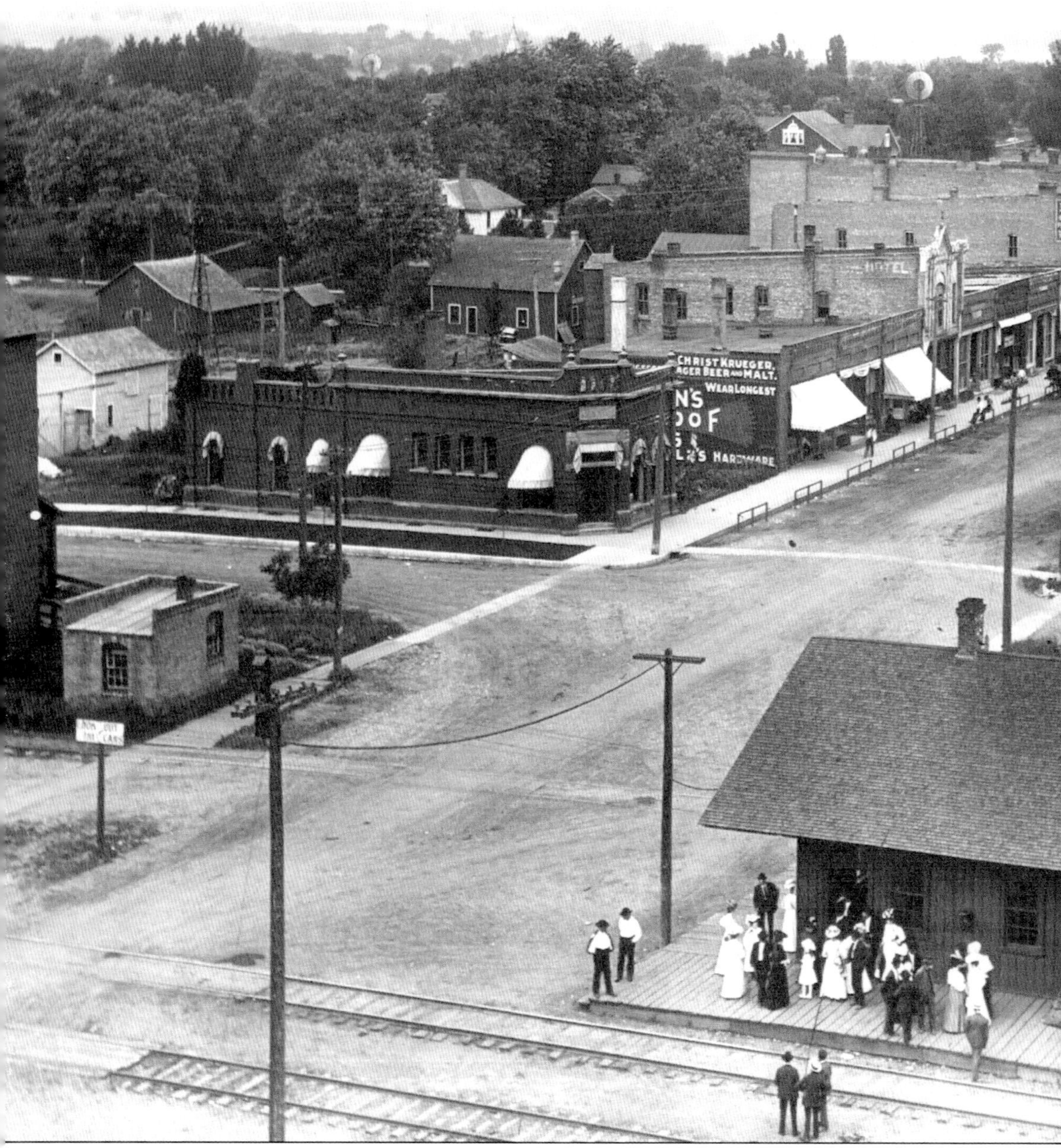

This view is of the city of Janesville looking north on Main Street. The arrival of every train

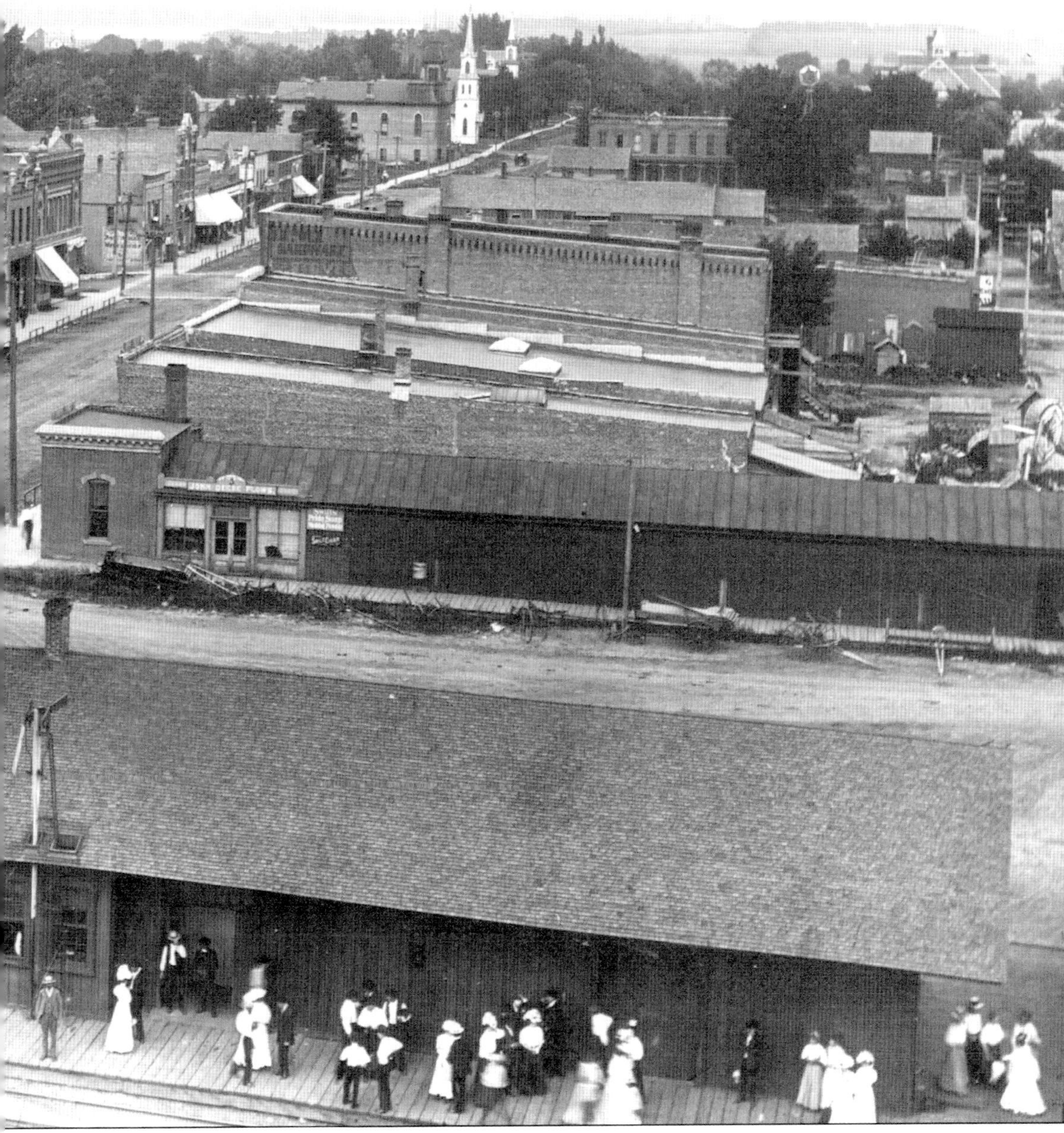

usually attracted a crowd.

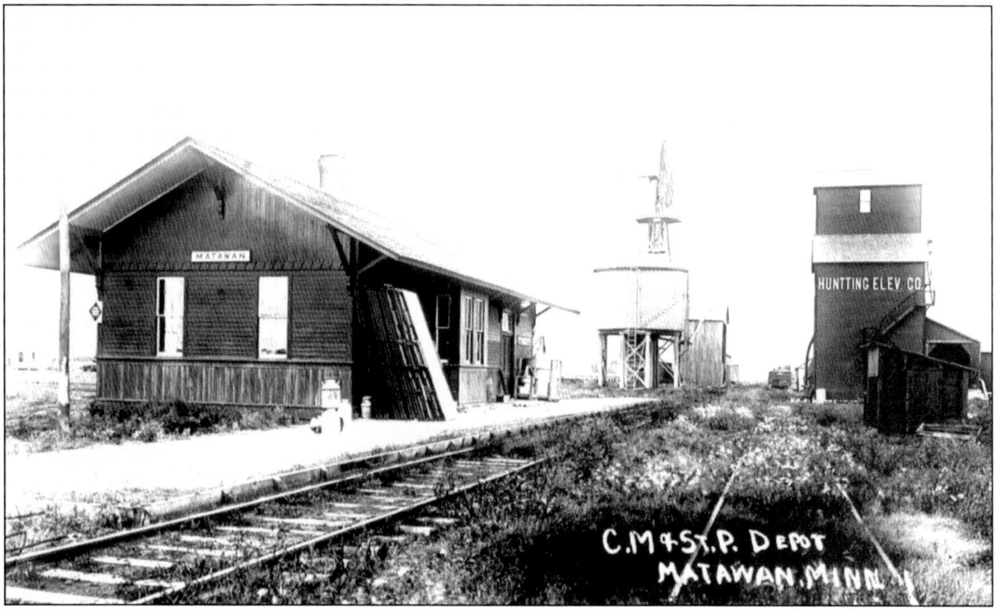

By 1907 the railroad tracks had expanded into Byron Township. Nicknamed the "Alphabet Railroad," it later became the Milwaukee Line. The railroad made possible an outlet to ship grain and livestock.

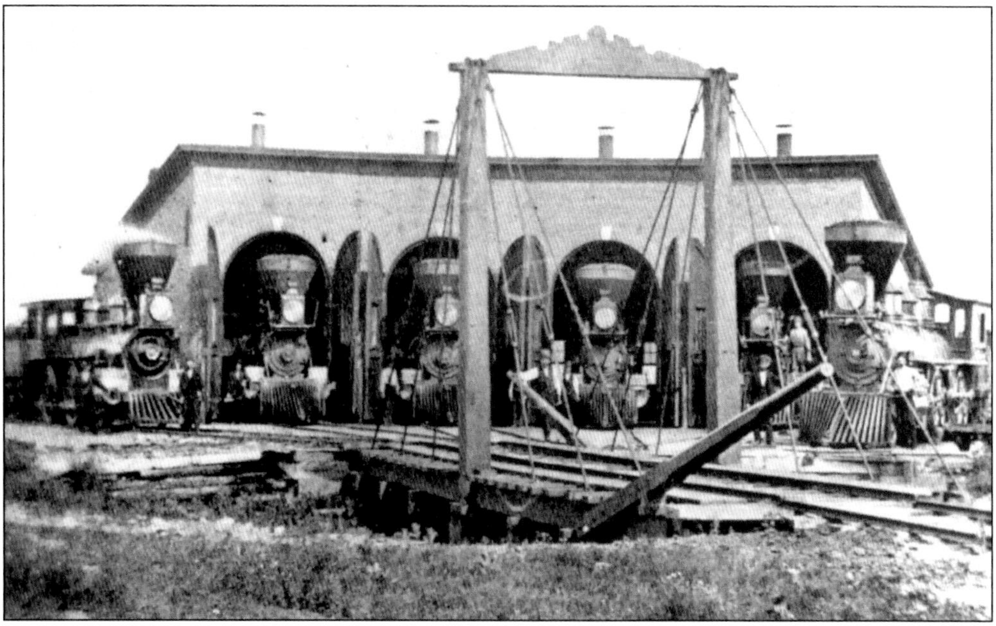

The roundhouse was built by the Chicago & Northwestern railroad in 1881 and was used to service and repair the engines. It was located in the railroad yards between West Elm Avenue and Fifth Avenue South West in Waseca. The engines were brought into the building and placed on a turntable in the center. The table would turn until the track lined up with the stall track it was to be repaired in. Each kind of repair had a stall. The roundhouse burned in 1953.

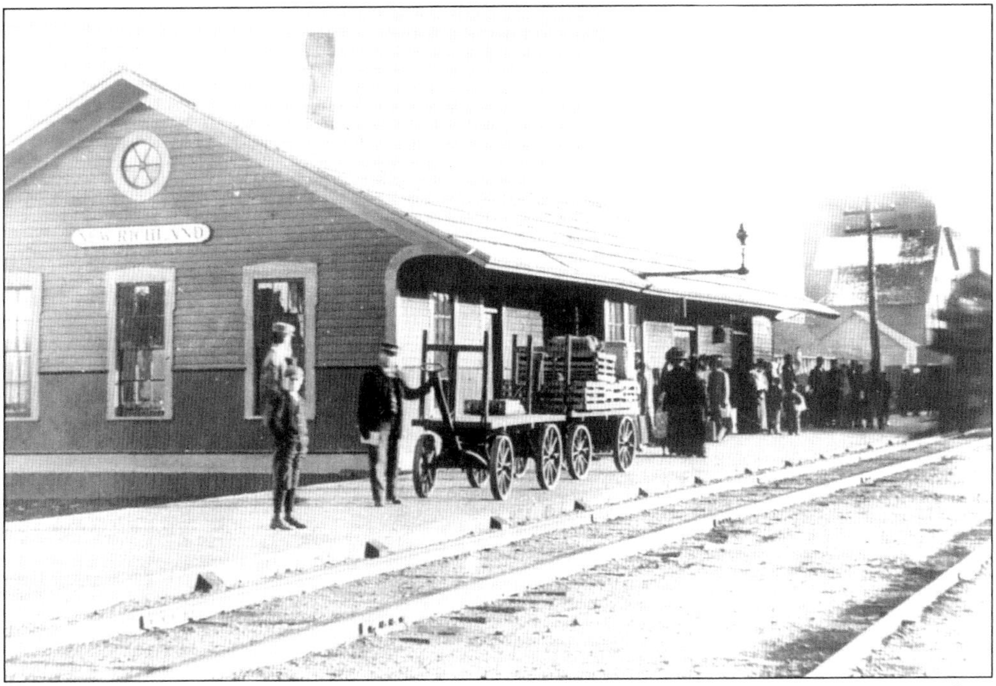

The railroad came to New Richland in 1877. The Minneapolis and St. Louis, or M.&St.L., line was operating between Albert Lea and Minneapolis. The first depot agent was E. Davis.

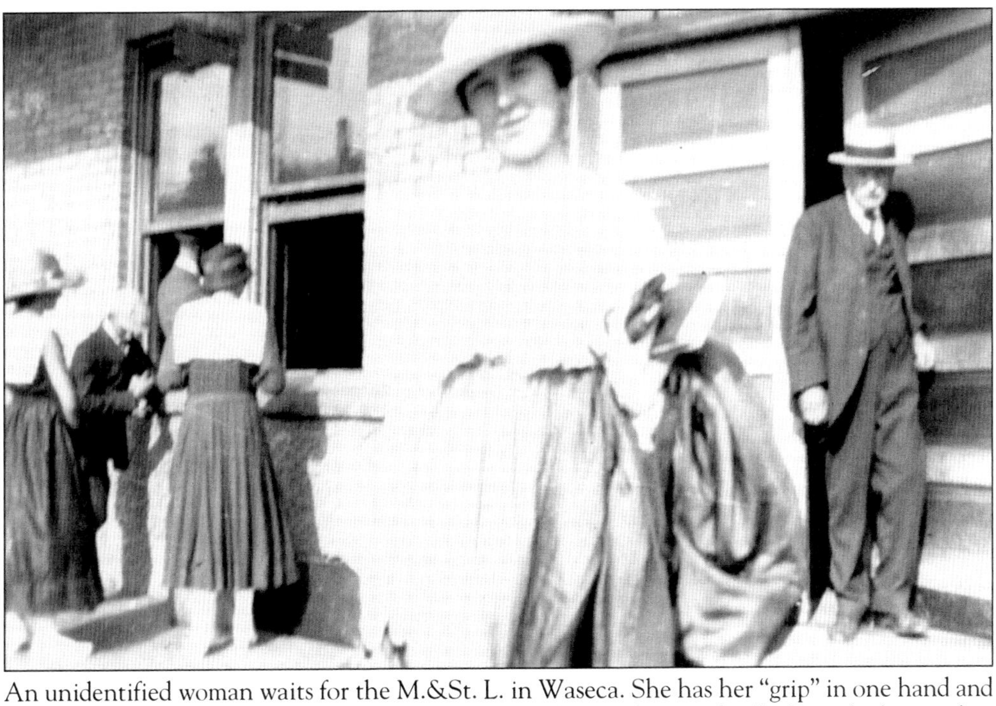

An unidentified woman waits for the M.&St. L. in Waseca. She has her "grip" in one hand and her reading material in the other. Others purchase their tickets and talk through the window while a man comes out of the depot to the platform—a typical beginning to a business or pleasure trip.

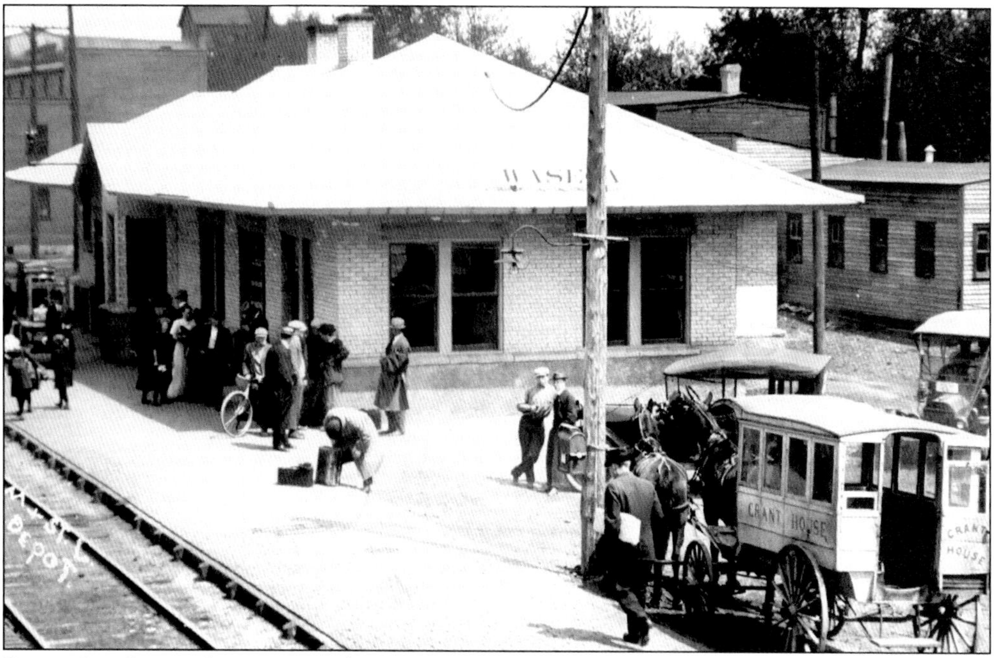

Pictured is the newly constructed M.&St.L. Depot. The hotels in Waseca hired passenger and dray vehicles (horse-drawn at first) to meet all trains. Both lines shared Union Depot, located at the intersection of Waseca's two railroads (M.&St.L. and C.&N.W.) until it burned in 1912.

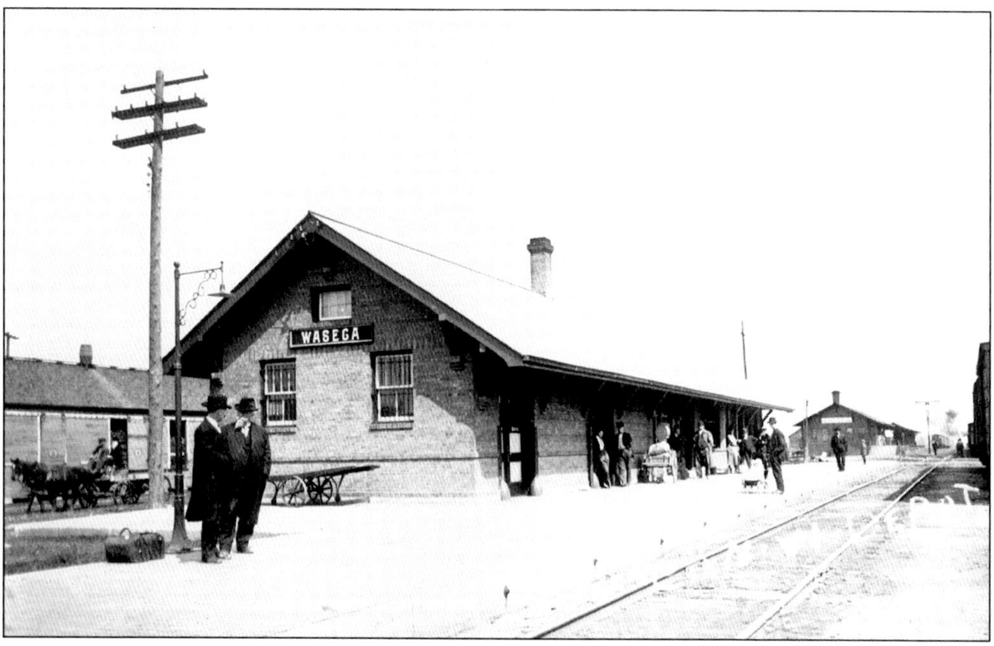

The Chicago & Northwestern Railroad purchased the Winona & St. Peter Railroad in 1867 but didn't change the name until 1900. The C.&N.W. Depot is still in use today by the D.M. &E.

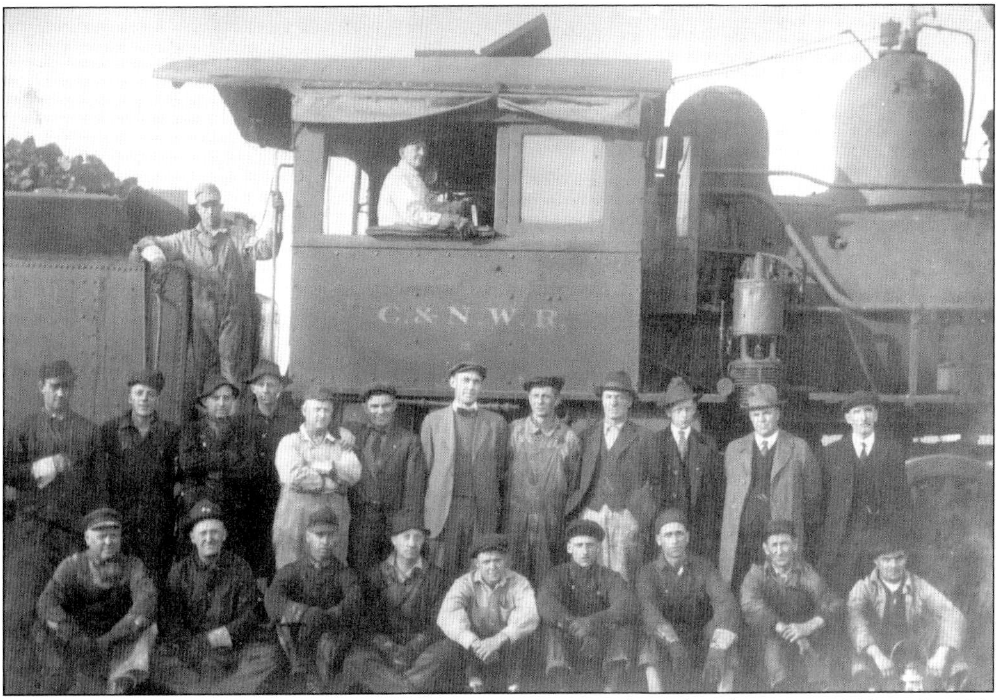

Here is a photo of a C.&N.W. steam engine and its tender taken between 1910 and 1920. Albert C. Neidt is fourth from left in the front row.

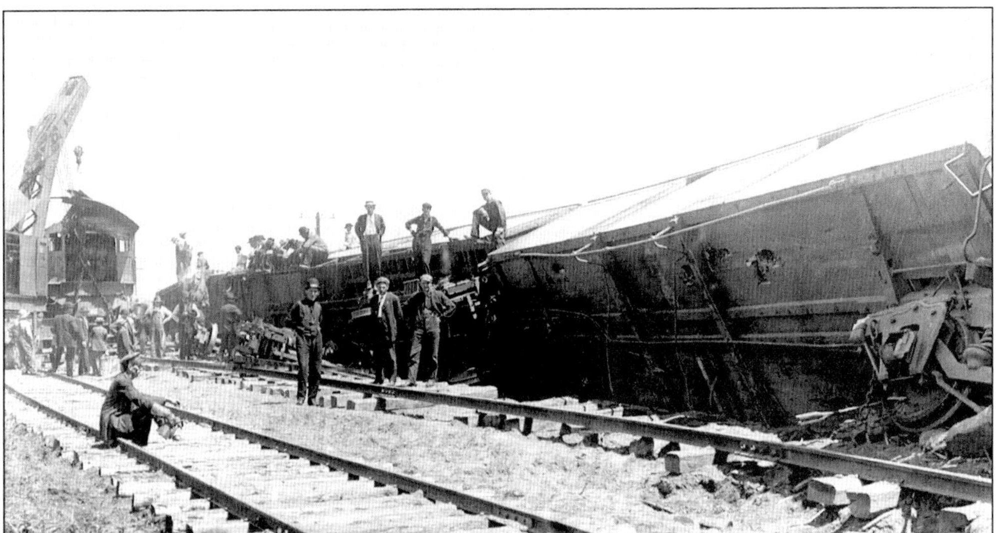

Train No. 1, due in Waseca at 4:22 p.m. on Saturday, July 9, 1910, jumped the track one mile south of Otisco. No one was injured. The engine, the mail car, and the baggage car derailed. Two passenger coaches remained on the track. By four o'clock Sunday morning, workmen had built a track around the wreckage while the original track was being cleared. The second train to pass over the new temporary track on Sunday morning, however, derailed on the scene of the wreckage. No damage was done. Some defective condition of the rails was thought to be the cause for the tender leaving the track and wrecking the train.

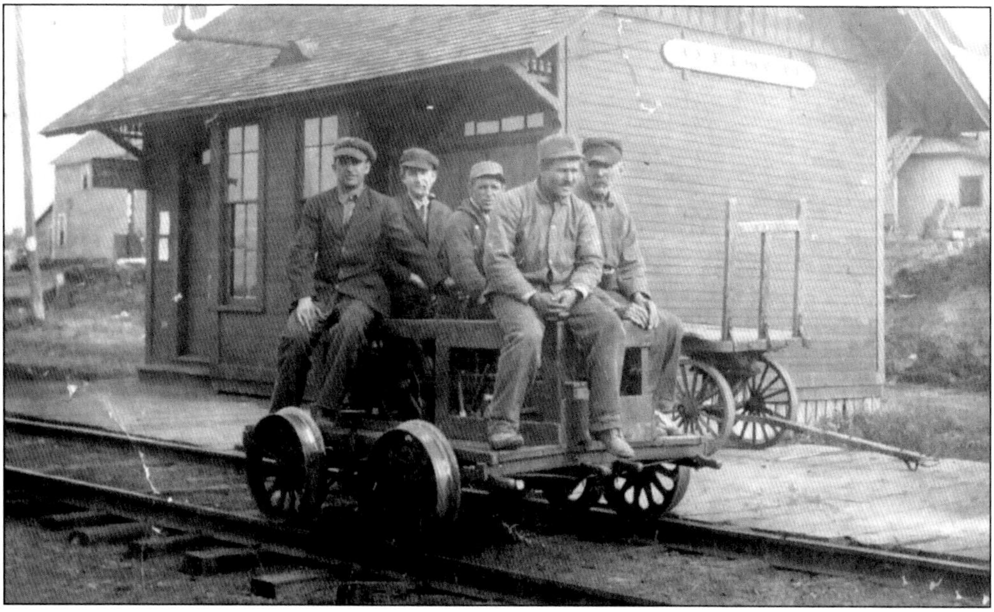

Lars Paulson, the section boss of the railroad crew, is pictured with four others on this handcar near the Otisco Depot. Railroads relied on each man to do his job. Some worked in the depots, assisting passengers and loading freight. Yardmen assisted trains in the yard and "blocked" them, readying them for final destinations. The train crew operated the trains from town to town. Section crews laid track, upgrading with heavier rails to carry heavier trains, and repaired them after derailment.

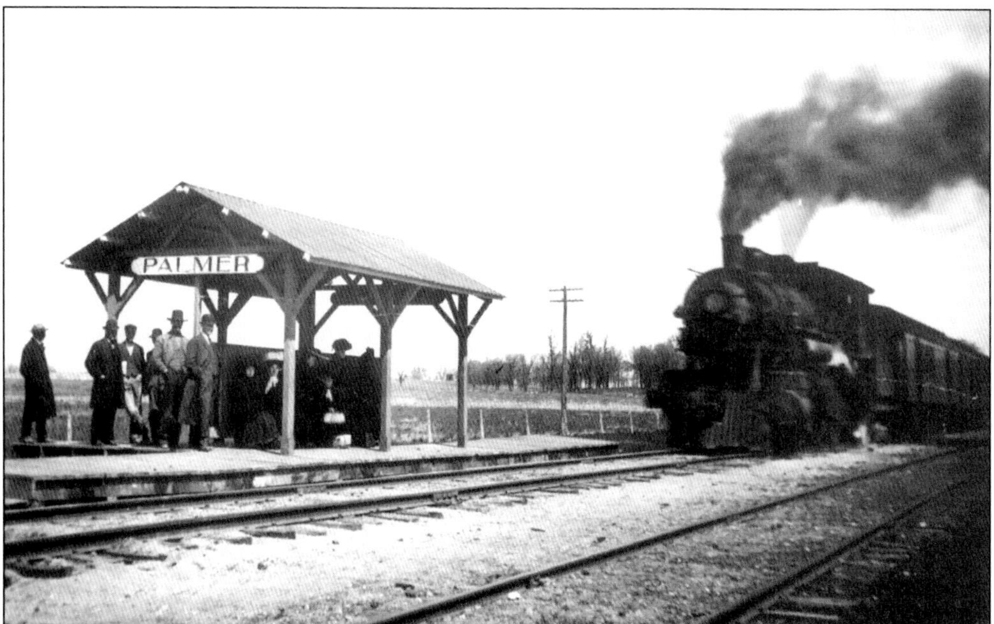

Several people await the M.&St.L. train as it pulls into the Palmer Station. This station was located one mile north of the railroad crossing running through section 13 of Iosco Township. The train brought the mail, which was sorted by Sigurd Jackson and distributed at his store.

Three

MAINSTREETS

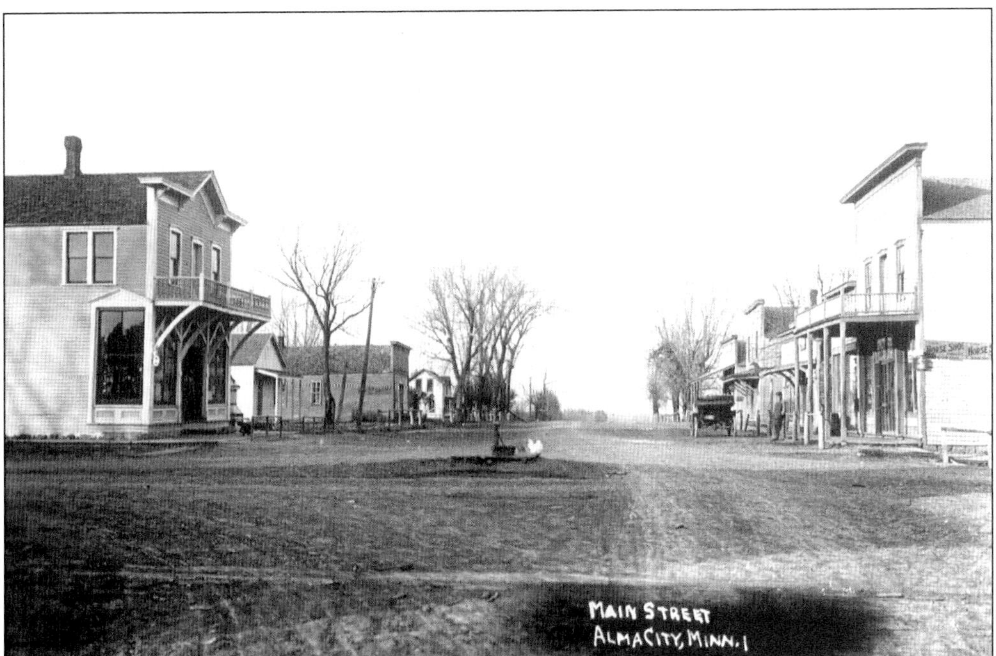

Here is a view of Alma City Main street. The water pump is in the middle of street with a chicken looking for a drink. An early automobile is parallel-parked on right side of street, with horse-hitching posts still evident in front of every building. Alma City was surveyed and platted in 1865 by S.E. Stebbins for "Uncle Sam" Larrabee, the "father of Alma City."

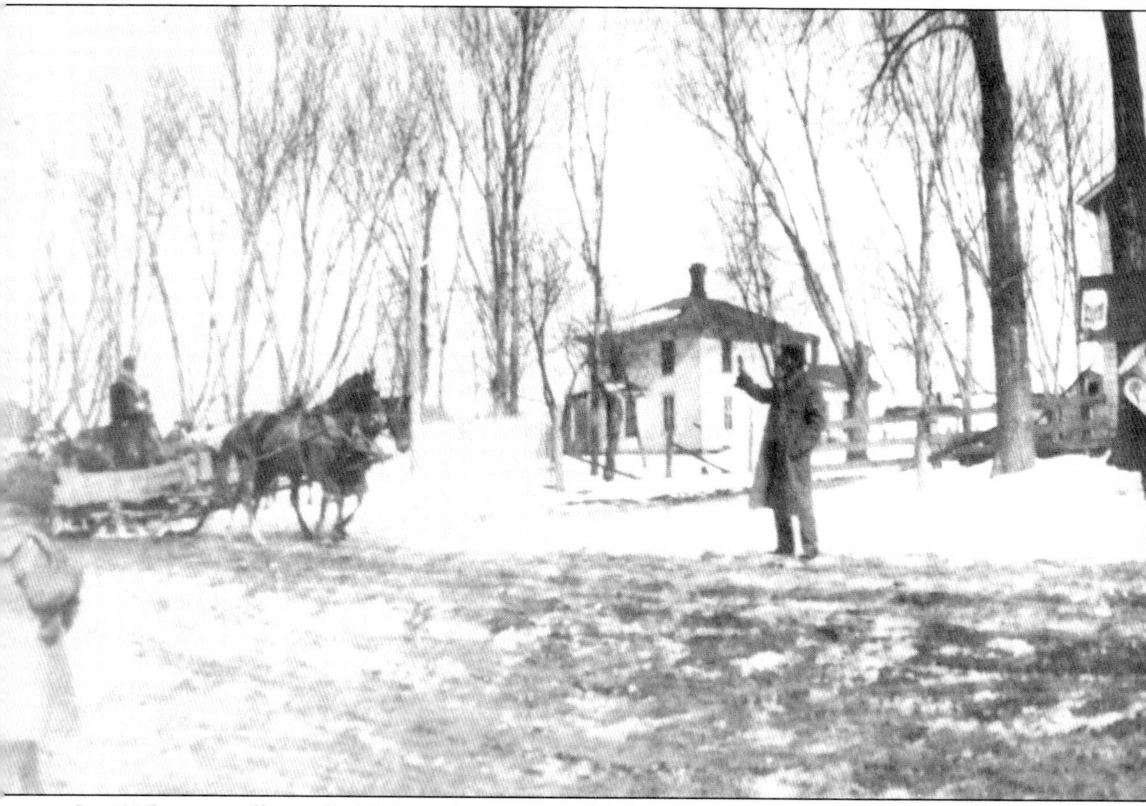

In 1895 a post office called "Cream" was established in the southeast corner of the northeast quarter of section 12 in Blue Earth County. As the town grew, its business spread into Waseca County since the town site was on the county line between Blue Earth and Waseca Counties. Waseca County had the distinction of having the lone Rural Free Delivery station in Minnesota.

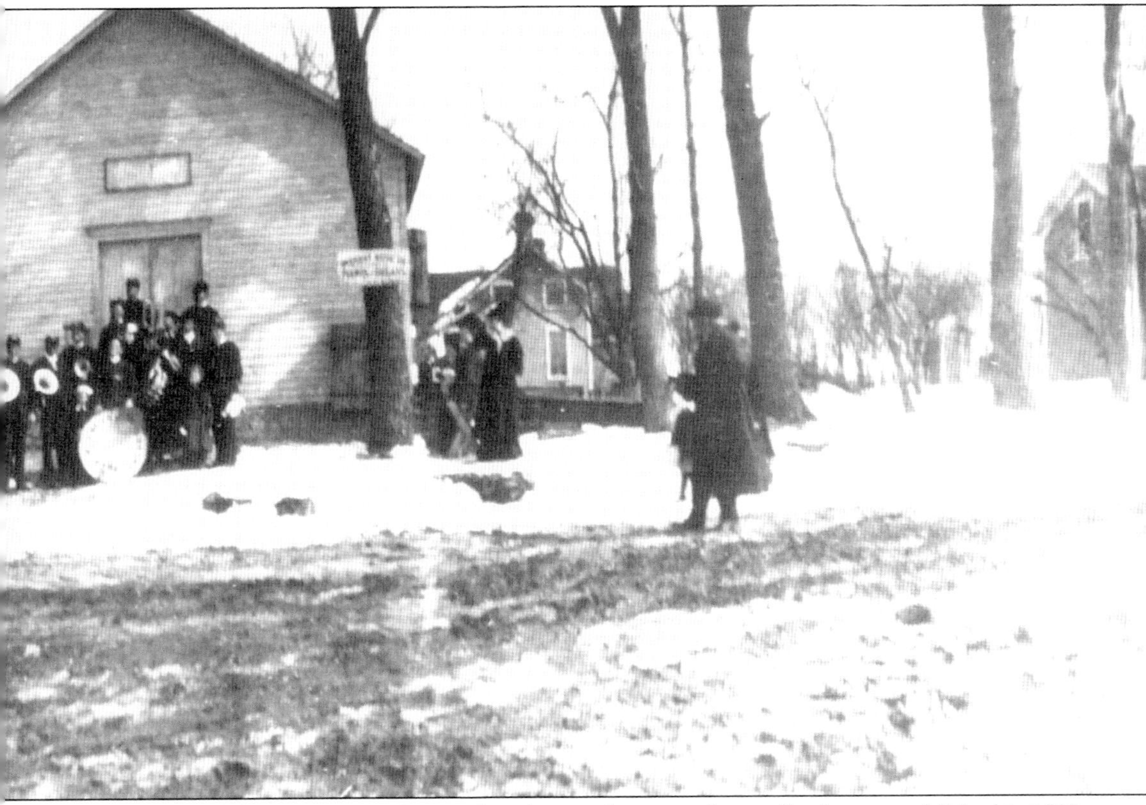

The name of this station was Cream, listed as a tributary to Janesville. It was established in 1902 and discontinued in 1904. In 1905 Cream was home to a creamery, cheese factory, general store, barbershop, box car depot, church, and the Modern Woodman Hall.

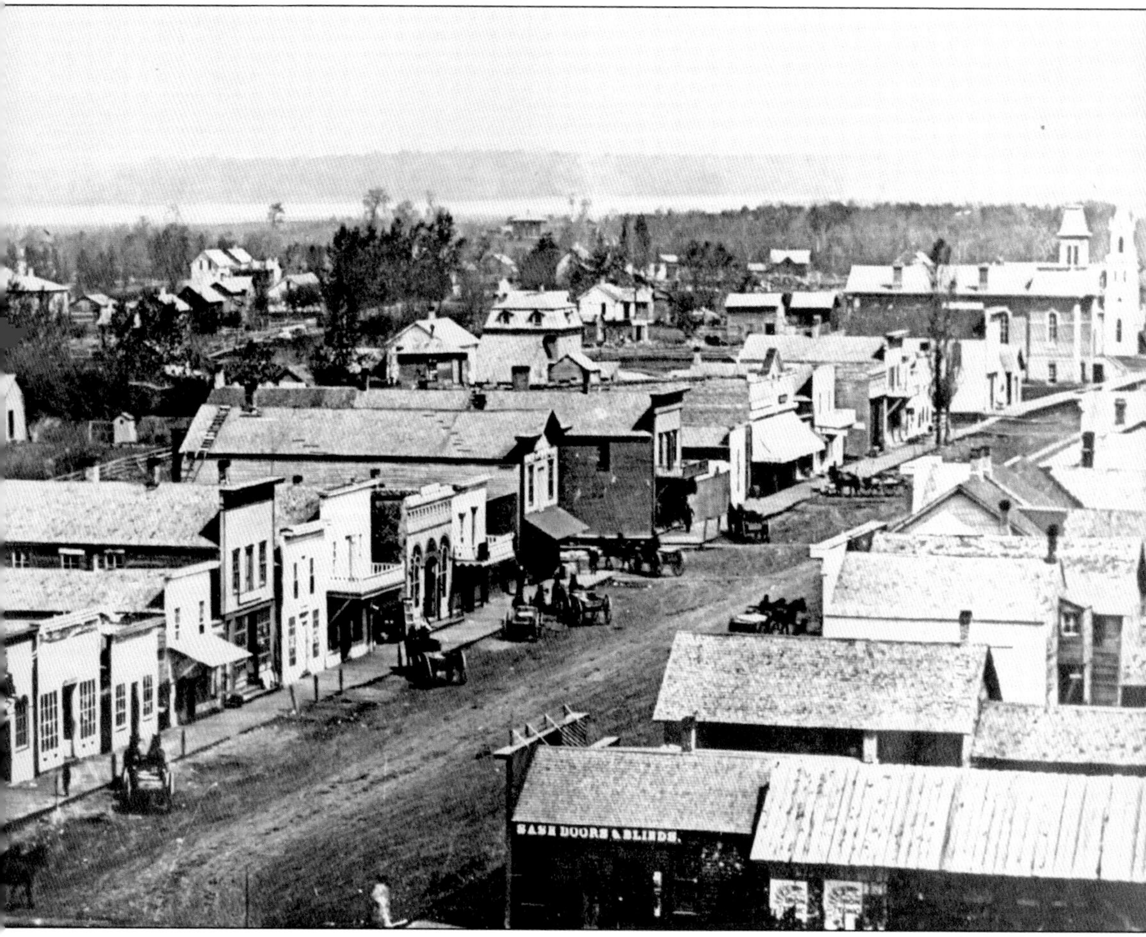

Seen here is new or "East Janesville" before the fire of 1887. Lake Elysian can be seen in the background. A steamboat used to carry passengers around the lake to Echo Island, Savage's Point, Elysian, and Okaman. Population of Janesville at this time was 1,054. A dam was put in later that removed the lake to its present site north of Janesville.

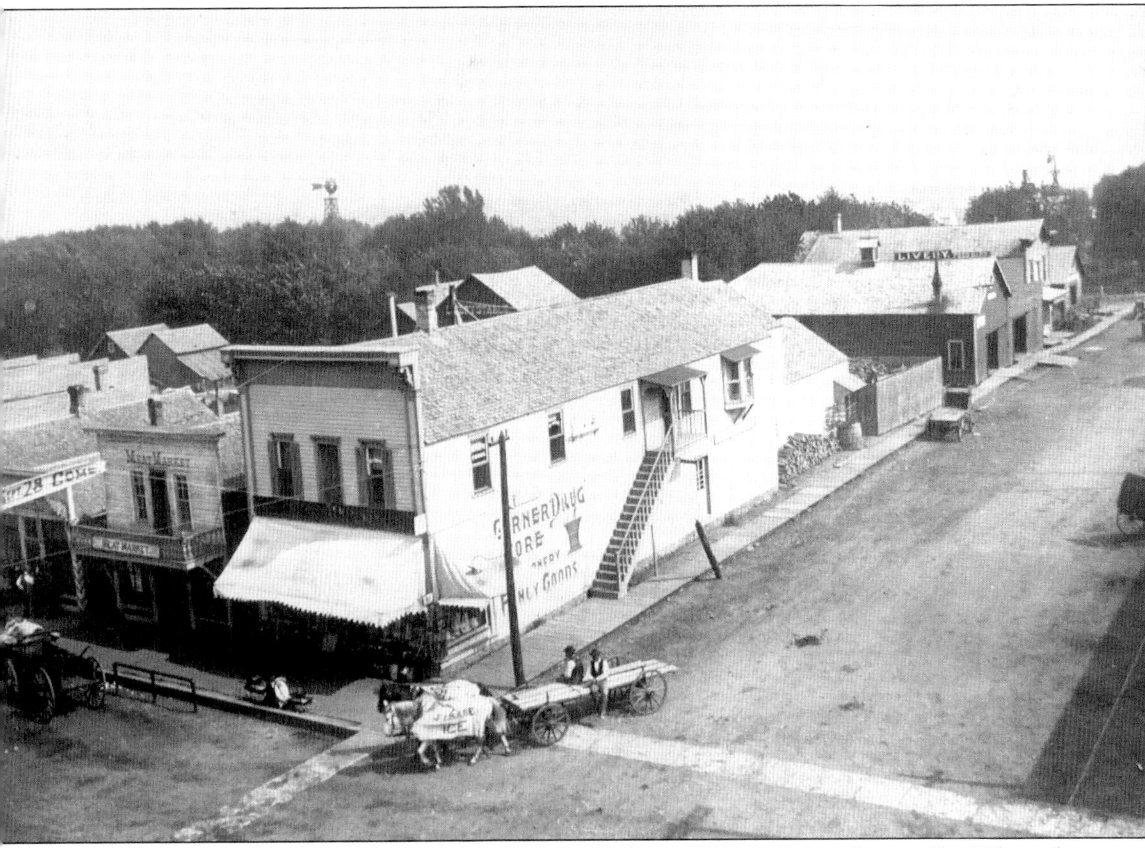

The original Janesville was located on a hill northwest of the present Janesville. When the Winona & St. Peter Railroad station was located directly west of Waseca, most of the "old town" buildings were moved over to the new site, called East Janesville. The town grew rapidly before the fire of 1887. This photograph was taken after the 1887 fire in approximately 1898.

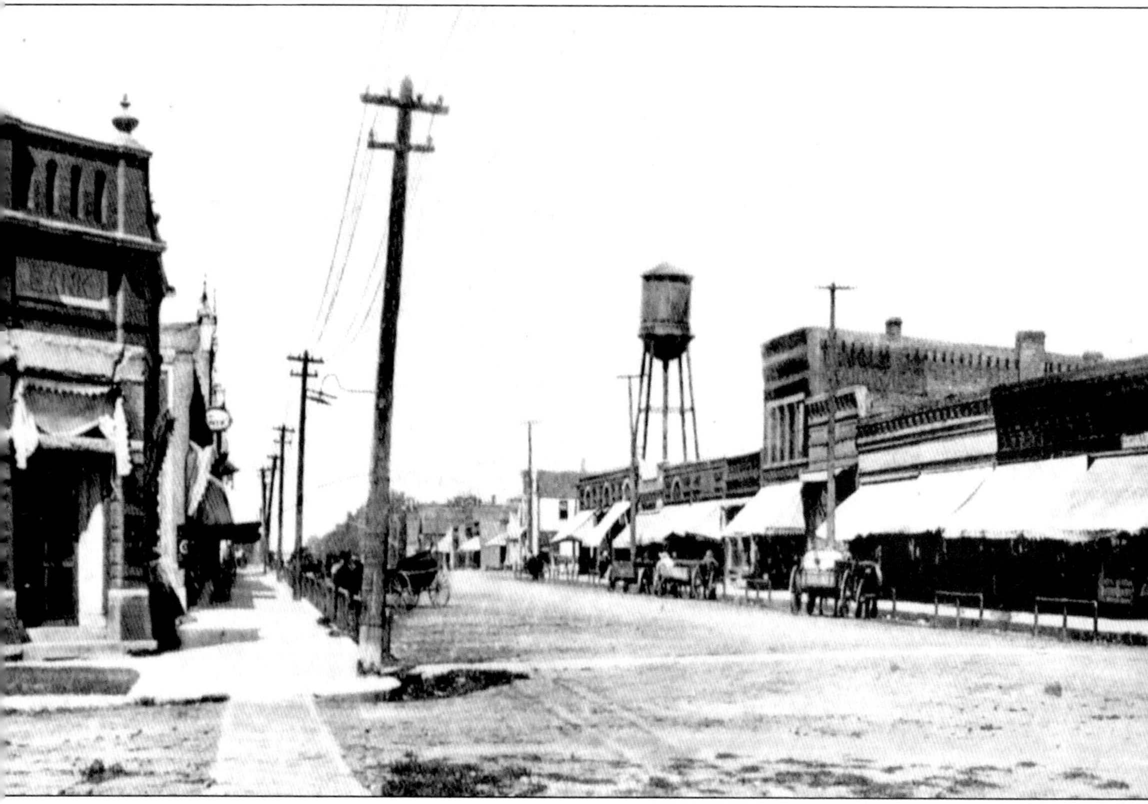

This photograph carries the postmark of 1913. It was taken looking north from the railroad tracks.

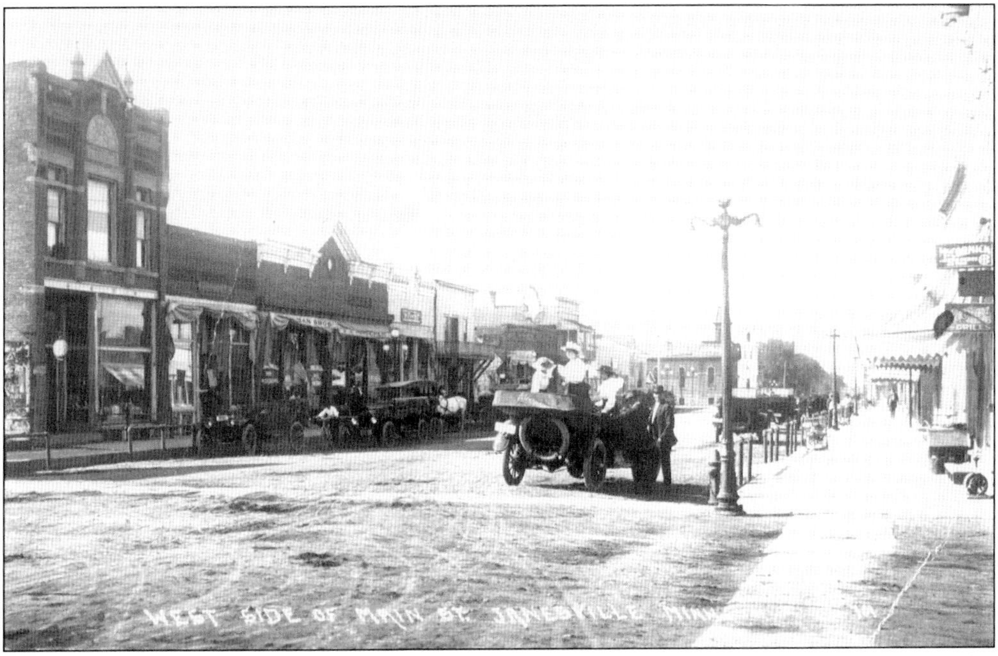

This photograph was taken from the corner of Main Street and Highway 14 in Janesville in the early 1900s. The streets are still dirt but electric streetlights are evident.

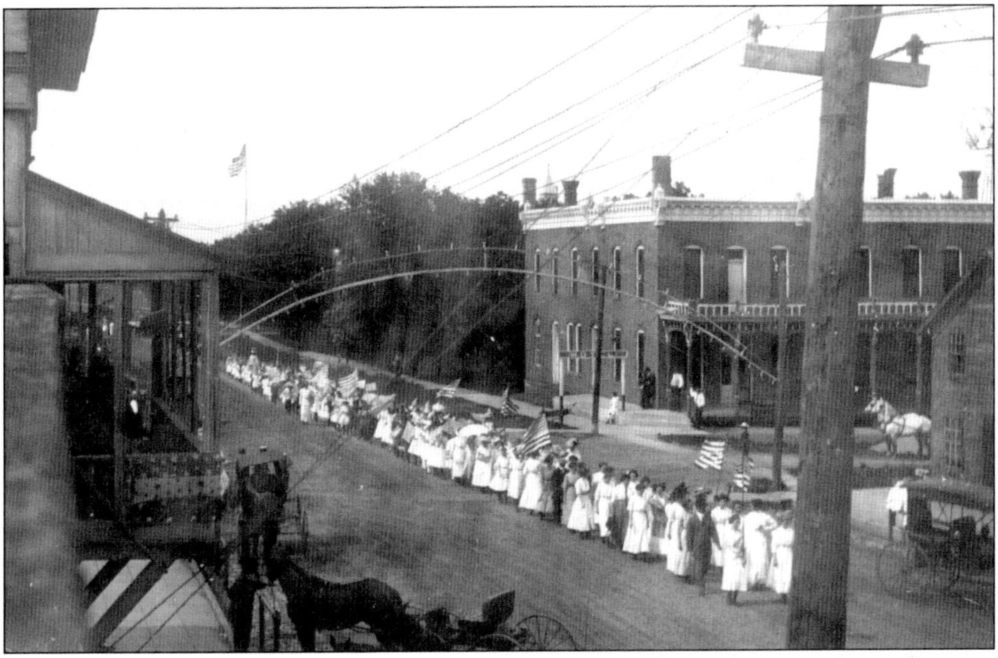

A parade of women is coming down Main Street in Janesville. Girls in parades at this time represented the states in the Union, one woman for each state. Behind them is the DeGraff House, which was on the northeast corner of Second and Main Streets. This hotel became a hatchery and finally a feed store before it was torn down in the 1960s.

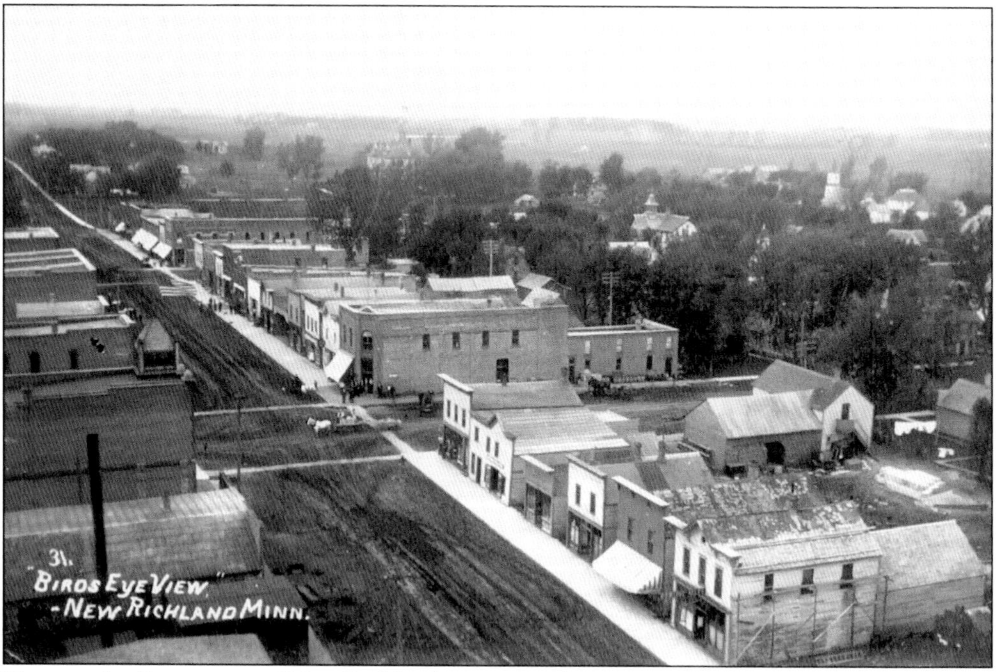

Here is a bird's-eye view of New Richland in 1910. There are no streetlights yet and the street is dirt. New Richland was laid out and platted by Henry T. Wells in August 1877, the same year the M.&St.L Railroad line arrived.

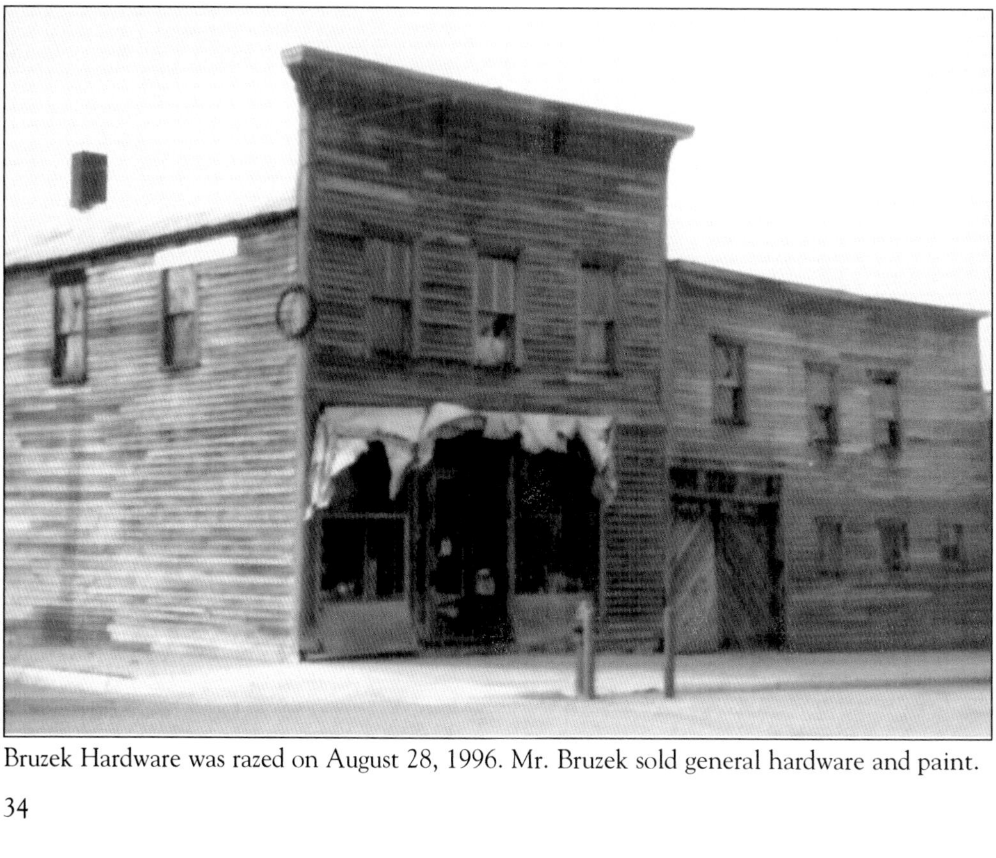

Bruzek Hardware was razed on August 28, 1996. Mr. Bruzek sold general hardware and paint.

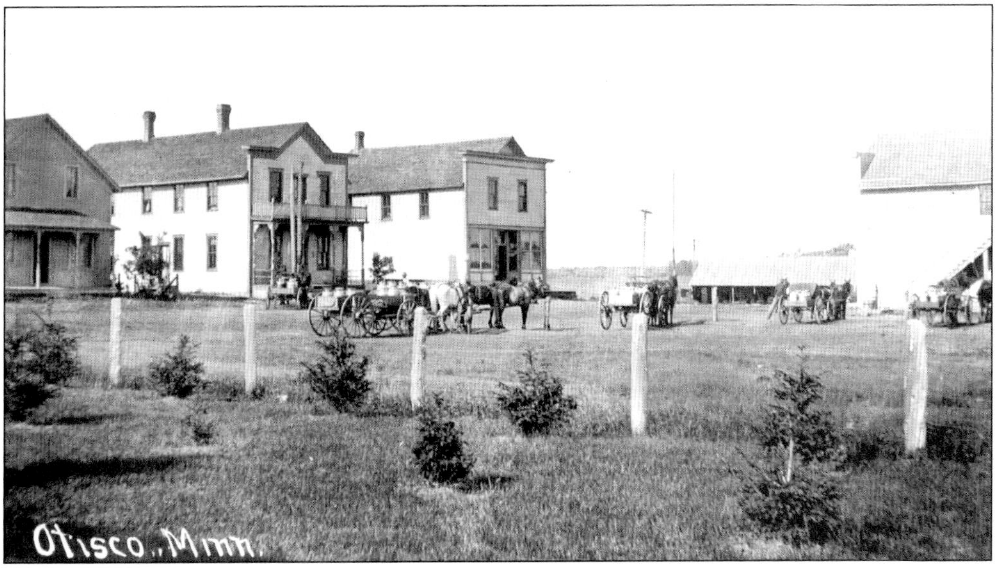

Otisco is seen here in about 1900. Pictured are the Otisco Hotel and the Johnson Store. Horses and wagons are hitched, carrying milk to the creamery.

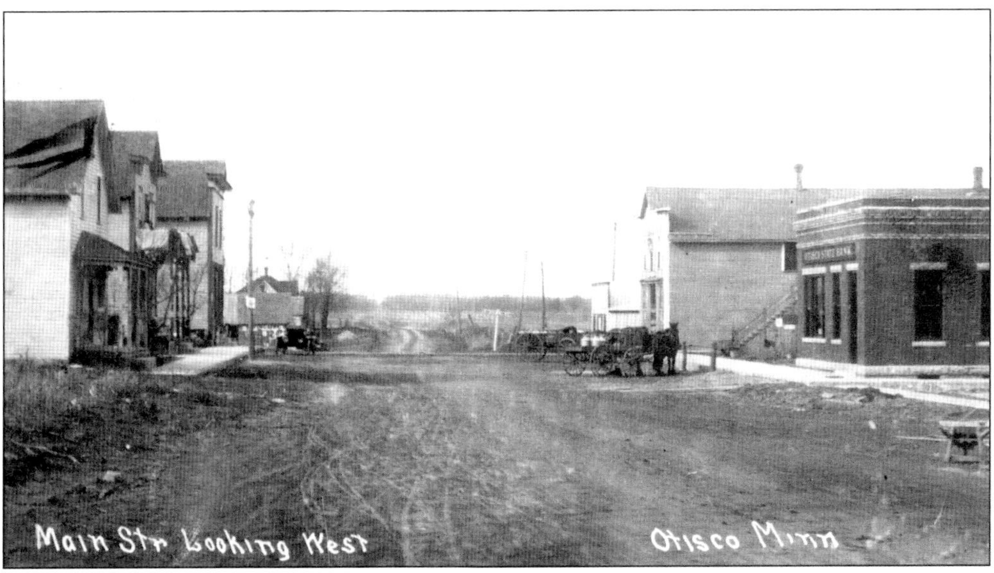

This view of Main Street Otisco shows the new bank building on the right.

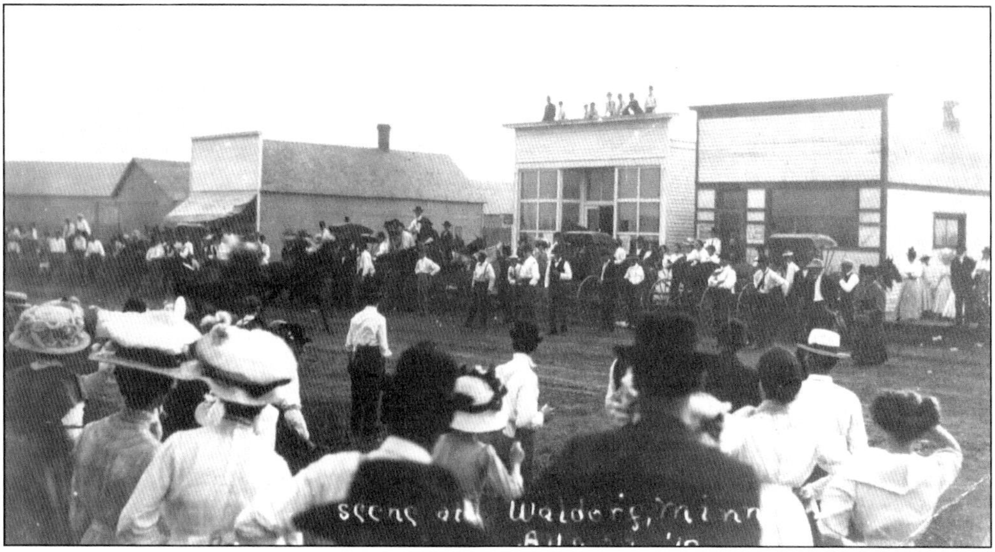

A horse race at "Picnic Day" in downtown Waldorf is captured in 1910.

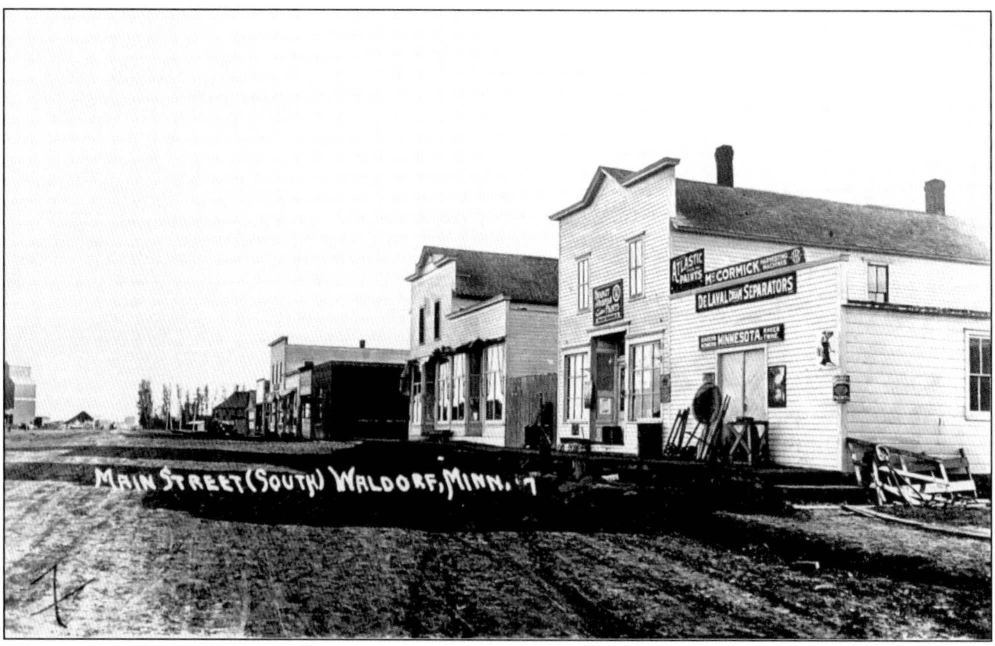

This image shows the view looking north on Main Street in Waldorf. Waldorf is located in section 16 of Vivian Township.

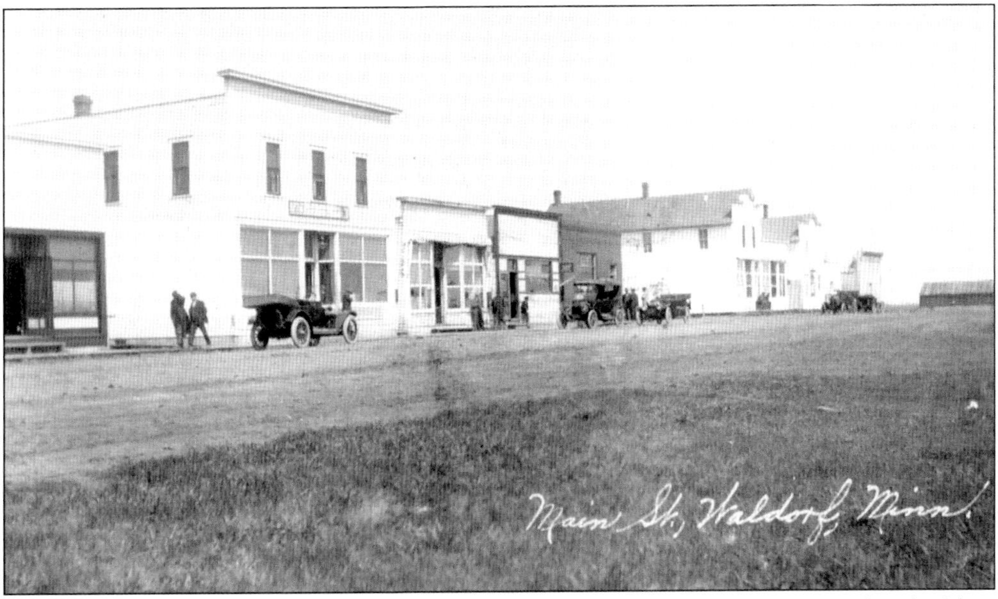

Pictured is an early street scene of Waldorf looking north. The signs on the first building read Atlantic Paints, McCormick Harvesting Machines, DeLaval Cream Separators, Binders, Mowers, Minnesota Rakes and Twine—one stop shopping for any farmer's needs of the day.

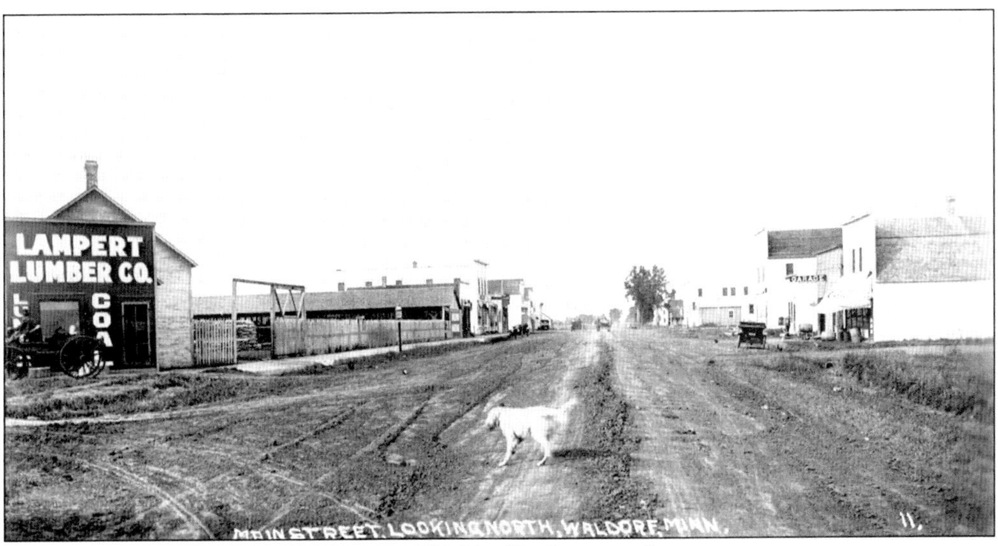

Here is another view of Main Street in Waldorf looking north.

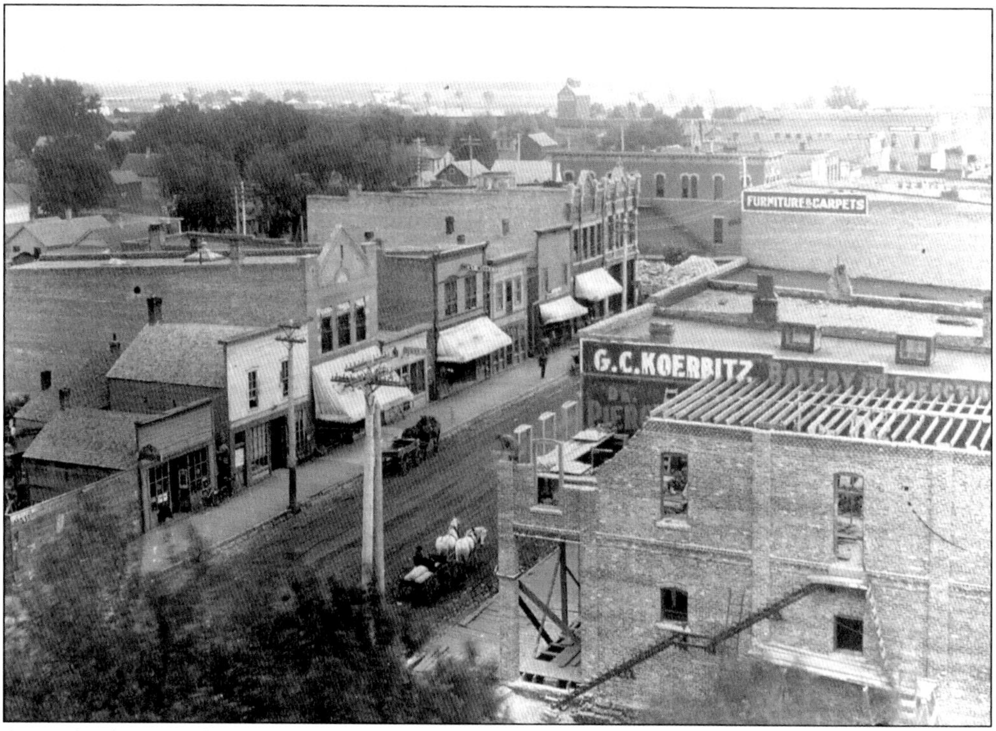

An early photograph of Second Street, now State Street, in Waseca was taken from the county courthouse. The building being built is one of four that was torn down in 2001. Several of the brick buildings along the street are still in use today.

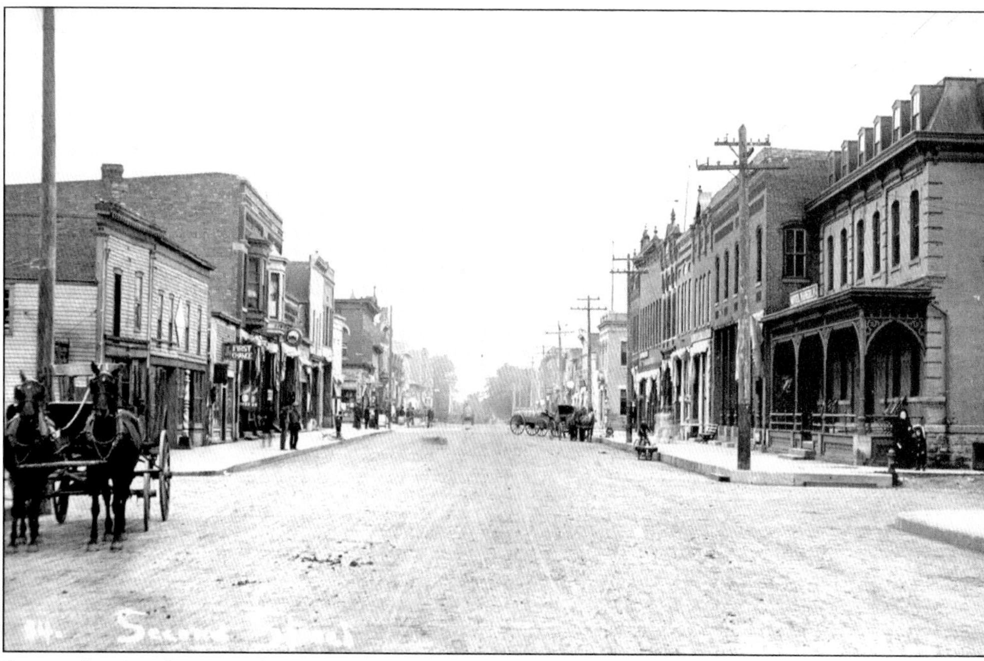

Pictured is South Second Street in 1908. This is presently the corner of South State Street and Second Avenue.

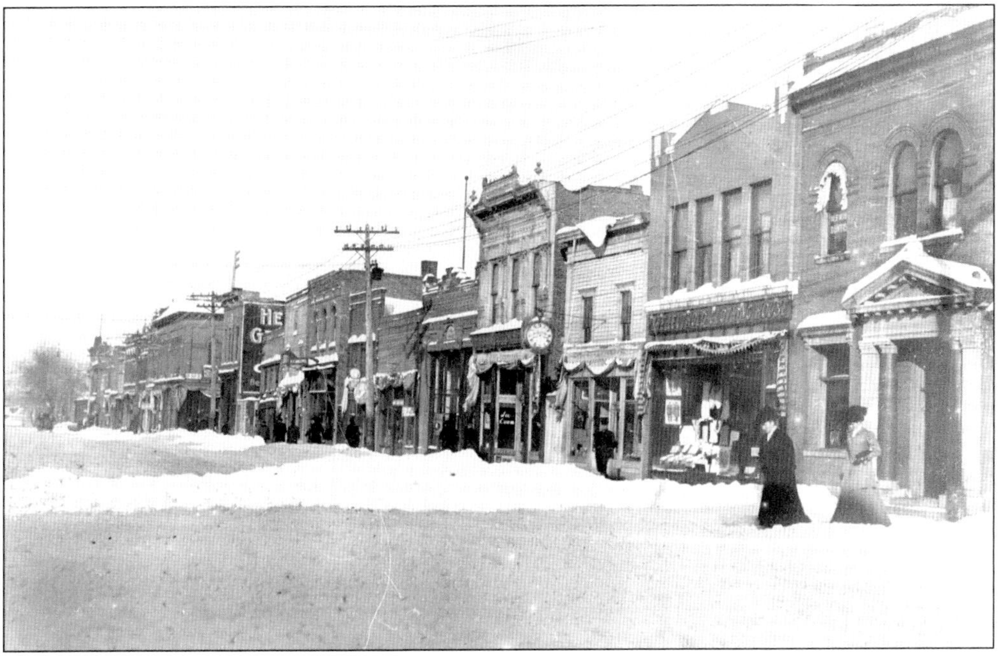

Today, North Second Street (seen here in 1908), is the east side of State Street in the 100 block.

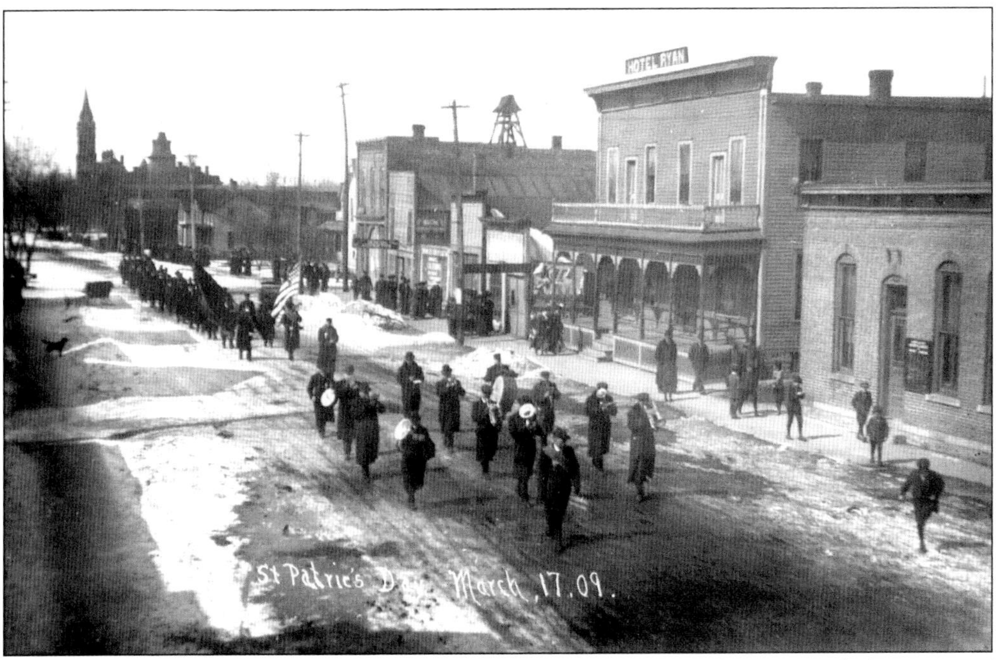

A St. Patrick's Day parade, coming east down West Elm in 1909, is about to reach the corner of State Street. This is a rare photograph of West Elm or Highway 14. The buildings to the right are where the the First National Bank and parking lot are now located.

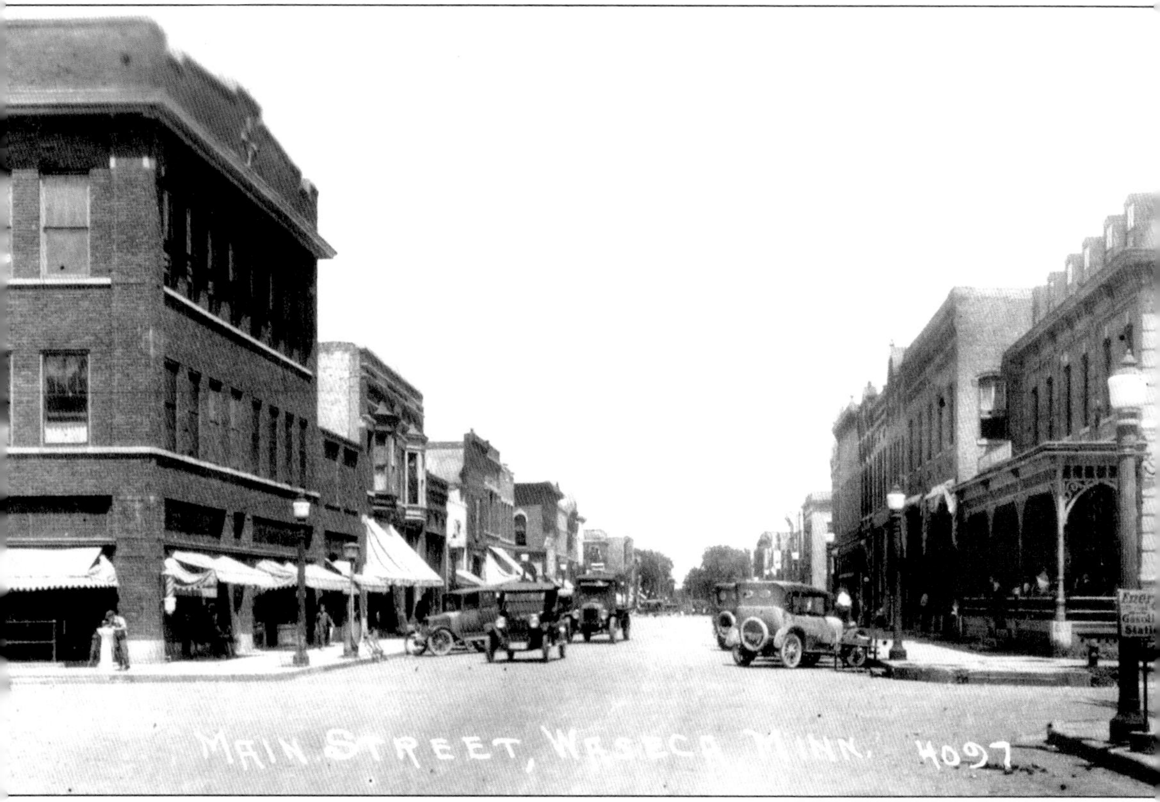

South Second Street, or State Street as it is known today, and Second Avenue are seen in this photo. The top floor of the brick building to the left burned, leaving a two-story building, which still stands today.

Four

BUSINESSES

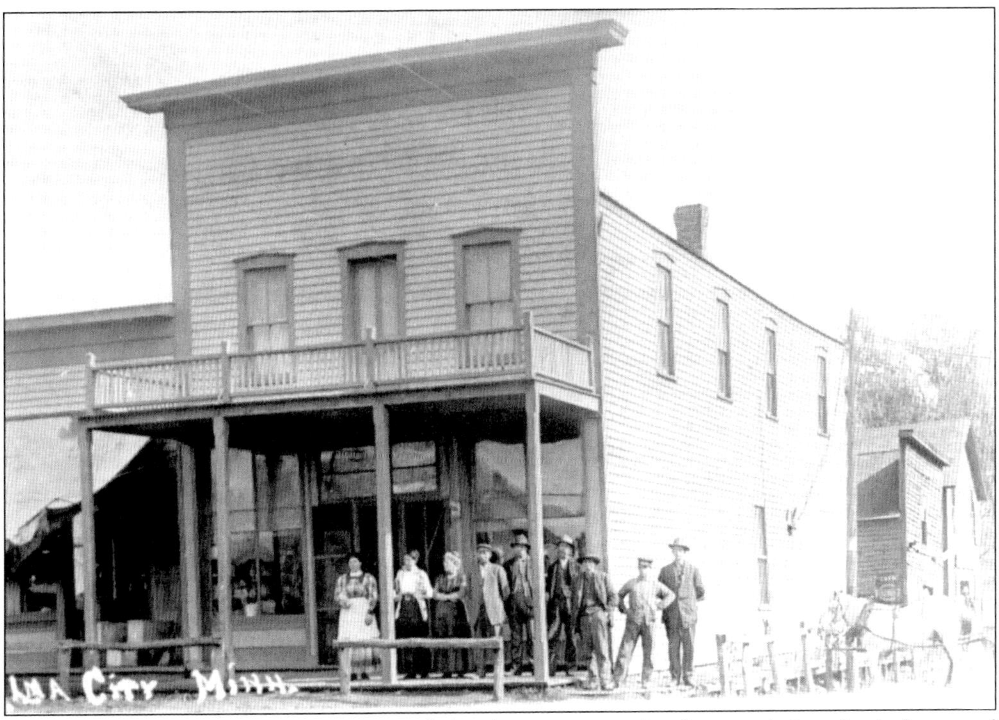

General Store in Alma City is seen with hitching posts and rails provided on both front and side streets. It is not known for sure which general store this might be. There were many in Alma City early in the city's existence. It was a growing, bustling community. On October 2, 1879, Bishop Milton Wright was in Alma City to lead the Four State Church Conference of the United Brethren Church. Bishop Wright was the father of the famous Wright Brothers.

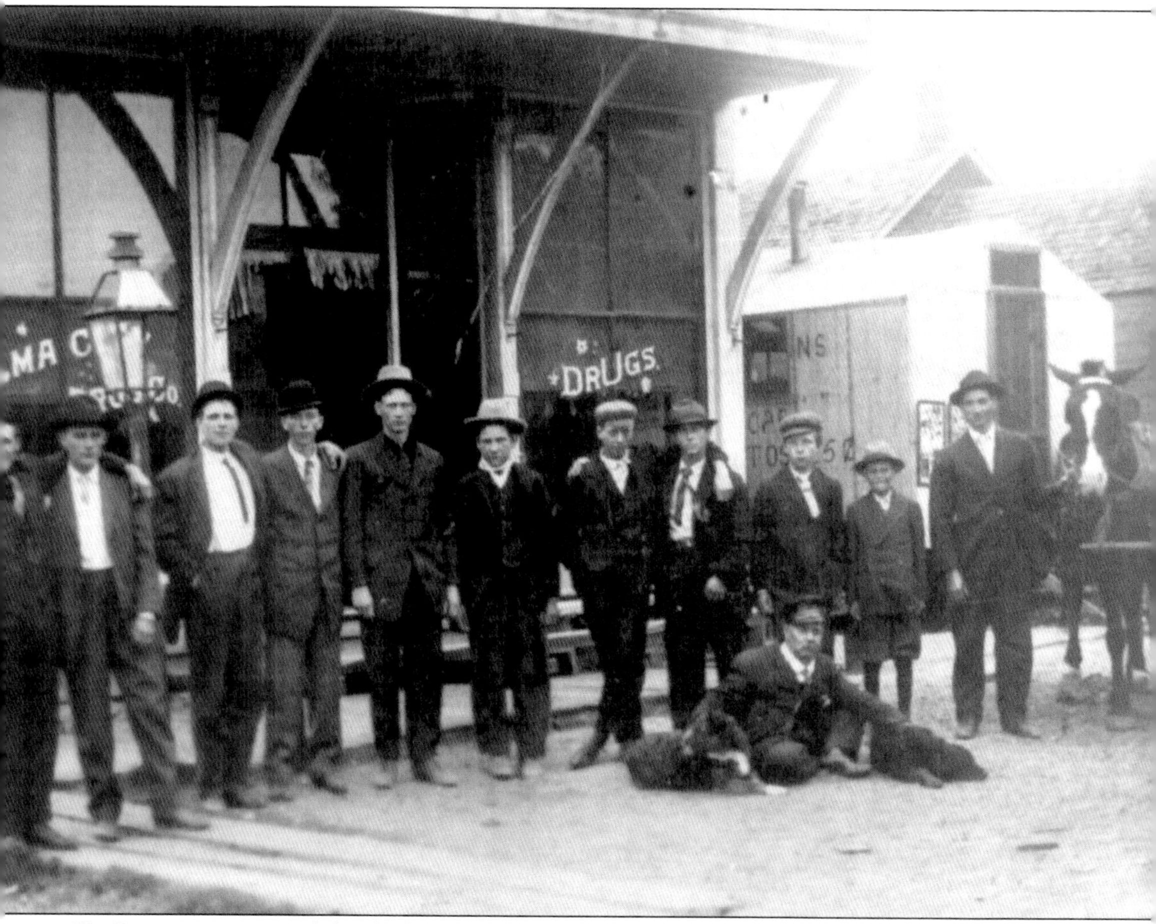

Dr. Remington erected this building in 1886 to use as his office, a drug store, and the second story for living quarters. Later the drug store was owned and operated by John H. Gallagher. Dr. O'Hara occupied the doctor's office for about three years until he moved his office to Janesville. Dr. Cory moved to Alma City from Janesville and purchased the drug store from J.H. Gallagher at the same time, taking over the pharmacy and the practice left by Dr. O'Hara.

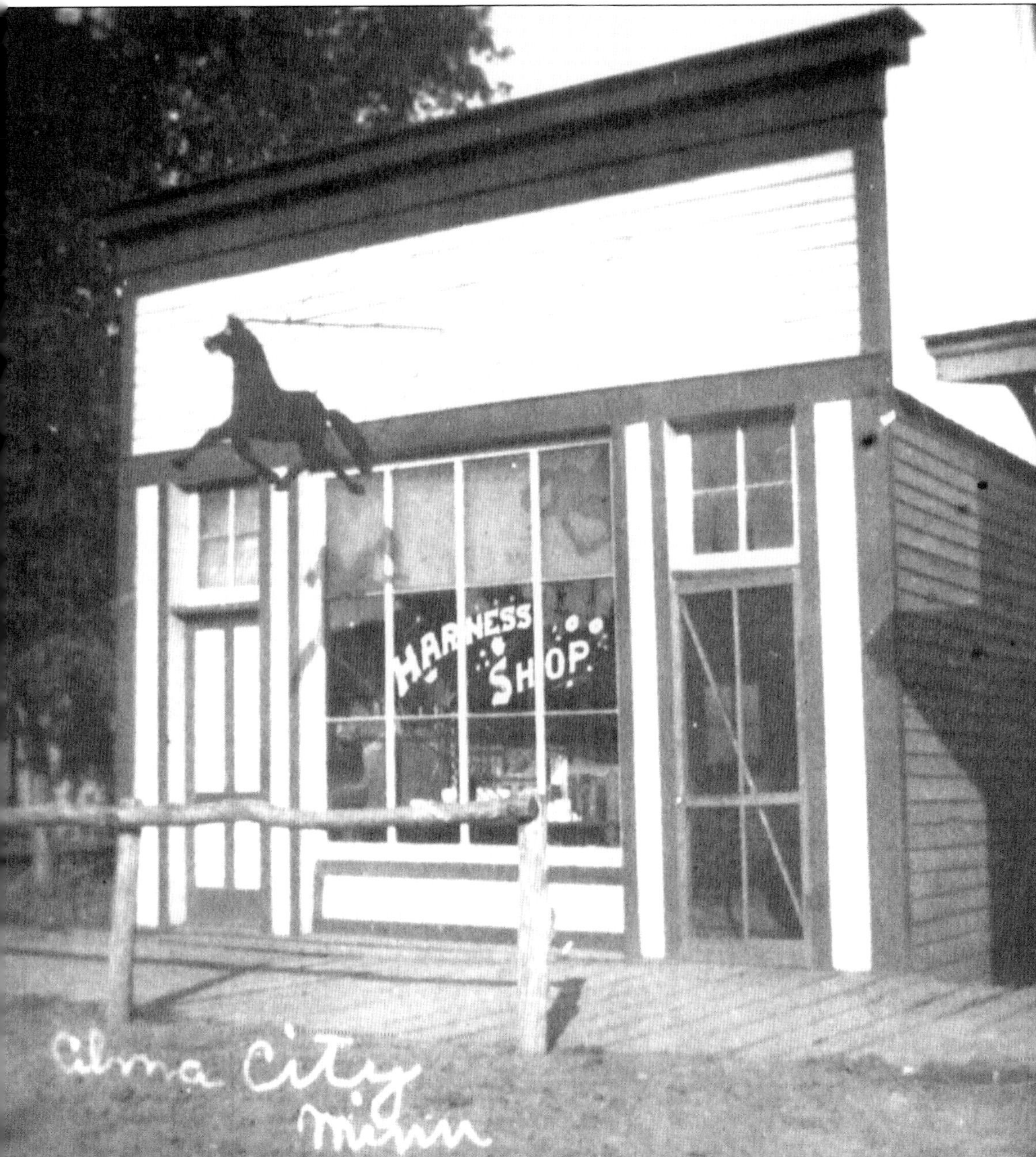

Theron Nettleton first owned the Harness Shop. He sold it to William Kraske. Kraske became the postmaster in 1920 and had both the Harness Shop and the post office in the same building.

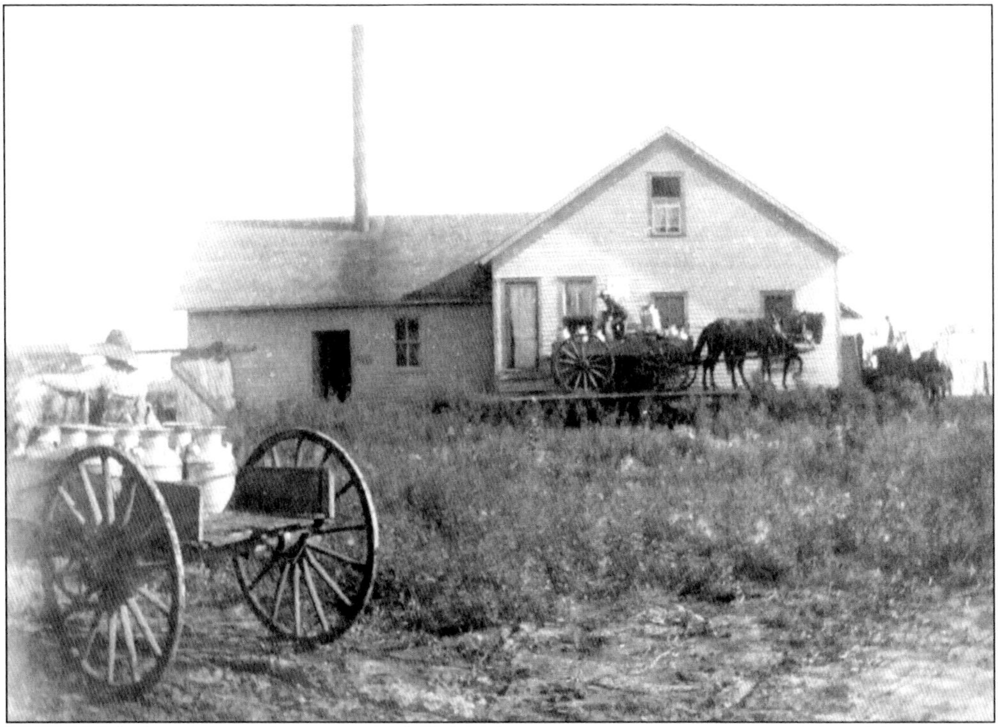

On December 1, 1894, the Alma City Dairy Association was organized to "manufacture and sell butter and other dairy products." The first officers were John Wilkinson, president; John Markham, treasurer; H.E. Gates, secretary; H.C. Bade, C. Doss, W. Thompson, and N. Witts; with W.V. Neal, buttermaker.

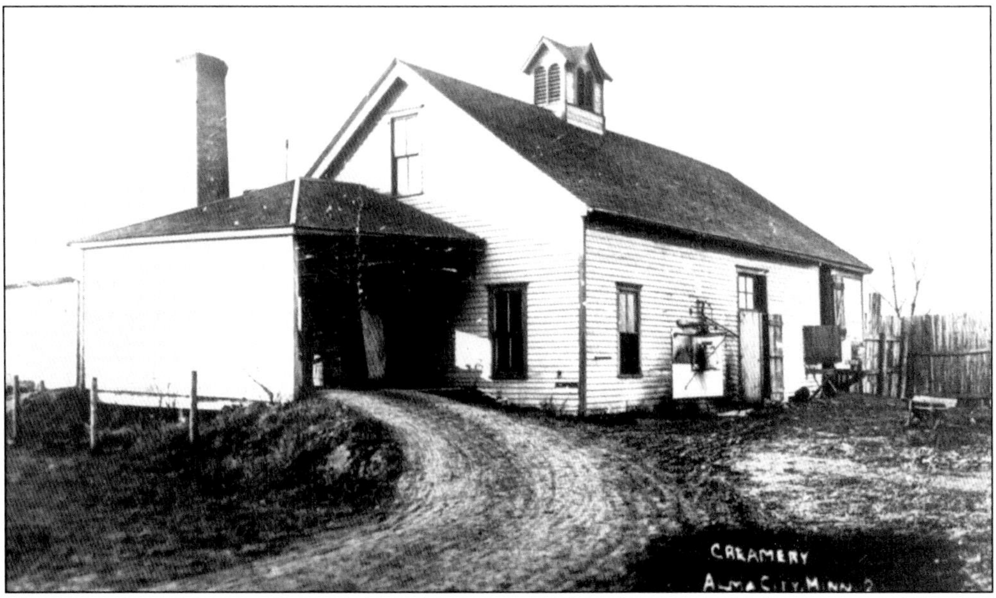

The first sale was butter, shipped directly to New York. After 1920 the butter was sold to the Minnesota Cooperative Creamery Association. In 1926 the Alma City Creamery became affiliated with the new Land O' Lakes Cooperative.

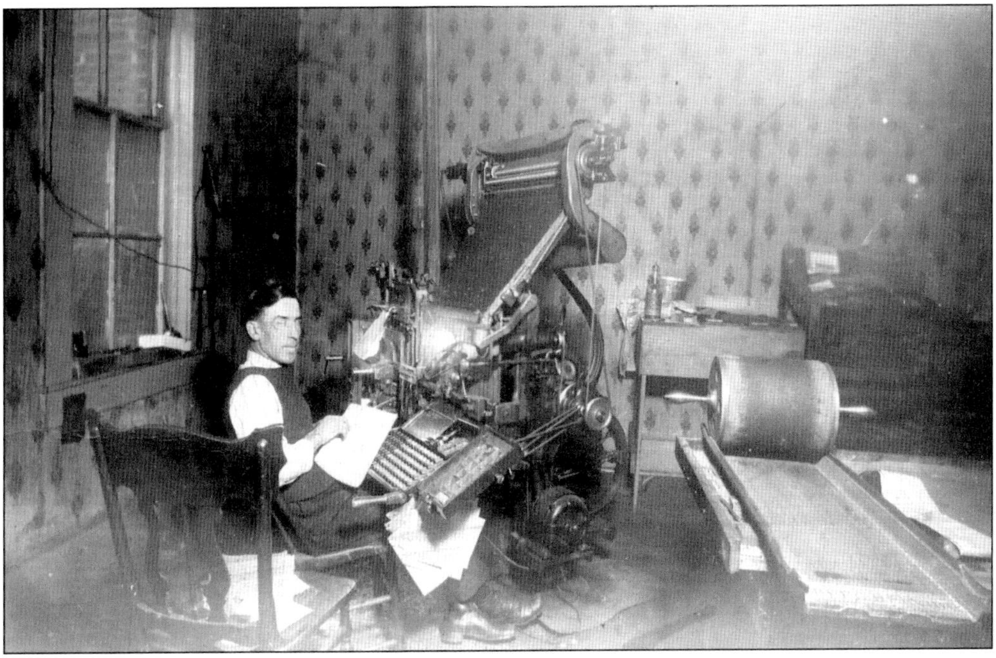

Anthony O'Grady Jr. is setting type at the *Janesville Argus*.

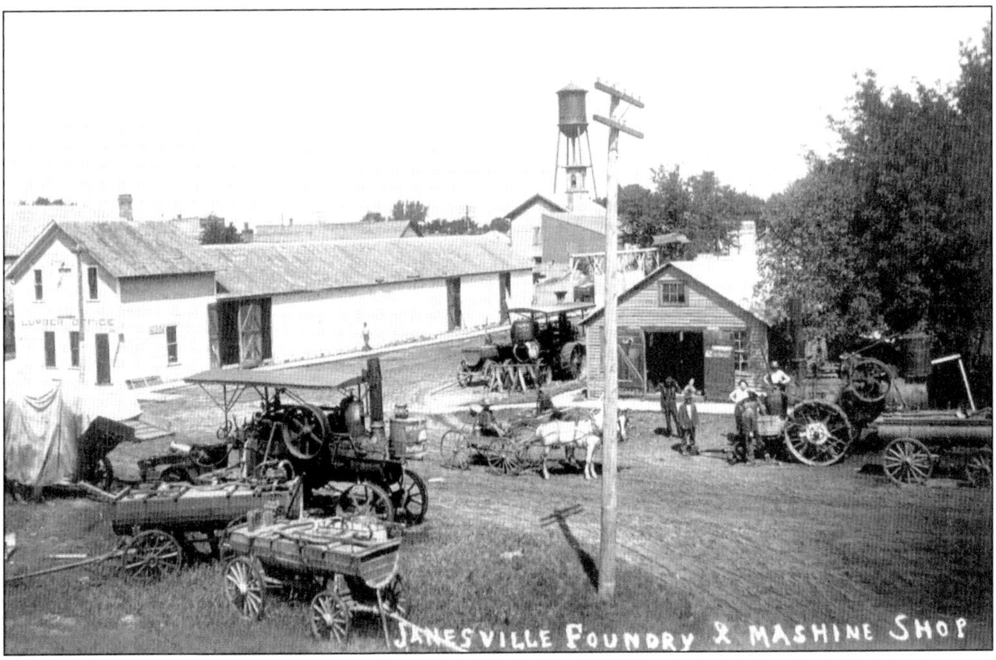

Janesville Foundry and Machine Shop bustles with activity.

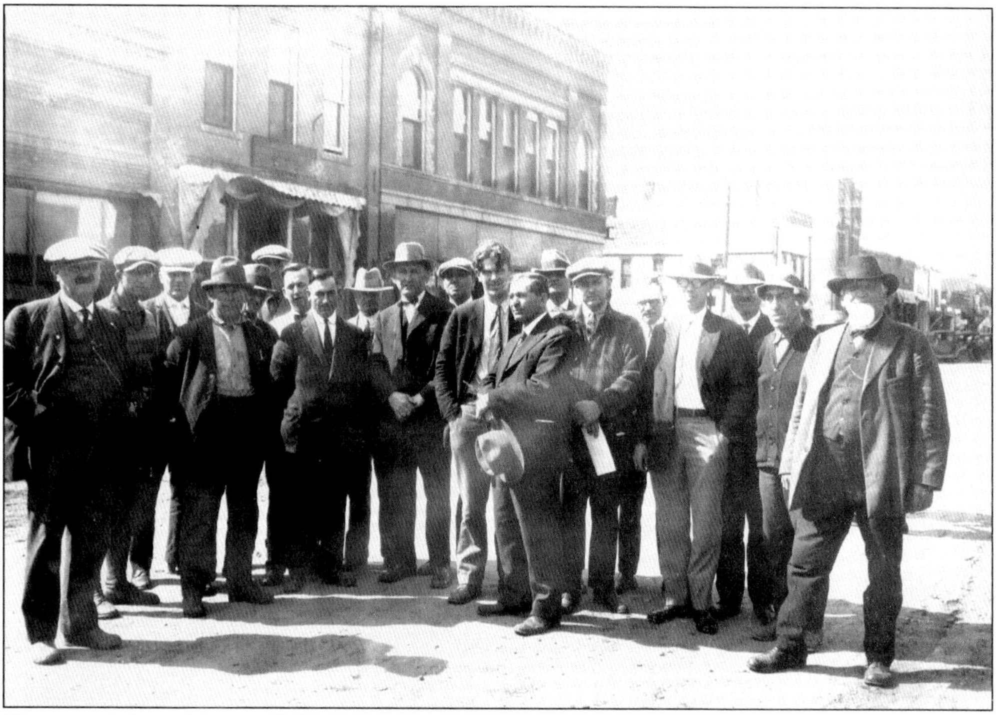

"Business Men of Janesville" in approximately 1923. Identified, from left to right, are W.R. Cahill, Monroe Schwandt, Emil Miller, Otto Schafer, Art Hagen, Harry Henry, Jay Nash, Otto Arnold, O.H. Tollefson, Eugene Cahill, Charlie Shafer, John Byron, Fred Veman, George Geiske, E. Werdin, Tom Foley, John Schwandt, and Ernest Miller.

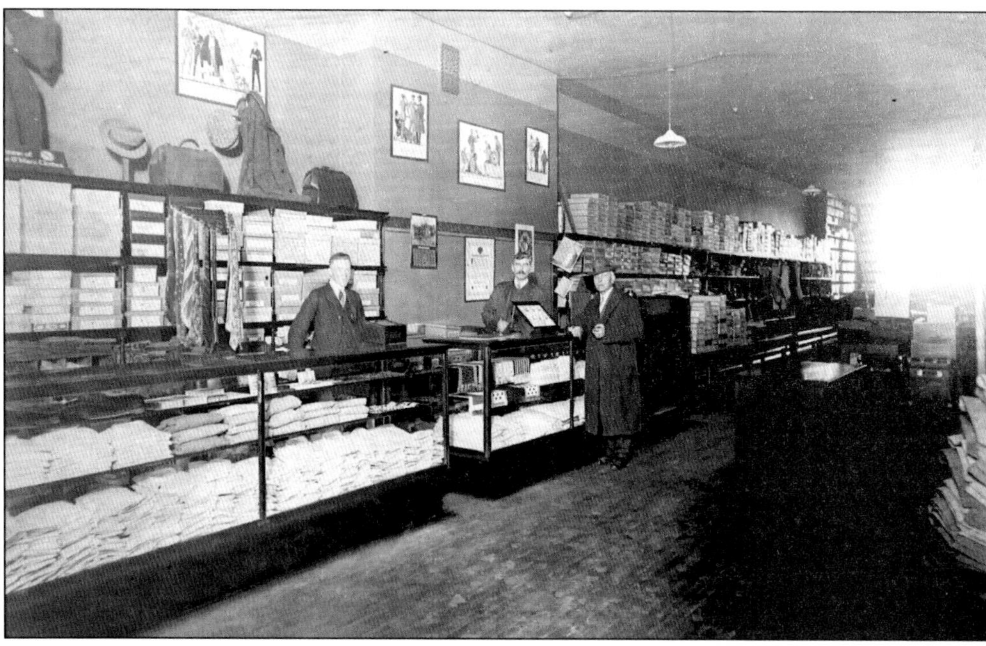

Ernst C. Werdin, proprietor of Werdin & Schmidt men's clothing, is standing on the left. This business was located on the south side of the Miner block building.

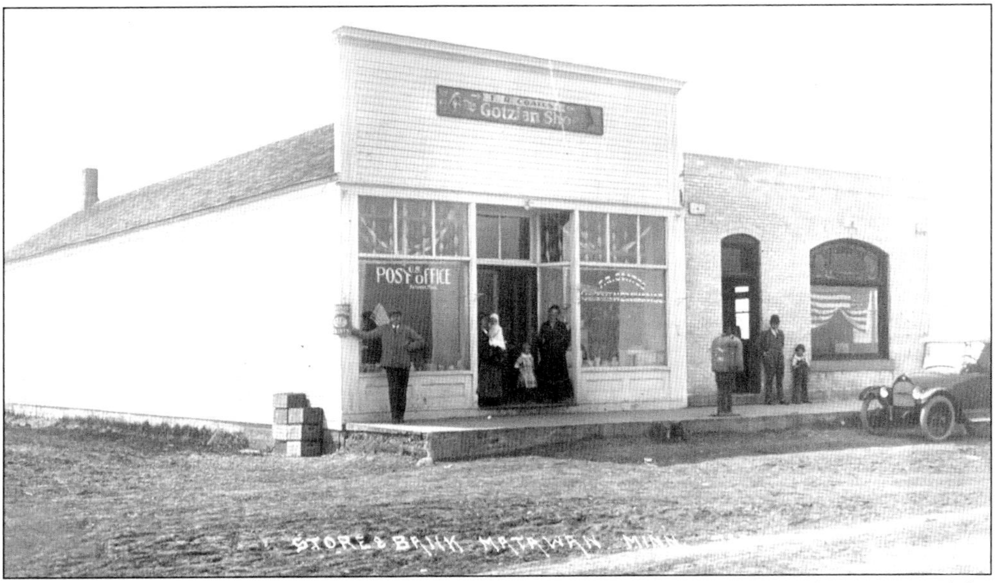

Matawan, which was located 17 miles southwest of Waseca in Byron Township, is one of the county's memory towns. The Farmer's Store was a general store owned by a group of farmers. It also housed the post office. To the right is the Citizens State Bank.

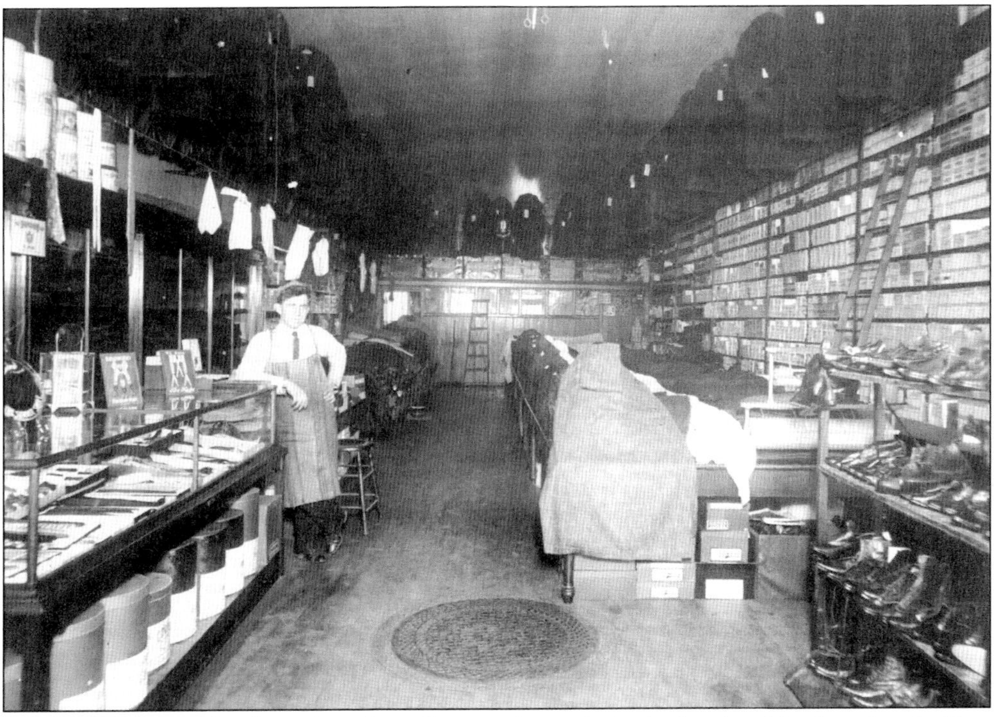
One of the Kreuzer brothers, Joseph or Raymond, stands in the brothers' leather shop in New Richland in approximately 1900. This shop also carried a full line of clothing and accessories. In the June 6, 1929 *Waseca Herald, it was* reported that J.W. Kreuzer of New Richland was elected president of the Retail Harness Dealers' Association. In his speech at the annual meeting in Saint Paul, he stated that the day of the horse is not past.

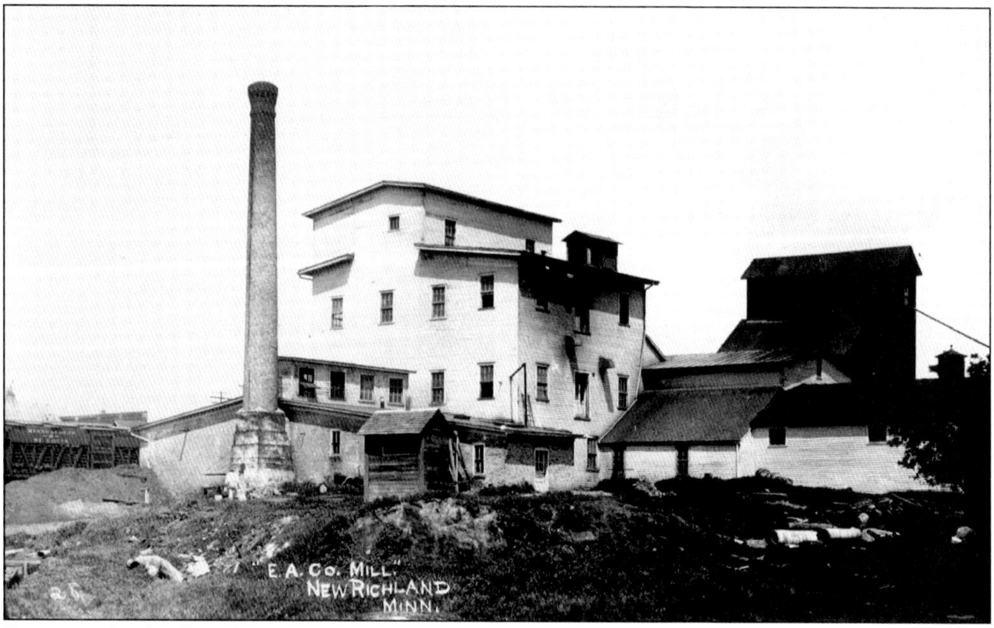

Everett, Aughenbaugh, and Company of Waseca purchased the New Richland Milling Company in 1894, which increased their capacity to 800 barrels a day in this county. In 1895 EACO also had elevators and flat warehouses at Otisco, Manchester, Hartland, and New Prague, Minnesota.

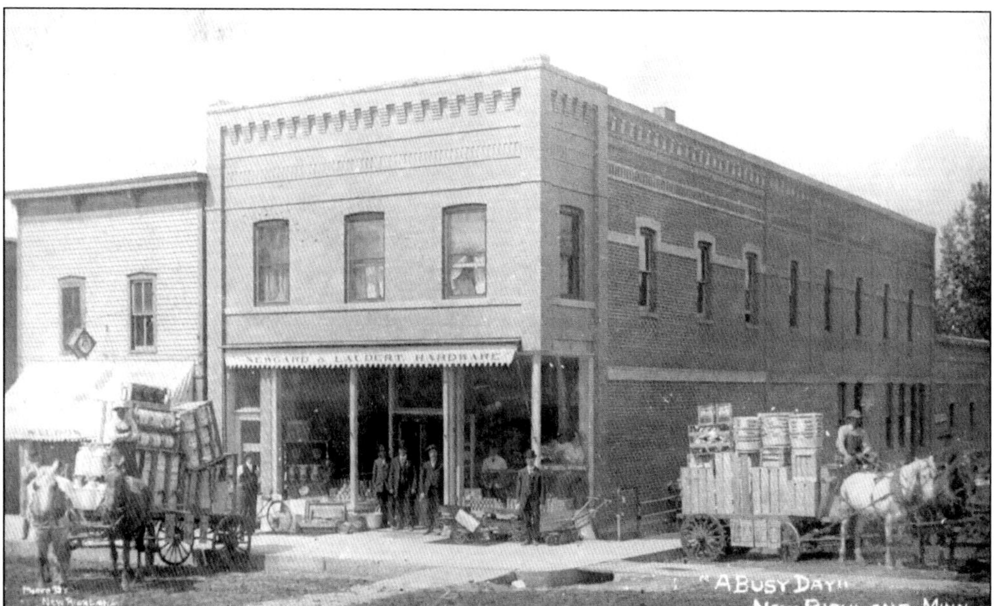

Pictured here is Newgard and Laudert Hardware of New Richland. This business was known to be in business in 1910.

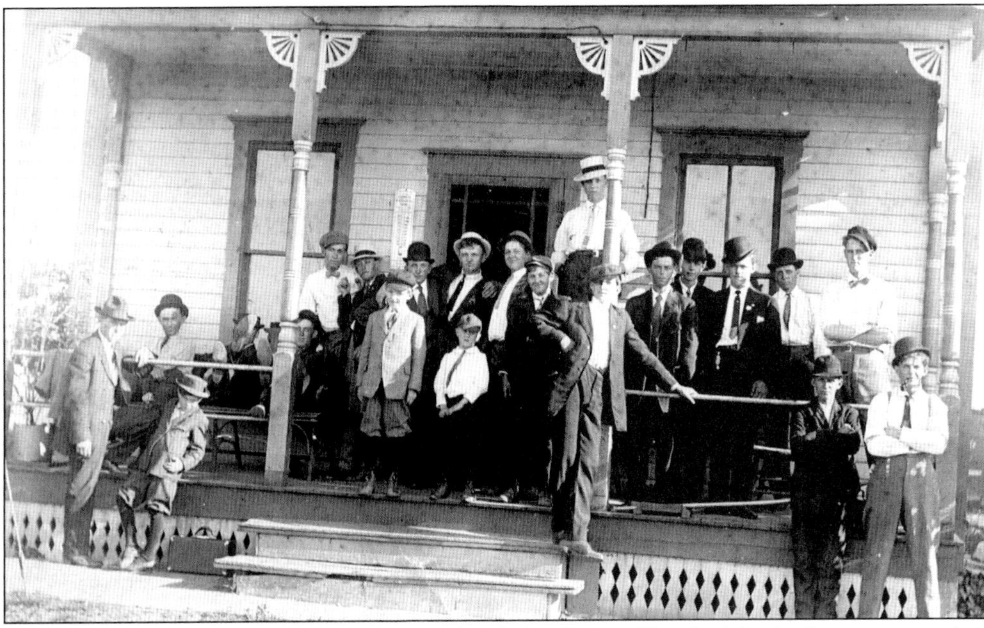

A group of young men stand on the porch of the Otisco Hotel. A.J. Anderson is standing by the post, wearing a straw hat. This could possibly be a later picture of the Otisco "Batchlers'" Club.

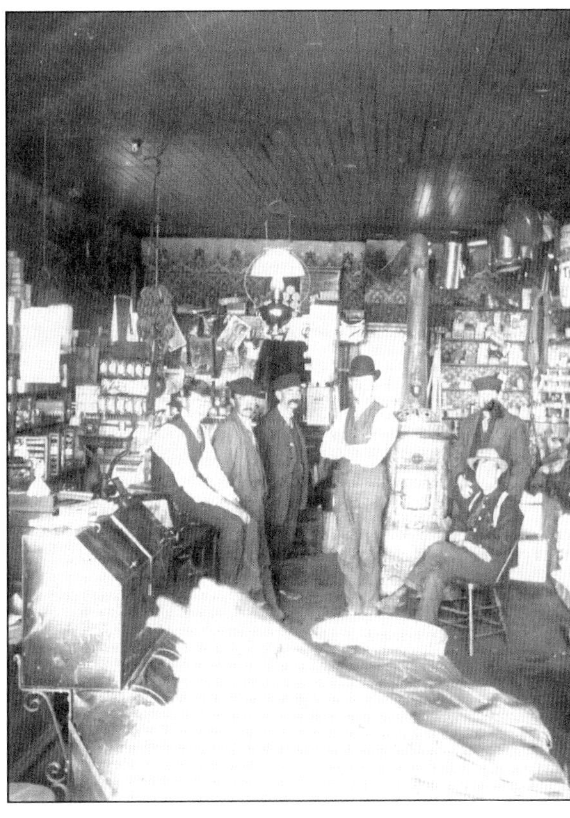

Hermas Johnson and Herman Peterson operated the Johnson Grocery store with Herman's brother Levene helping out. John L. Hanson built the building as a general country store in Otisco. Pictured in 1910 in the grocery, from left to right, are Herman Peterson; Hermas Johnson; C.W. Bigham, elevator manager; and Levene Peterson (seated). The fifth man is unknown.

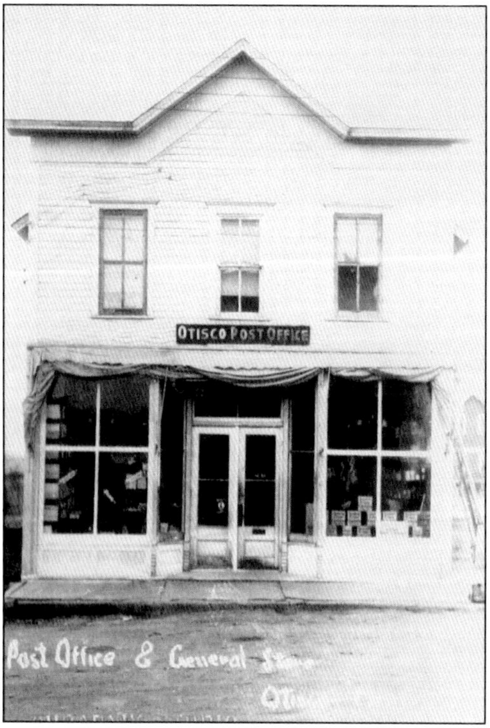

John Hanson erected the Otisco Post Office and General Store in 1895, the first building in Otisco. Before 1895 mail was handled at the Adam Bishman Log House in Otisco, located about one half-mile east of the M.&St.L. railroad tracks. Mailbags were thrown from the train at the Bishman house and collected by daughter Lizzie. Local residents collected mail there until 1895, when the new post office was built.

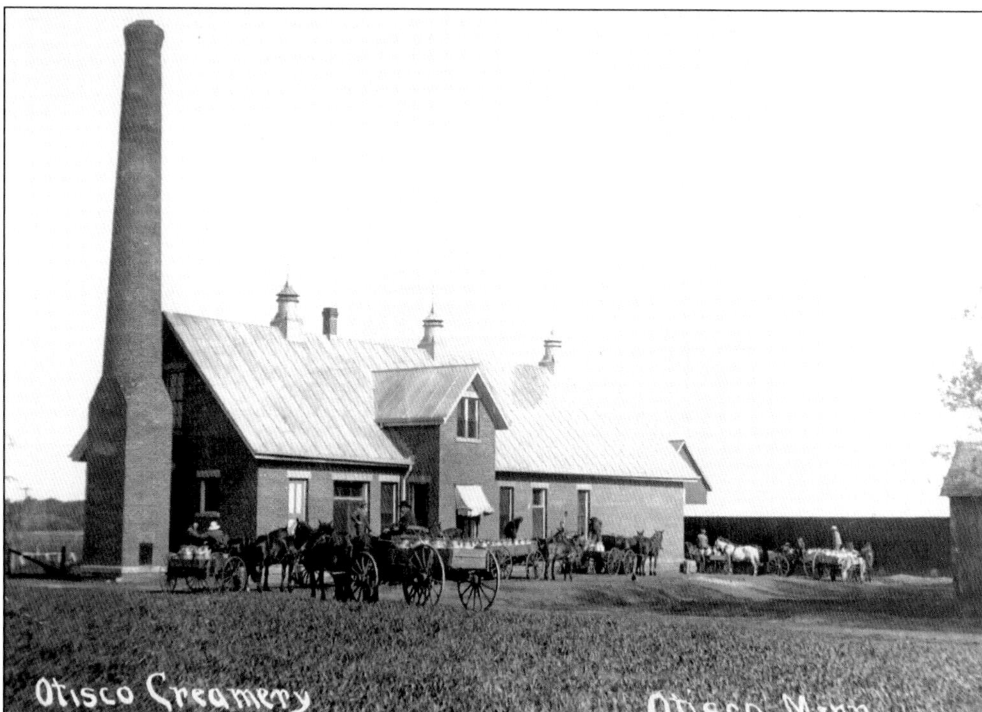

The teams of horses wait patiently beside their milk carts at the creamery in Otisco c. 1910. The building was erected in 1906. Early buttermakers in Otisco were Nels Christenson, H.C. Anderson, and A.J. Anderson.

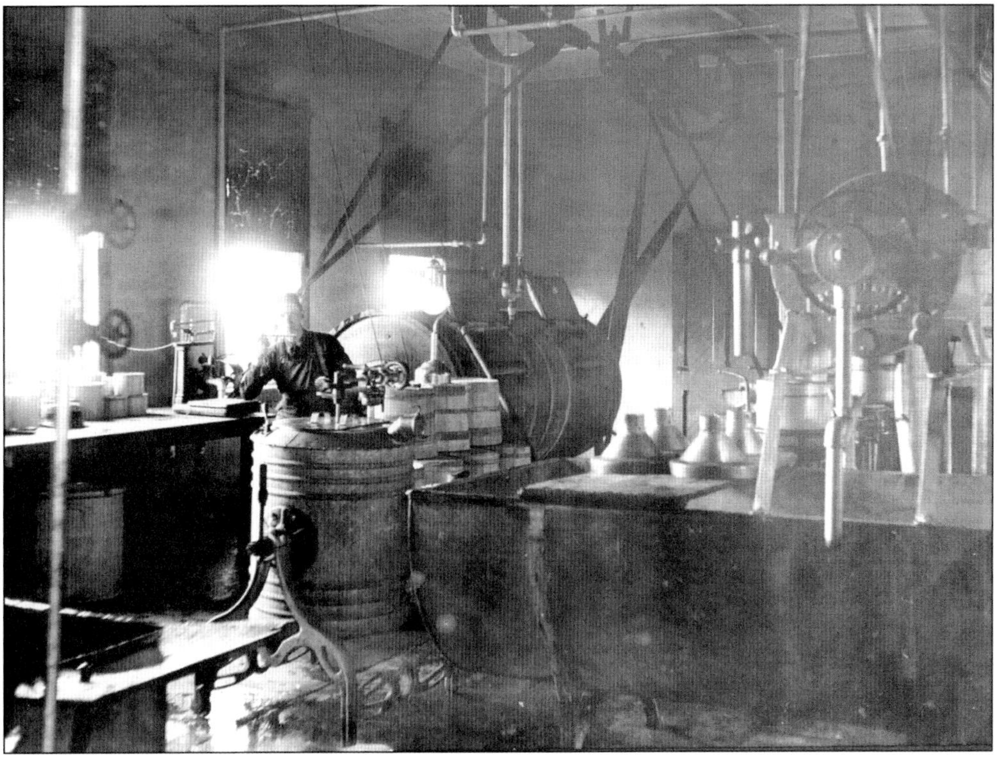

Award-winning buttermaker, A.J. Anderson, is pictured inside the Otisco Creamery.

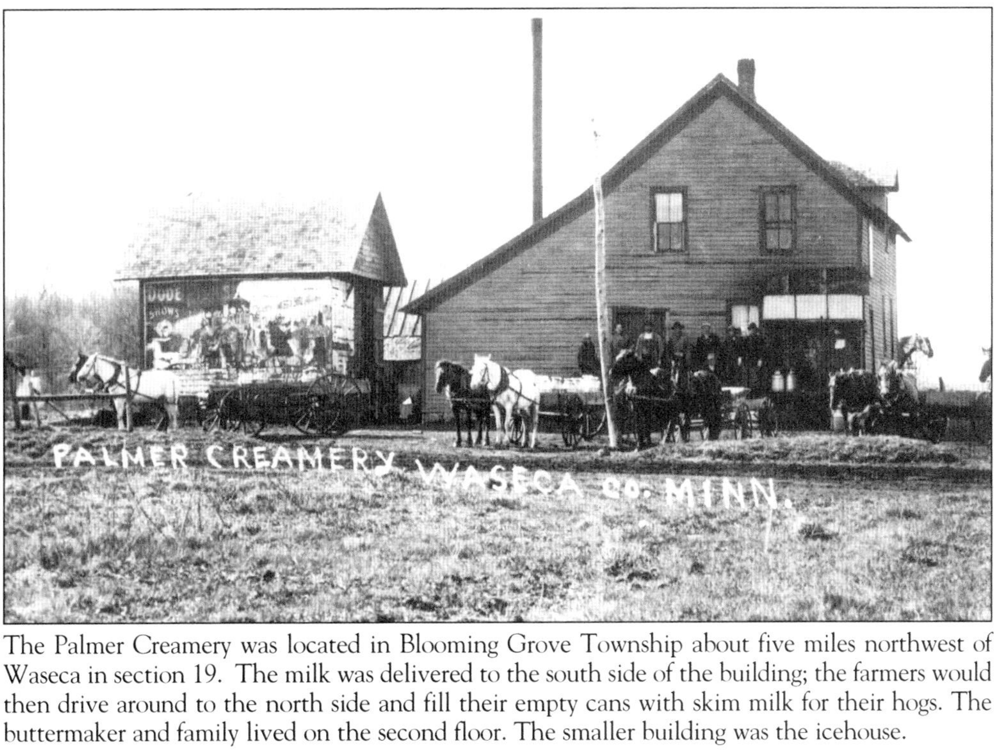

The Palmer Creamery was located in Blooming Grove Township about five miles northwest of Waseca in section 19. The milk was delivered to the south side of the building; the farmers would then drive around to the north side and fill their empty cans with skim milk for their hogs. The buttermaker and family lived on the second floor. The smaller building was the icehouse.

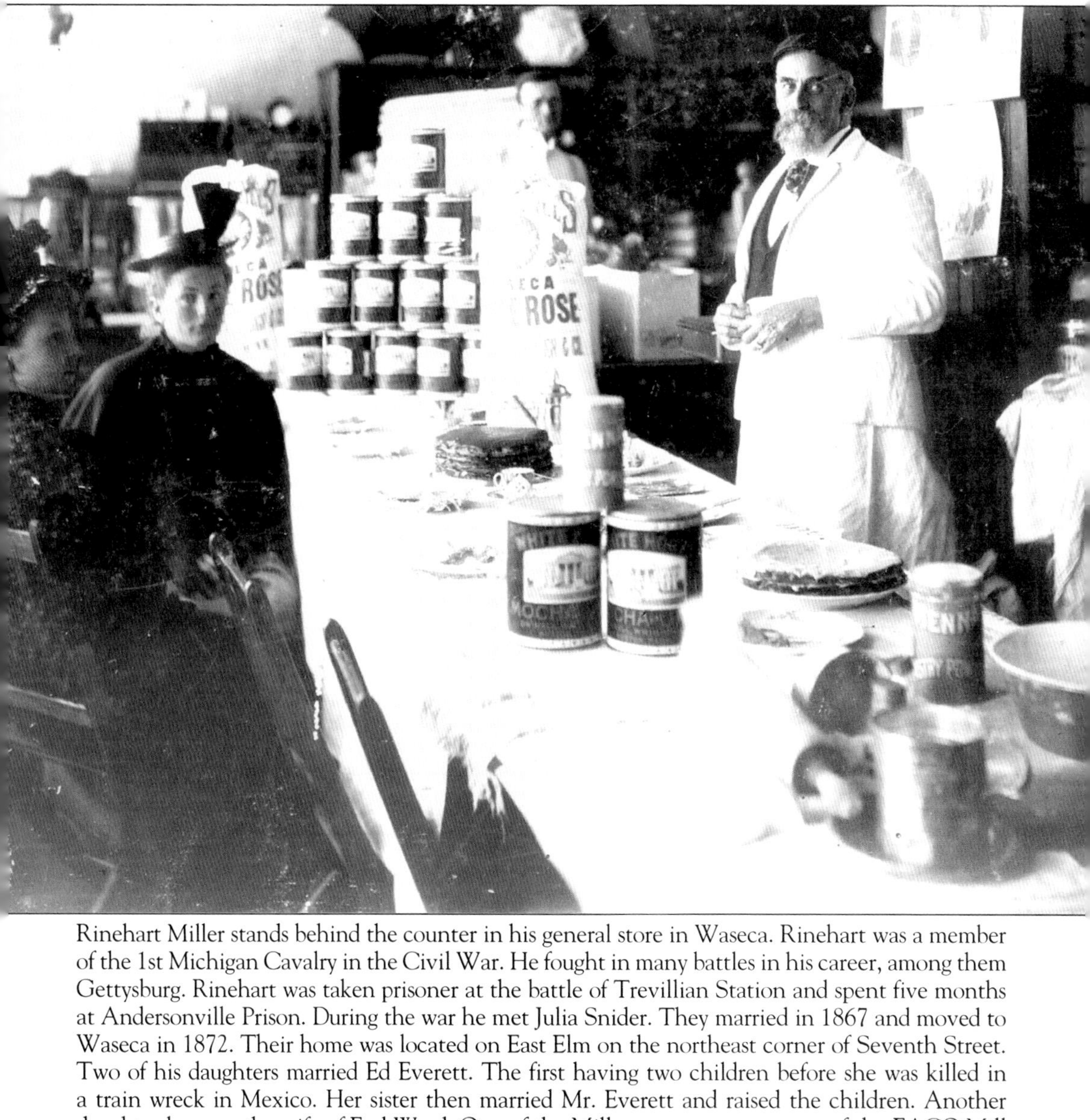

Rinehart Miller stands behind the counter in his general store in Waseca. Rinehart was a member of the 1st Michigan Cavalry in the Civil War. He fought in many battles in his career, among them Gettysburg. Rinehart was taken prisoner at the battle of Trevillian Station and spent five months at Andersonville Prison. During the war he met Julia Snider. They married in 1867 and moved to Waseca in 1872. Their home was located on East Elm on the northeast corner of Seventh Street. Two of his daughters married Ed Everett. The first having two children before she was killed in a train wreck in Mexico. Her sister then married Mr. Everett and raised the children. Another daughter became the wife of Earl Ward. One of the Miller sons was a manager of the EACO Mill in Lakeville and another married Daisy Aughenbaugh and worked for the milling company.

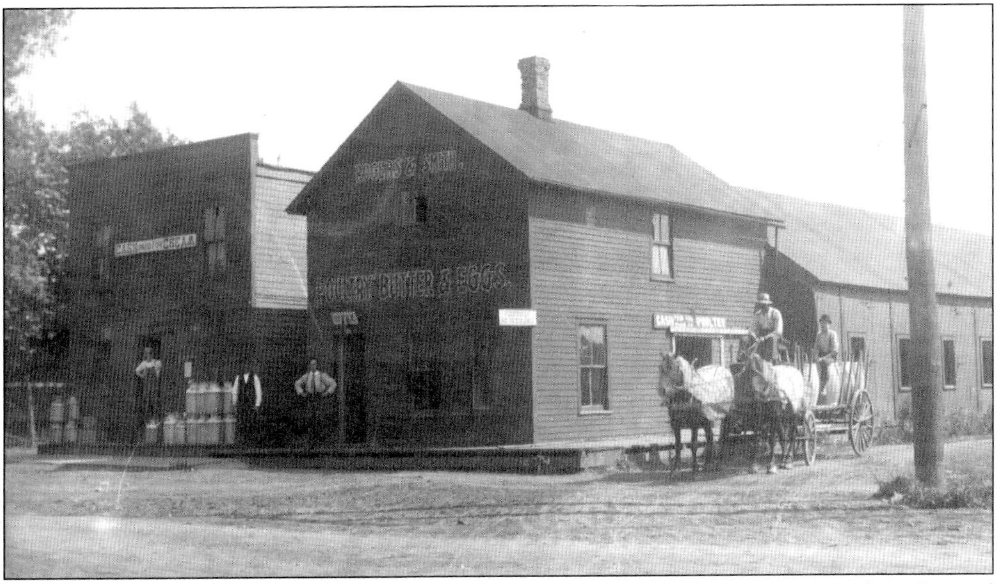

This Waseca business was thought to be located where Swift and Company was later located on West Elm. It is Rogers and Smith Poultry, Butter, and Eggs. They are advertising "cash paid for cream." The small sign jutting out on the front corner of the building announces there is "Positively No Retailing." The back sign says "Blaesers Dray Line."

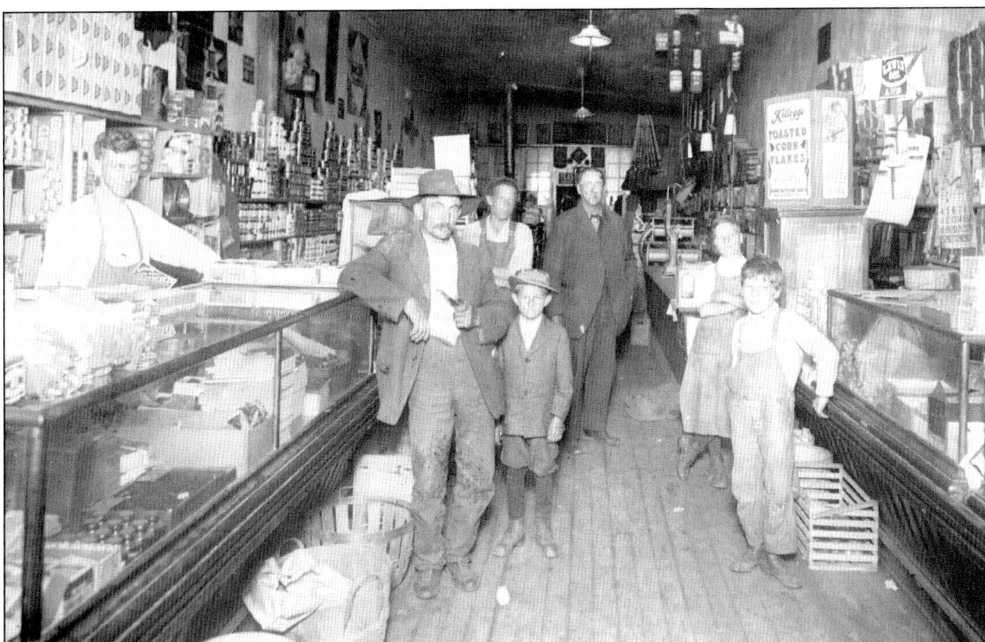

Pictured is William Herbst's grocery store in Waseca. At far left is Hjalmer Anderson, a clerk waiting on his customers.

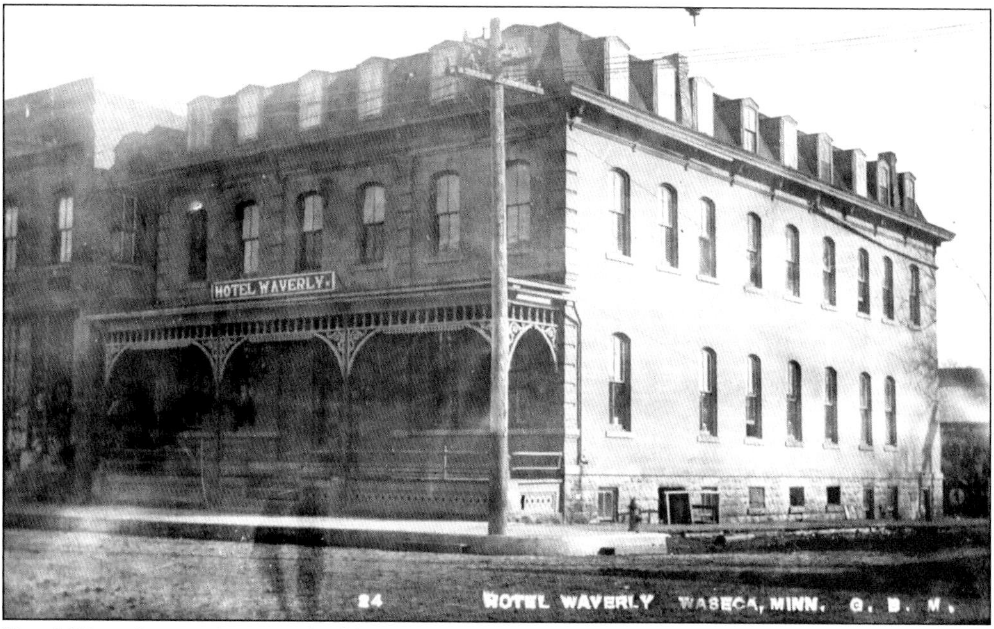

Hotel Waverly was photographed by G.B. Mellby. Patrick Moonan built the Sheridan House, as it was originally named, in 1882 and ran it until 1887. In 1897 J.A. Morse operated the hotel and the name changed to the Waverly Hotel. The last operator of the hotel was Mrs. (Ma) Emmons H. Smith. They ran the hotel from 1925 to 1928. It was then sold to F.J. Conway and converted into offices and apartments.

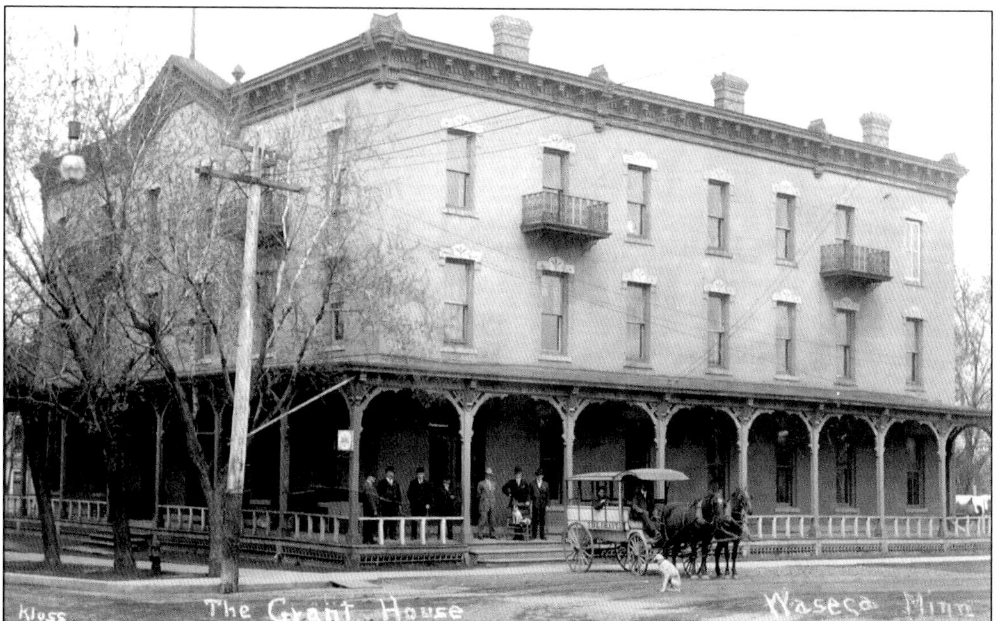

The Grant family was among the earliest settlers in southern Minnesota. The Grant House was built in the summer of 1882 for the sum of $15,000. The building was a showcase and a modern structure for its time. The hotel offered breakfast, dinner, supper, and lodging for the cost of $2 a day.

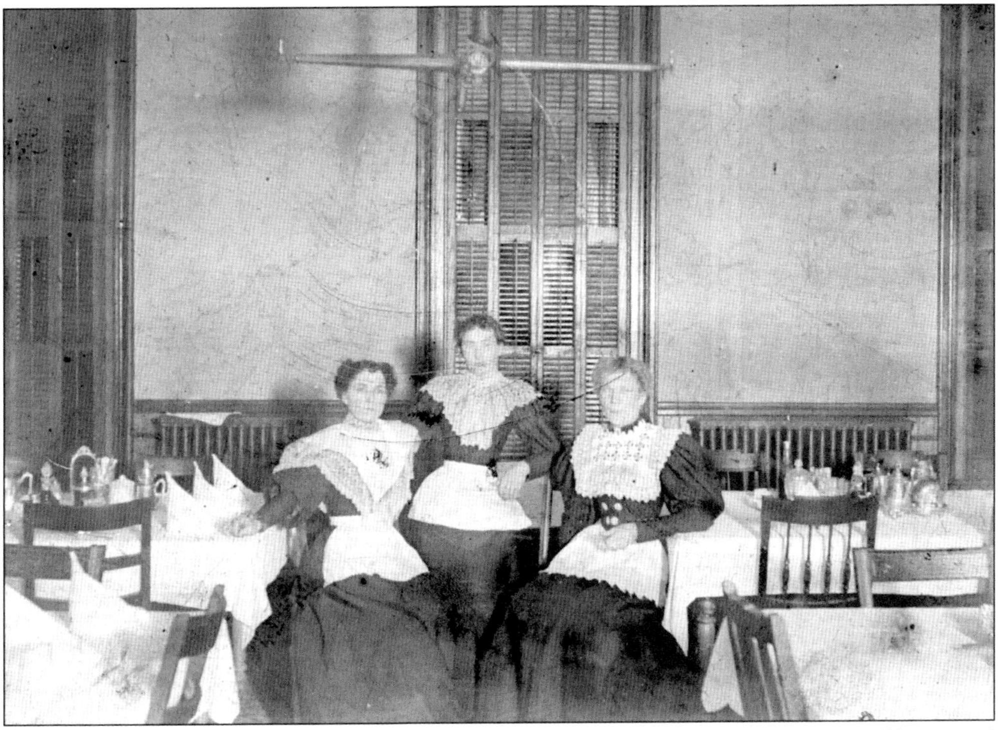

The Grant Hotel was furnished with quality hand-carved walnut furniture, marble-topped tables, commodes, and dressers. It was also equipped with indoor bathrooms for an extra charge of 25¢. The water for the toilets and baths was hand-pumped to a large tank on the roof. It had to be filled daily and it took quite a bit of time and strength to accomplish the task.

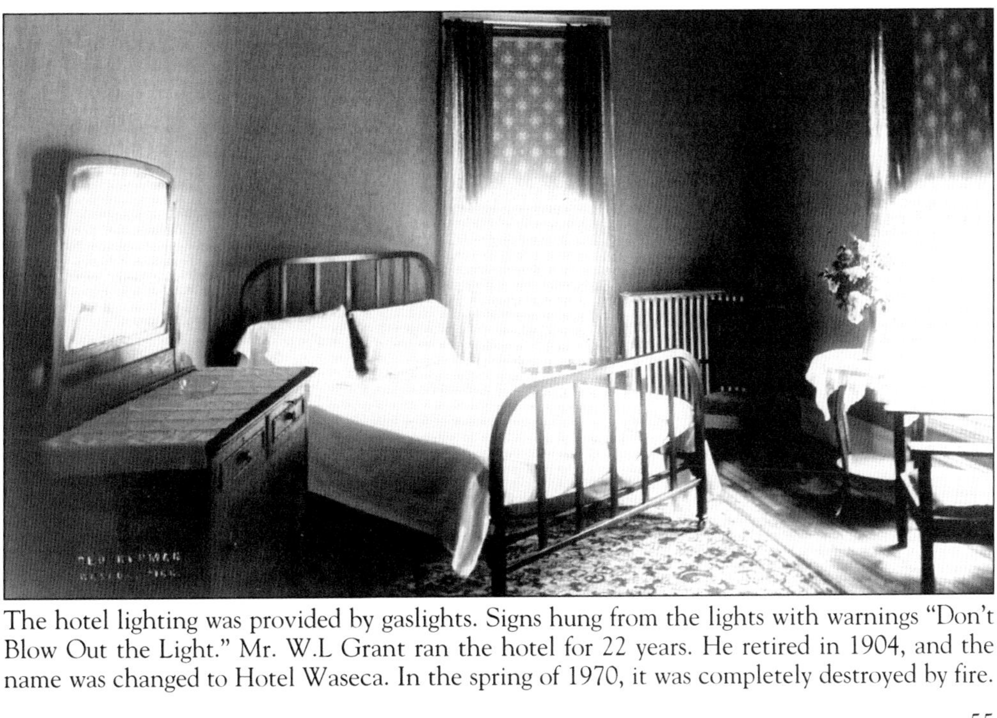

The hotel lighting was provided by gaslights. Signs hung from the lights with warnings "Don't Blow Out the Light." Mr. W.L Grant ran the hotel for 22 years. He retired in 1904, and the name was changed to Hotel Waseca. In the spring of 1970, it was completely destroyed by fire.

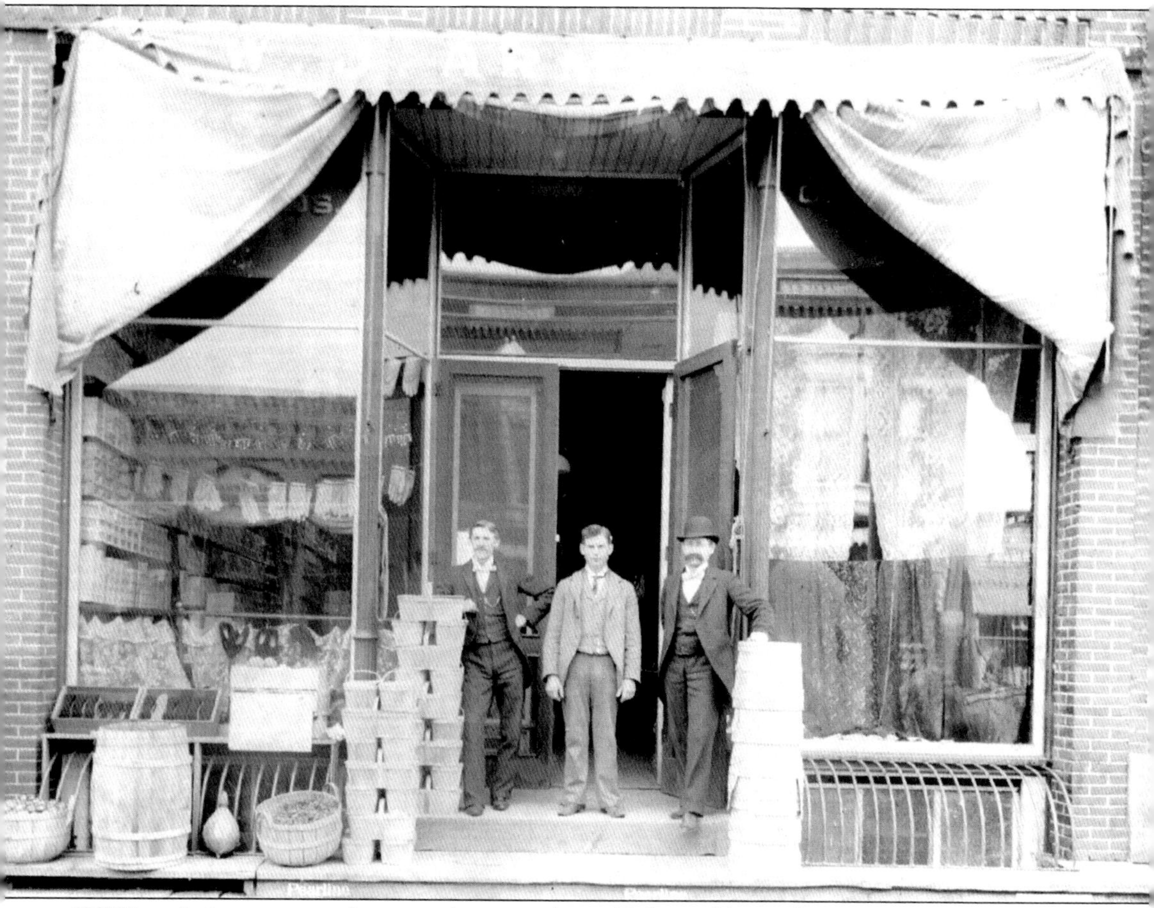

"William J. Armstrong is fitting up his new place, (Fishers old stand) in nobly style. Look for Armstrong in his new store on Saturday, May 13, 1891." W.J. Armstrong stands to the right in the doorway of his "nobly" store. In 1895 he added a second story to his building. He stated he had to go up or back toward the alley, so he built up.

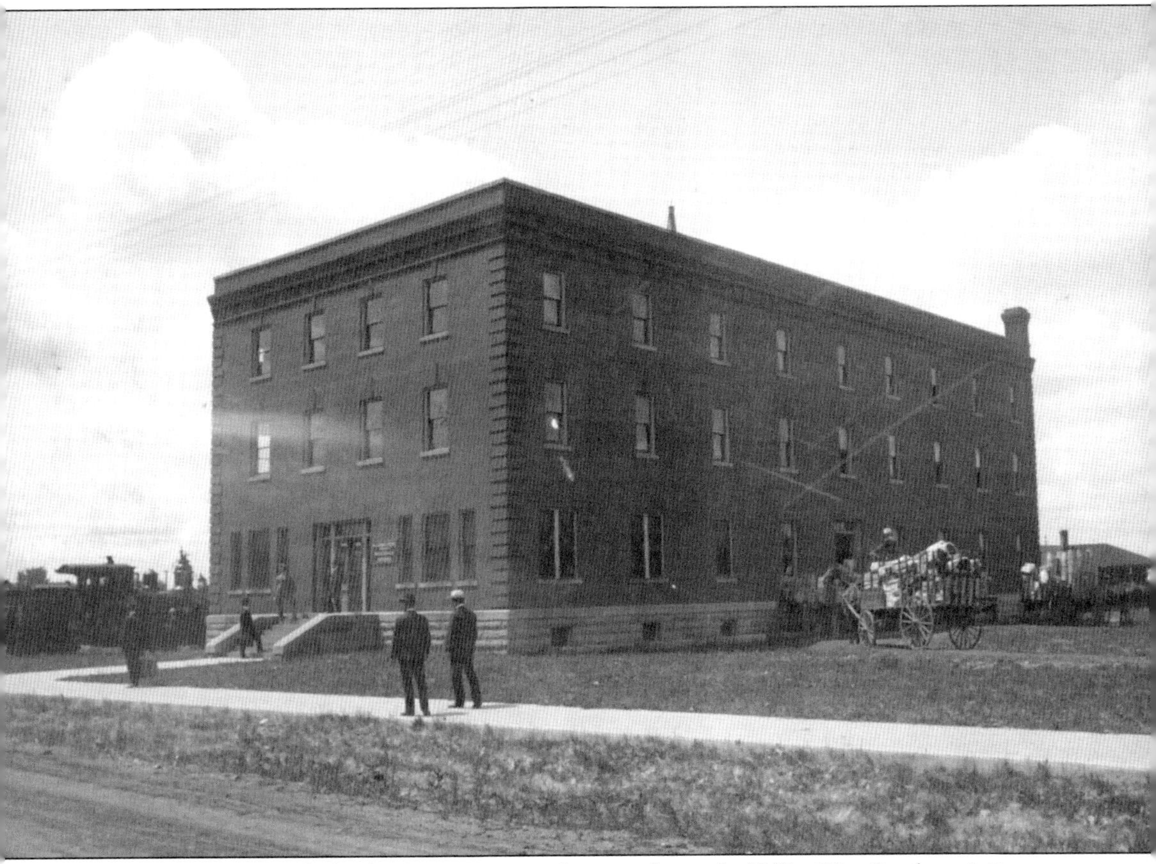

W.J. Armstrong's Wholesale Grocery is seen here in the early 1900s. The Southern Minnesota Grocery Co. once shipped completely by rail, sending goods to Minnesota , Wisconsin, North and South Dakota, and Iowa. W.J. Armstrong added other buildings off the back—this is where two bottling companies existed. The first one was owned by Armstrong and was called "Armstrong Bottling Company," the second was called "ABC" brand. W.J. and his son W.G. Armstrong started the later one. They continued operation until one year after W.J.'s death in 1948. Another division of the company was a cigar factory, operating in 1914. The company produced hand-rolled cigars using imported and domestic tobacco and trained local workers to master the craft. They also manufactured ice cream and packed and distributed tea with the brand name "Bluejay." This building is one of nine on the National Register of Historic Places in Waseca County.

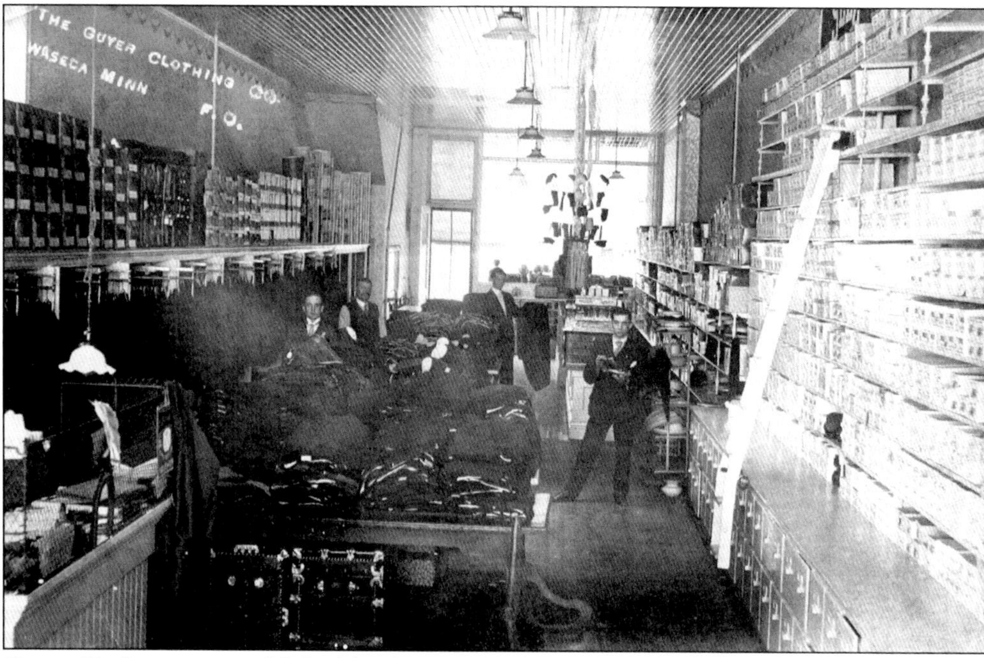

Guyer Clothing was established by Anton Guyer. Anton came to Waseca County in 1883 and first engaged in the saloon business. In 1886 he rented the brewery producing some 20–25 barrels of beer per week, sold in and around Waseca. After he left the liquor business he went into clothing and operated Guyer Clothing until 1926, when he turned over the business to his son and son-in-law.

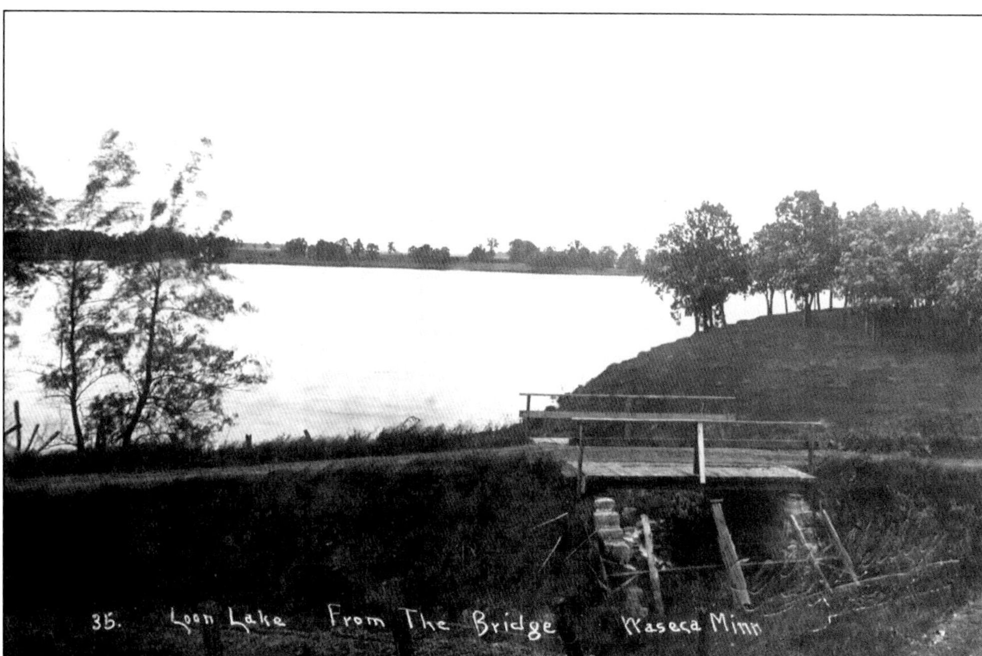

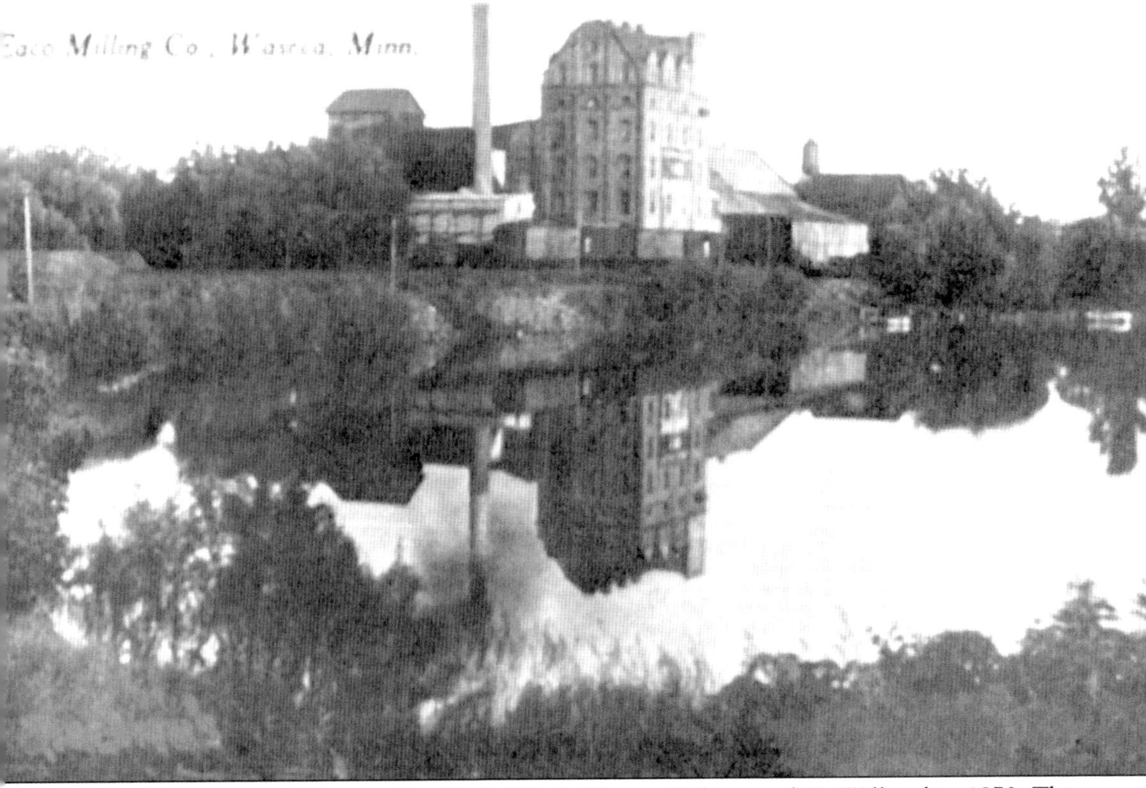

The flouring mill was erected by W.G. Ward, Thomas White, and H. Willyard in 1870. This firm continued in business but a short time, when Mr. Willyard disposed of his interest to his partners. About the year 1872, Mr. Ward purchased the interest of the remaining member of the firm, and for about three years operated it alone. In 1874 William Everett purchased a half interest therein, forming the firm of Ward & Everett. Two years later Mr. Everett rented the interest of his partner for ten years. Associating with himself J.W. Aughenbaugh, the firm name was changed to Everett & Aughenbaugh. Everett and Aughenbaugh re-leased the interest of Mr. Ward in 1886. It is not exactly known when Everett & Aughenbaugh bought out W.G. Ward. Apparently W.G. Ward had sold his share of the business to the partnership in 1888 when William Everett's son Edward was taken into the partnership and the name was changed to EACO.

Opposite: Pictured is the bridge on the east side of Loon Lake. The bridge spanned the outlet of the lake that formed the slough connecting Loon and Clear Lakes. The recorded history of Loon Lake is vague. Most of what we know has been handed down through stories and recollections from our early citizens told generations ago. Loon Lake was first used commercially by the railroad and milling industries in the 1800s. In 1867 the east-west tracks were laid and Waseca grew around them. The engineers drew water for their steam-powered engines from the south shore of Loon Lake. Mills were strategically built on the lake to utilize the fresh water. Warm water was then discharged back into the lake, keeping it from freezing over the winter months. The bridge was filled in during the summer of 1901.

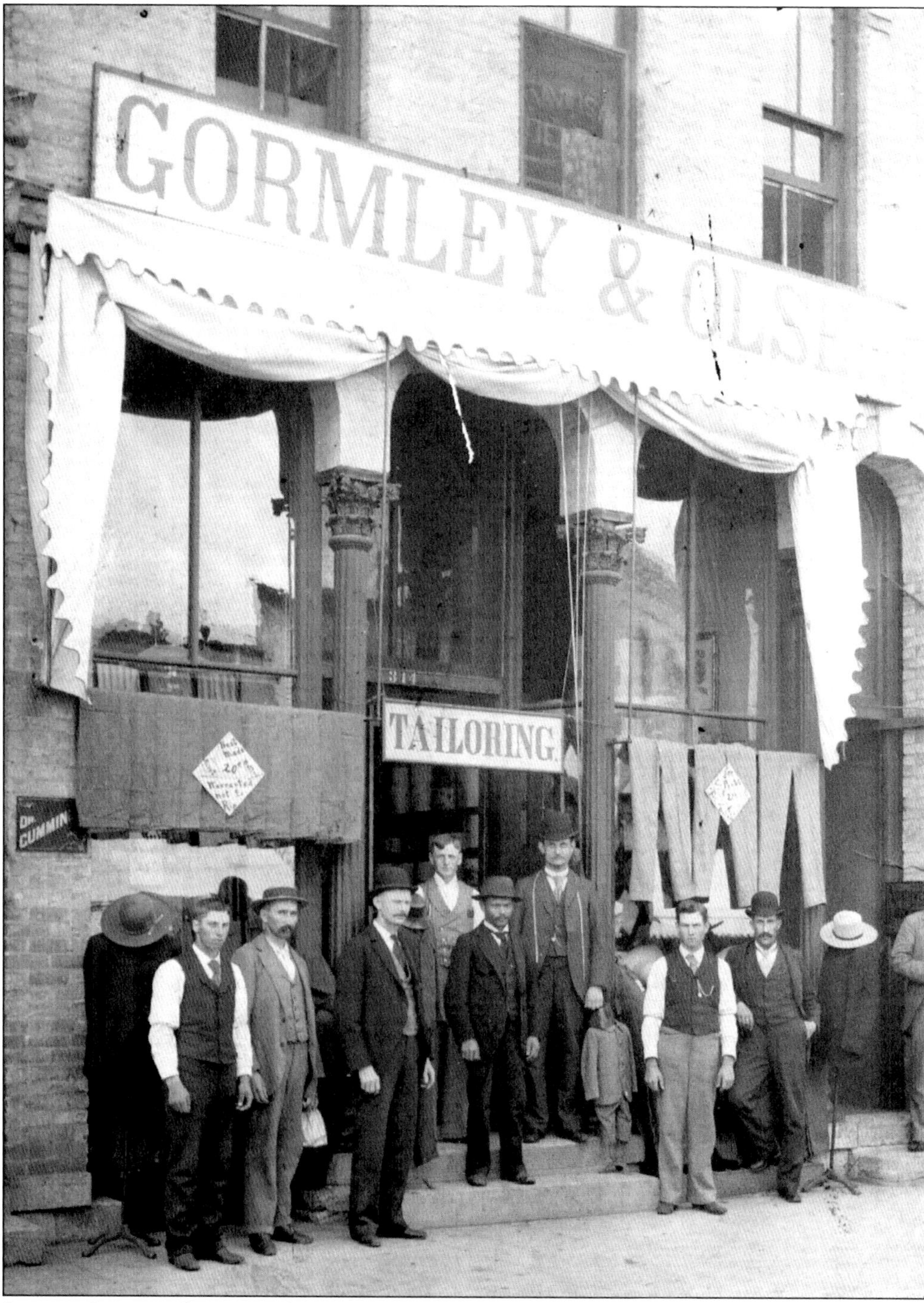

It is not known when Gormley & Olsen Tailoring was in business. Upstairs, Dr. Cummings practiced medicine and Dr. Davidson practiced dentistry. This photograph dates to the early 1890s.

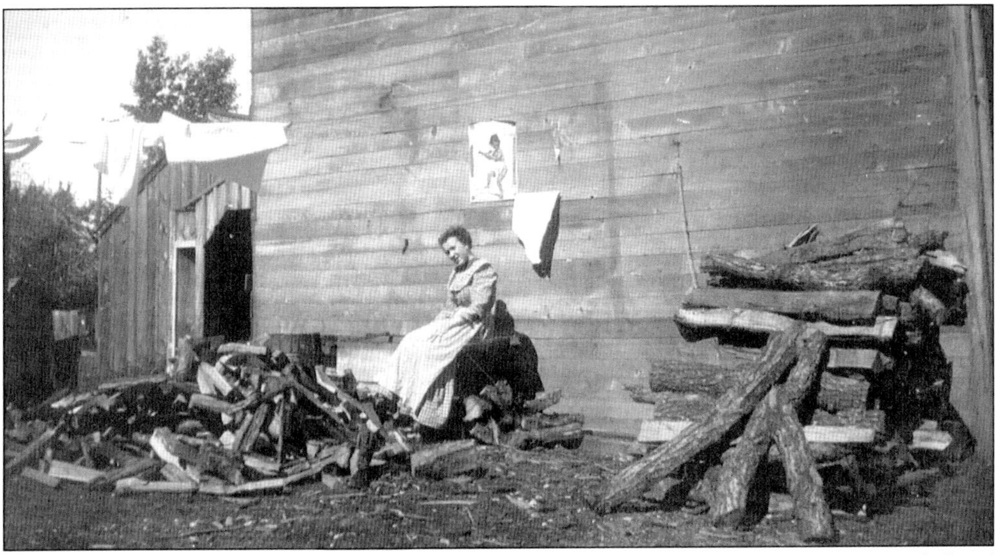

A woman sits beside a woodpile in back of the Ryan Hotel in 1897. She would be sitting behind the new and improved Ryan Hotel. It was reported in the July 25, 1894 *Waseca Radical* that "the Ryan Hotel was badly scorched Sunday night, the kitchen destroyed and the furniture consumed or badly damaged. The loss falls principally on Paul Billiard who owned the building and most of the furniture, while loss is fully covered by insurance $1,950.00 on the building and contents. Mr. Ryan the proprietor was lucky in having just completed the fitting up of the building on Elm Street which building he at once proceeded to occupy."

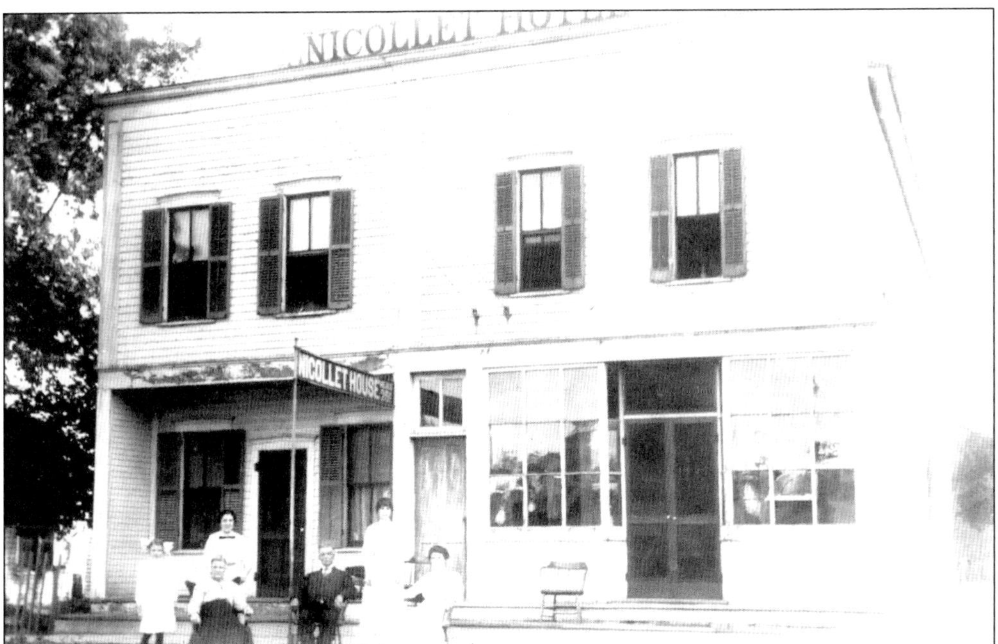

The Nicollet Hotel was also known as the Nora's House, Miller's House, and the Billiard Hotel. It was located at 217 West Elm Avenue in Waseca. In front of the hotel, from left to right, are Pearl Billiard (Boje), Mary (Radloff) Billiard, Lulu Billiard (Miller), Paul Billiard, Esther Billiard (Vogt), and Adeline Billiard (Rogers), c. 1909.

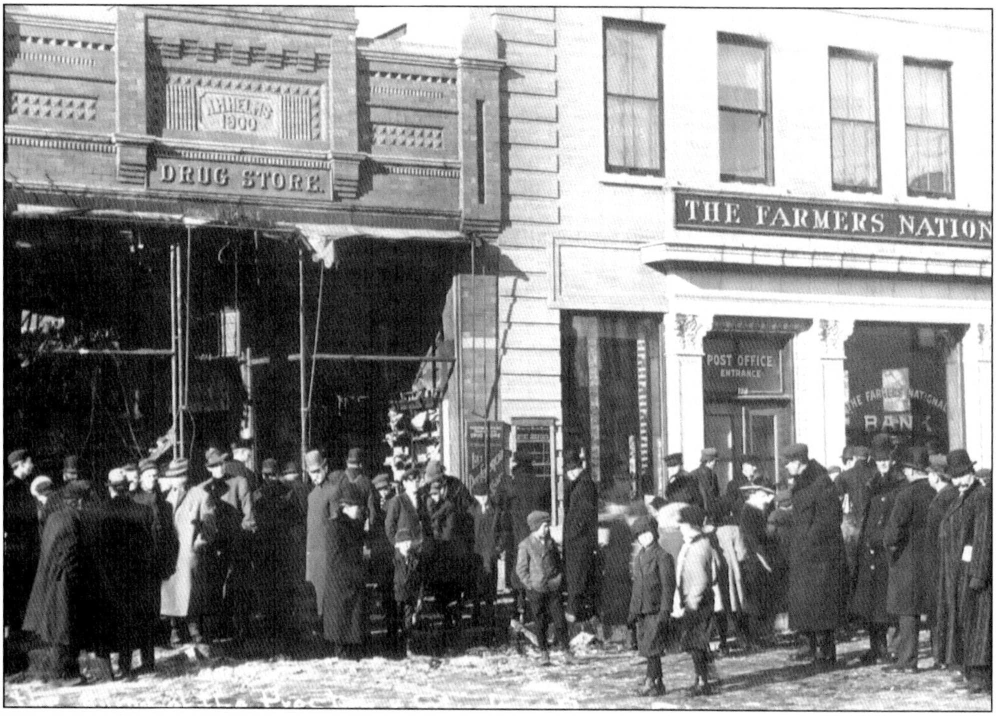

The crowd is gathered to look at the Preston & Stucky Drug Store after its fire on December 9, 1908. This business started under the name of Middaugh and Tarbell Drug. H.H. Suddeth and S.H. Preston purchased it in 1878. In 1899 Anton Stucky bought into the business and it was named Preston and Stucky Drug. In 1915 Preston died and the store was re-named Stucky's Drug. A branch was started in Waterville by Anton Stucky's son in 1926, and is presently running under the name Berg Pharmacy and Drug.

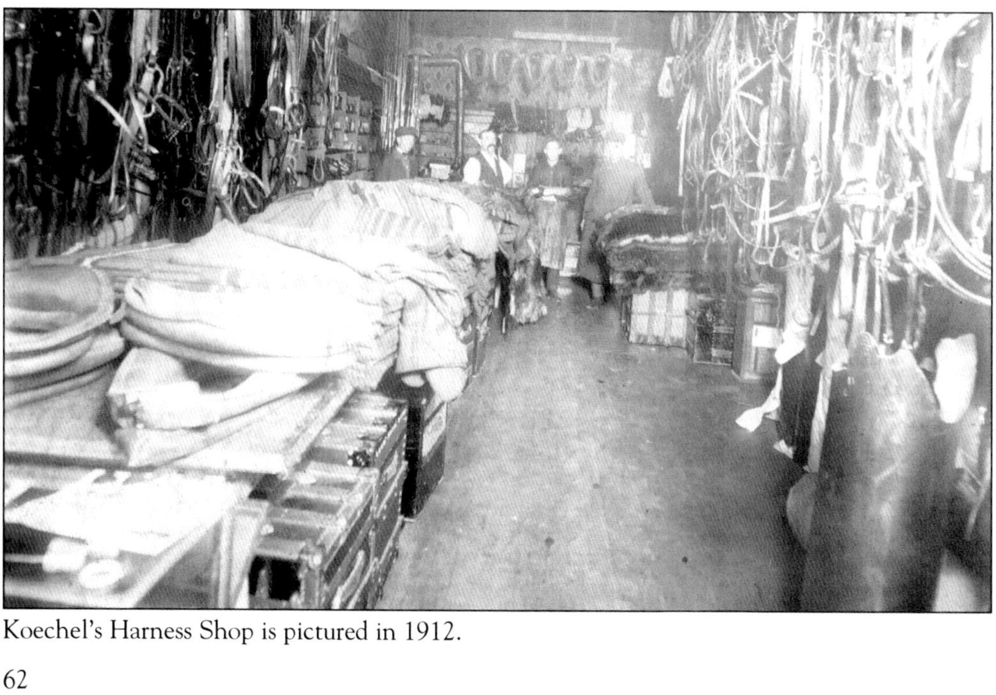

Koechel's Harness Shop is pictured in 1912.

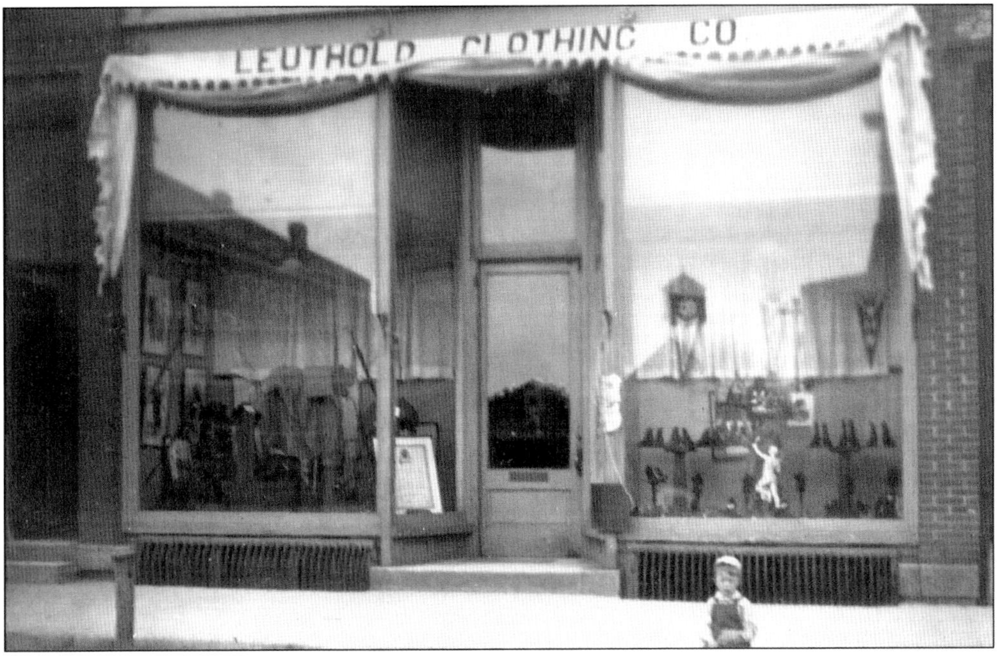

The Leuthold Clothing Company in 1910, was one of fifteen stores in the state of Minnesota owned and operated by the five Leuthold brothers.

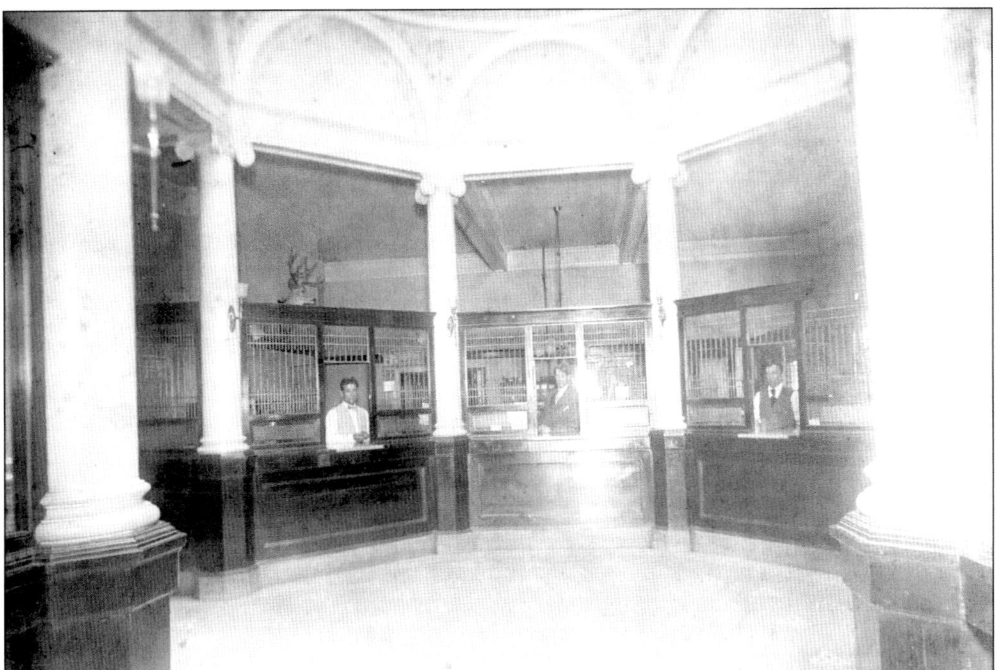

The interior of the First National Bank is shown in 1908. It was located on State Street across from the present First National Bank.

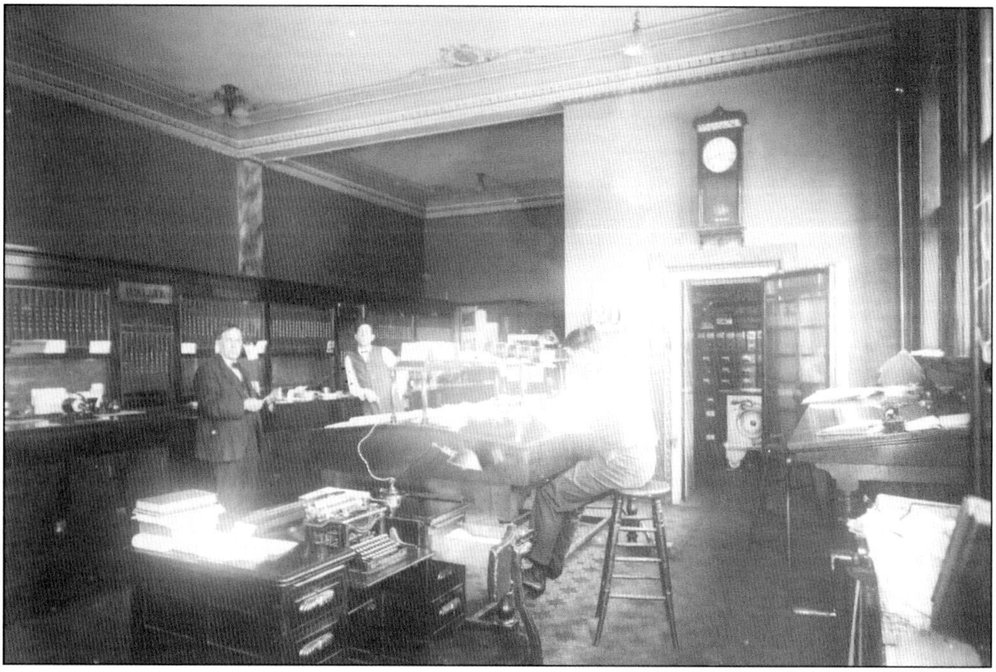

Pictured is Farmers National Bank in 1913. From left to right are Charles H. Bailer, Cleveland Turnacliff, and Emil J. Priebe. This bank is now operating as the Roundbank.

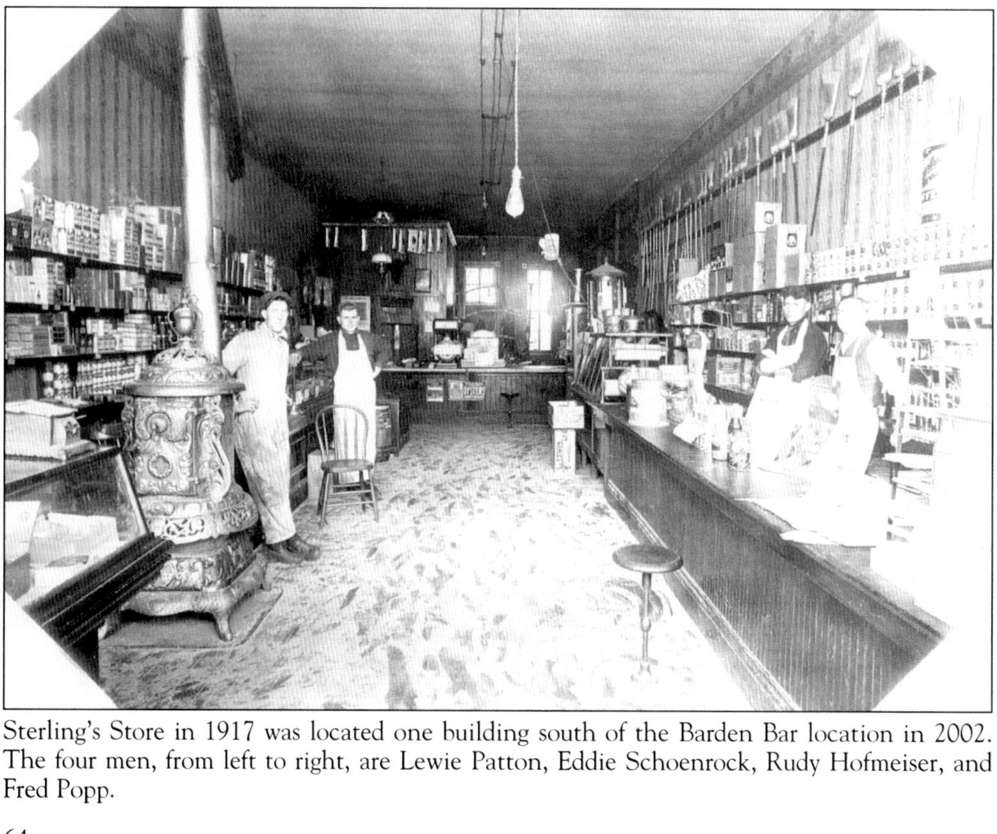

Sterling's Store in 1917 was located one building south of the Barden Bar location in 2002. The four men, from left to right, are Lewie Patton, Eddie Schoenrock, Rudy Hofmeiser, and Fred Popp.

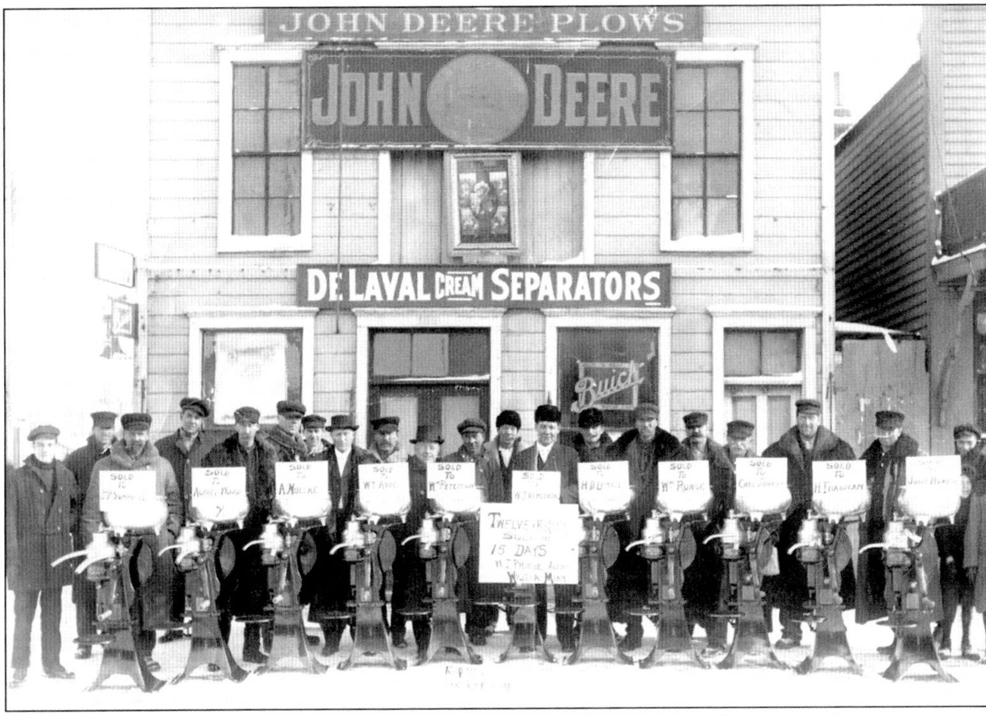

Twelve DeLaval separators were sold in fifteen days by W.J. Priebe, agent. The customers, from left to right, are J.P. Sommers, Alfred Wood, A. Noeske, Wm. Abbe, Wm. Peterson, W.J. Armstrong, H.D. Lewer, Wm. Runge, Charles Johnson, H. Frahman, and John Buker. This store was located where the First National Bank parking lot is located today.

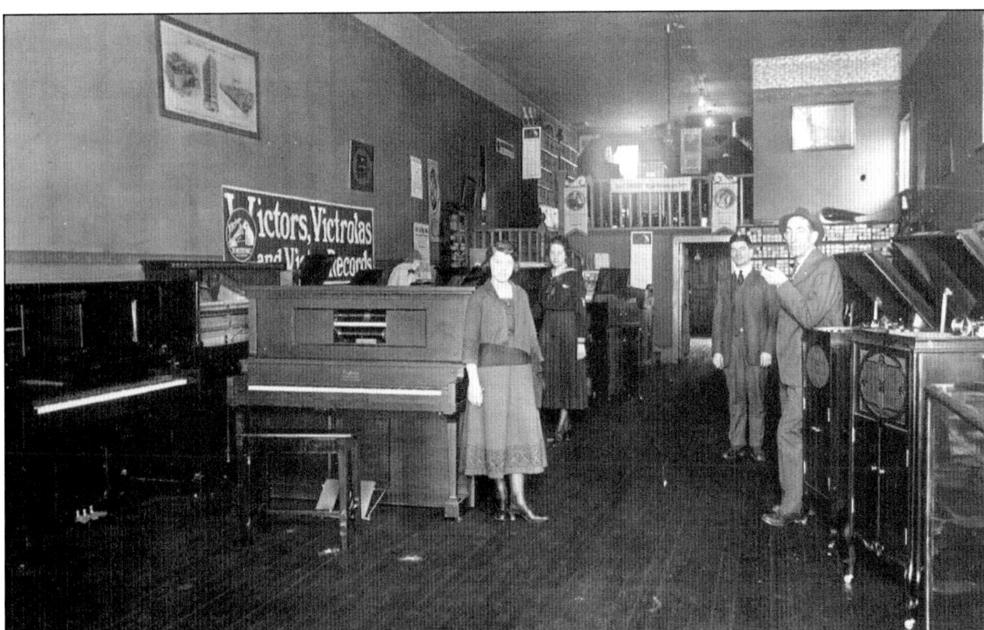

Pictured is the D.E. Perrin Music Store in approximately 1920. This store is located where the present Waseca Music continues to operate.

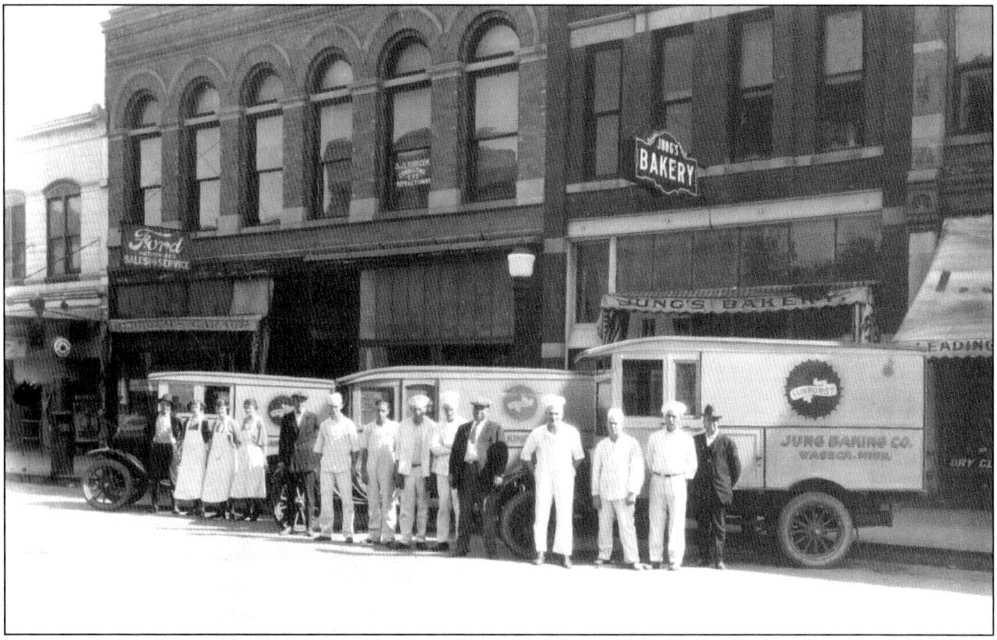

Jung Bakery began in 1913 by leasing the Koerbitz Bakery Building.

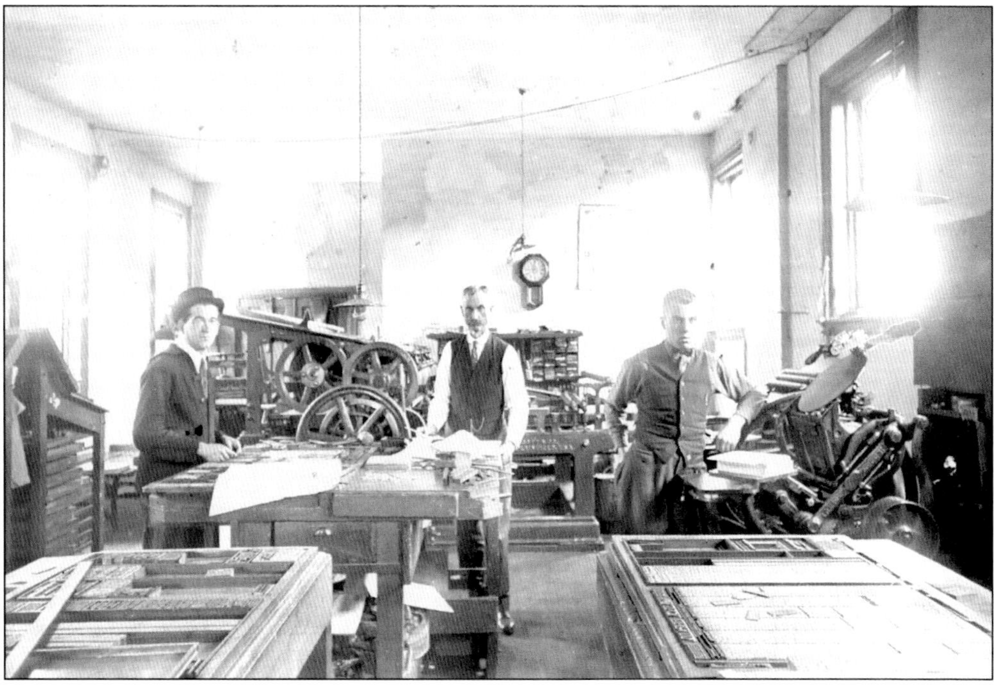

John P. Coughlin purchased the *Waseca Herald* in the fall of 1911 from Child Publishing Company for $3,500. Frank Goodspeed was the president of Child Publishing at the time of the sale. John's son D.M. Coughlin joined his father in the business in June of 1923. Mr. Coughlin worked everyday for 34 years until his death in 1945. The *Herald* combined with the *Journal* on October 1, 1948, when Donald C. Brown purchased it. Lem Reeves, John P. Coughlin, and A.J. Fullerton are shown here.

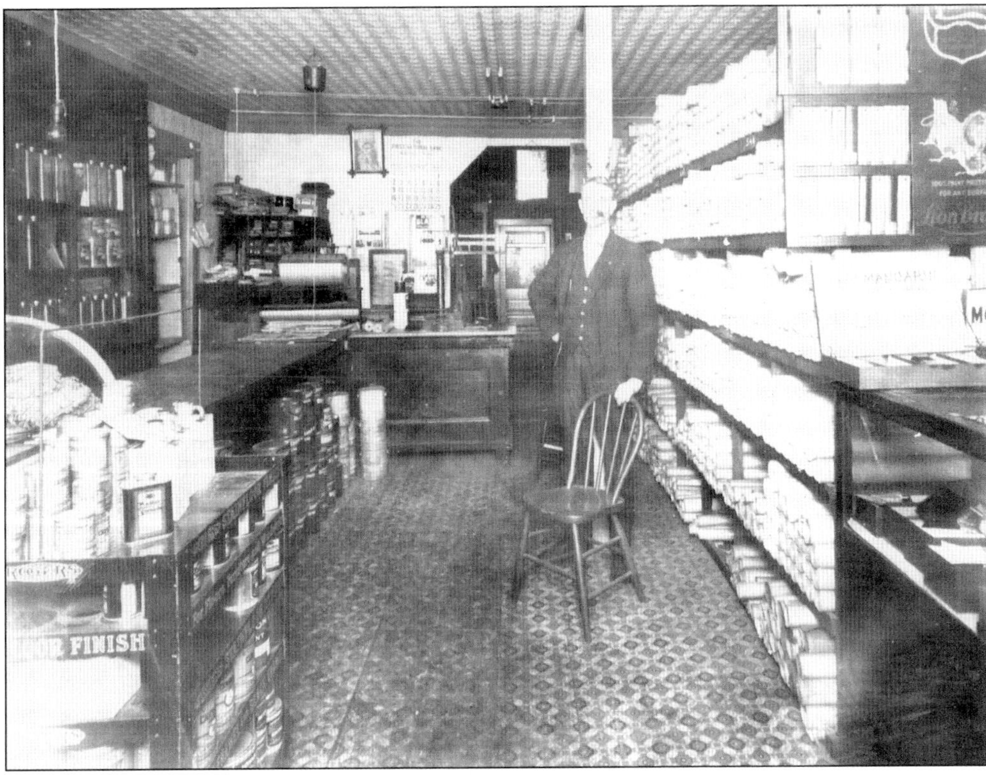

Philip Gehring in 1927 stands in Gehring and Son Paint store located at 204 South State.

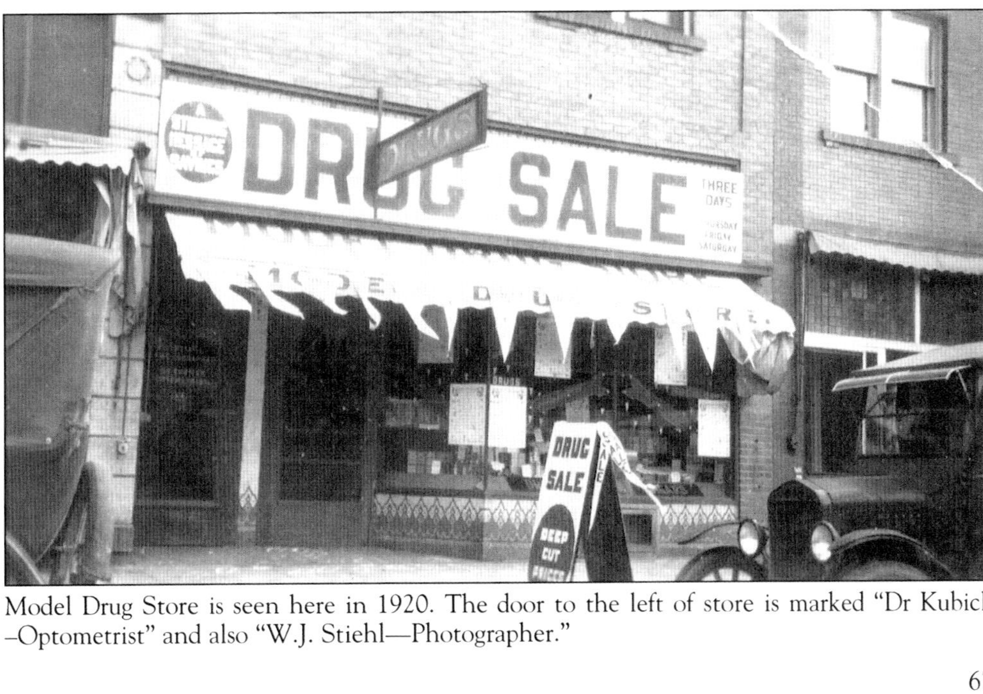

Model Drug Store is seen here in 1920. The door to the left of store is marked "Dr Kubick –Optometrist" and also "W.J. Stiehl—Photographer."

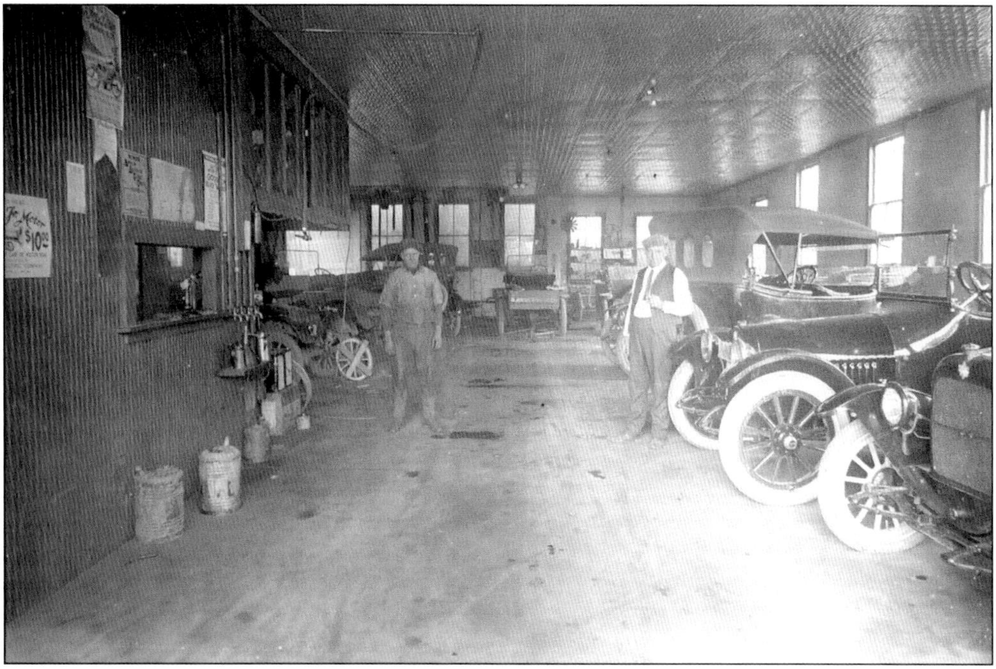

William J. Priebe's garage is seen here on Second Avenue in Waseca. Priebe sold Buicks, Chevrolets, and Maxwells.

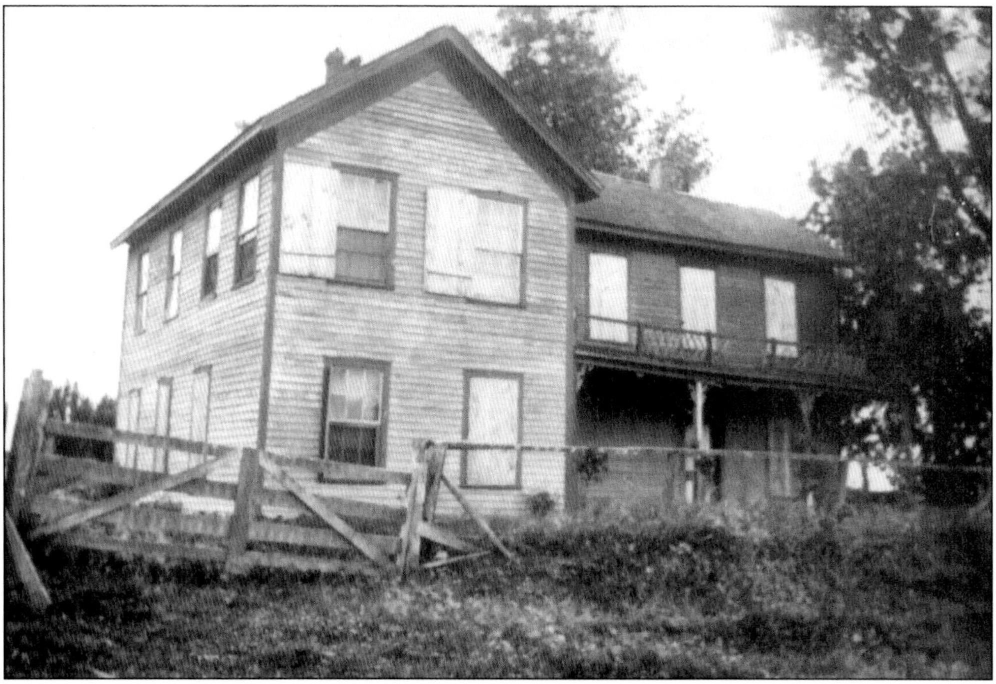

Wilton Hotel, built by A.J. Woodbury and Sons, was the first in the county. It was built during the winter of 1856–57. A.J. and his sons George H. and Henry C. assisted in running the hotel until about 1882. Other known hotels in Wilton were the Globe, built and run by E.A. Rice, the Eureka, built by B. Arnold in 1861, and the Winship Hotel, built in 1861.

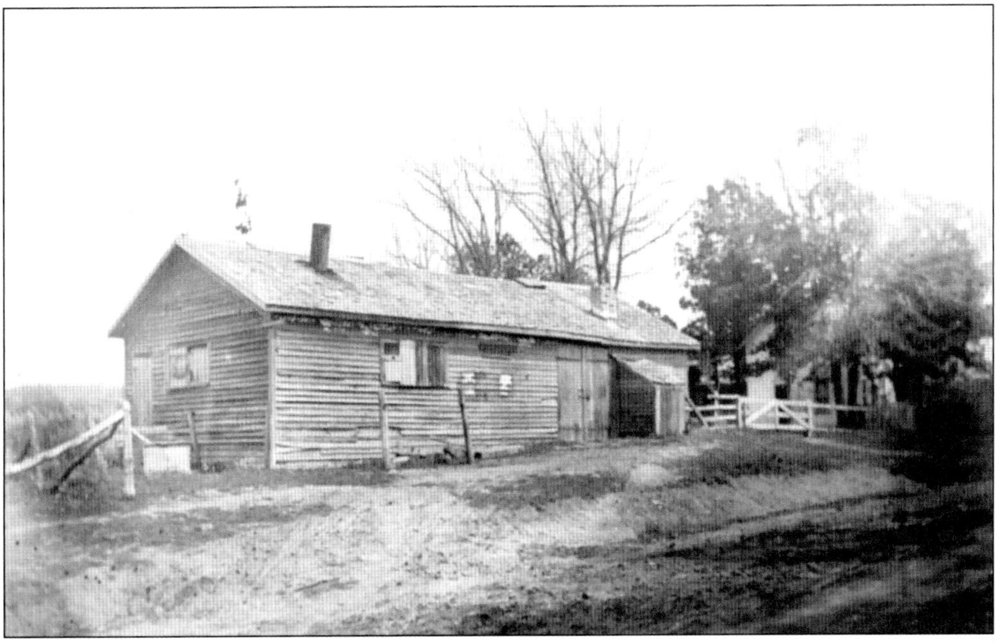

The first blacksmith shop in Waseca County was built in Wilton in 1856 by H.P. Norton of Yates County, New York. H.P. worked across the country at his trade, finally locating in Wilton. He and a younger brother ran the blacksmith shop until 1859, when he was elected clerk of the district court.

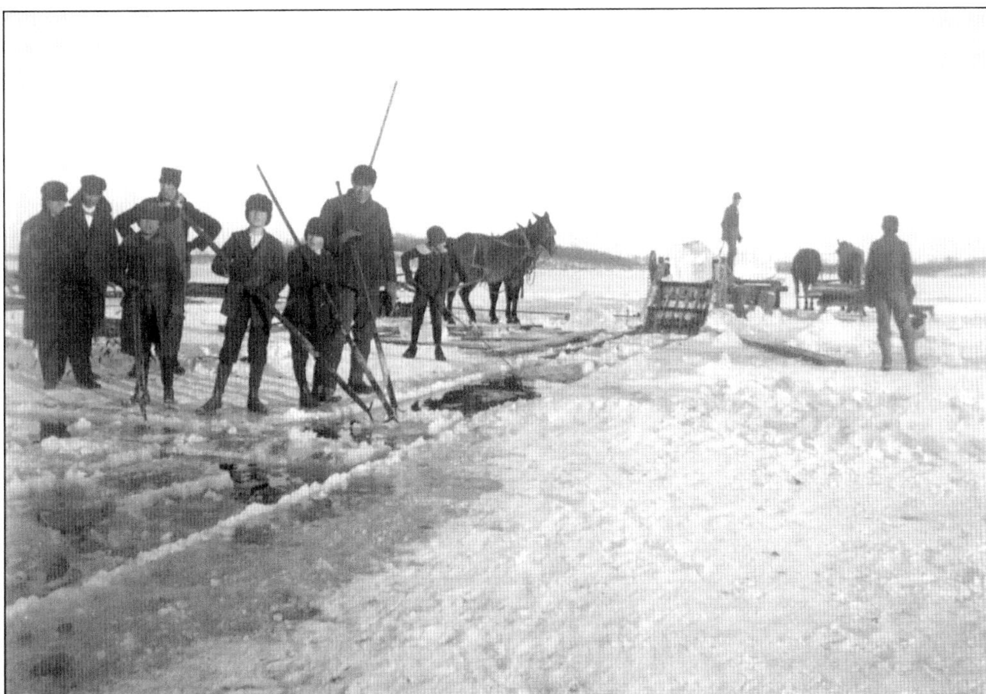

W.C. Johnston and Malecha Sheehan started the ice business in Waseca in 1894. It was located on the southeast shore of Clear Lake on what is now the Kiesler property.

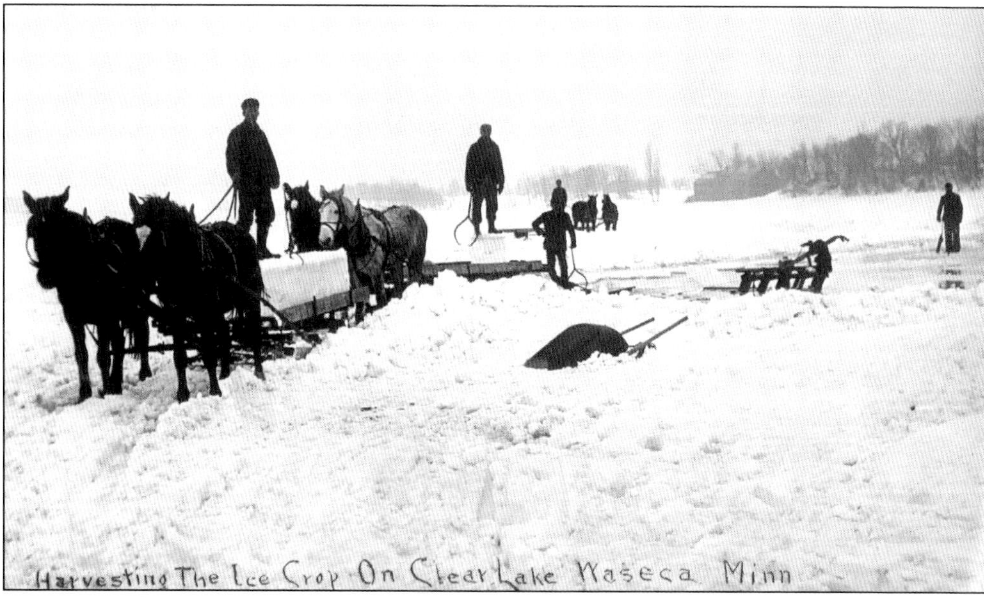

Ice was cut from Clear Lake in cakes weighing from 400 to 600 pounds depending on the thickness. Cakes were transported from the lake to the icehouse for storage by horses and large bobsleds. Fifty teams and sleds were often involved in the hauling operation. Horses gave way to trucks in the early 1930s.

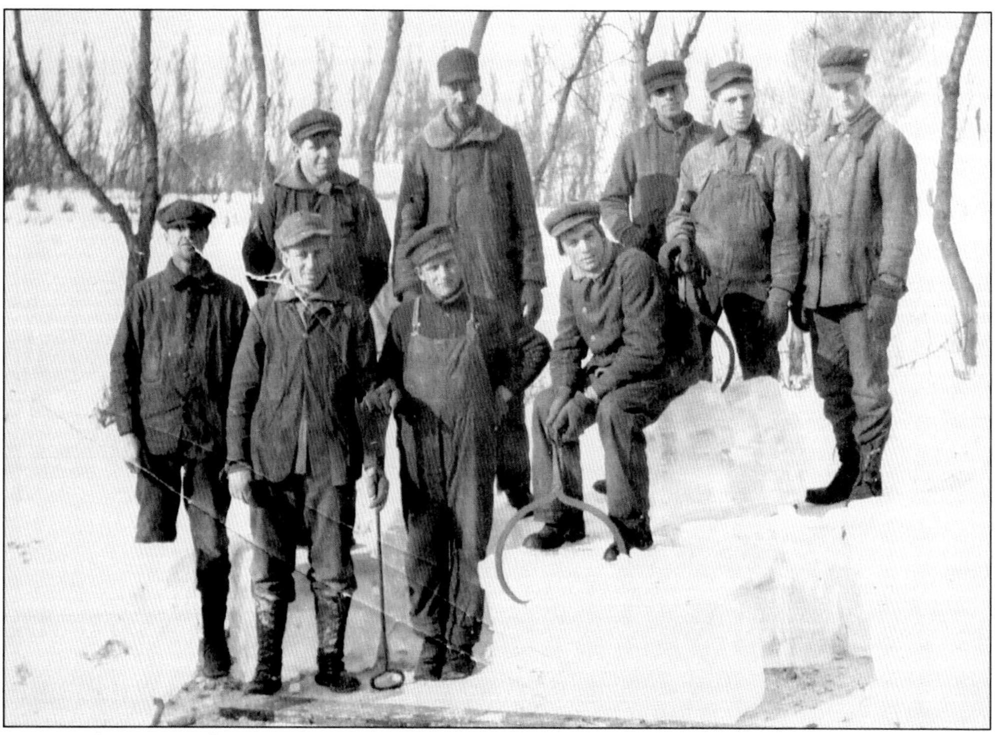

In 1935 the W.C. Johnston Ice Company of Waseca was given the contract to furnish 5800 tons of ice for the C&N.W. Railroad Company. They also needed 1,500 tons for their icehouse. This would take some 15 men working about 3 weeks or more.

Five

RESIDENCES

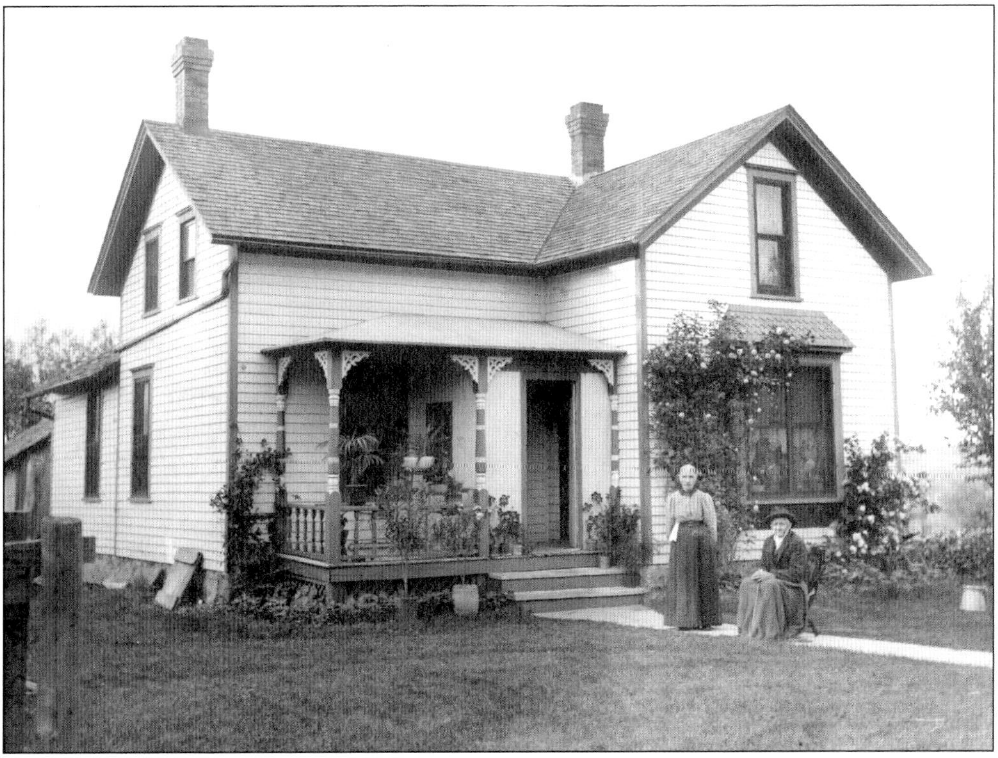

Seen here is the Martin and Wilhemina (Panzram) Grundeman Helwig home in Janesville. Wilhemina was the stepmother of Herman Panzram. Pictured in front are Wilhemina (standing) and Martin (sitting in the chair). He died in February of 1910, and she in August of 1911. They lived in Peddlers Grove for many years and spent their last years in this house.

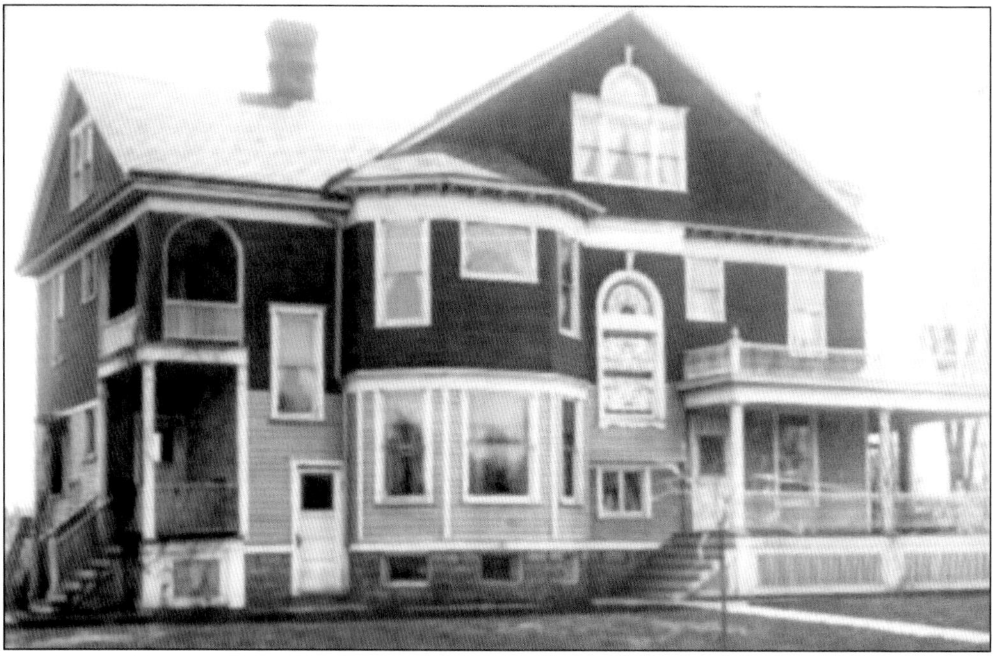

Dr. Martin J. Taylor and his wife, Stella (Carpenter) Taylor, contracted with Theodore Hoverson of Medo to build this Queen Anne-style three-story house in Janesville in 1903. William Strunk laid the foundation and did the cement work. Charles Schafer installed the boiler and the plumbing. It has been restored and still stands on the corner of Second and North Mott Streets.

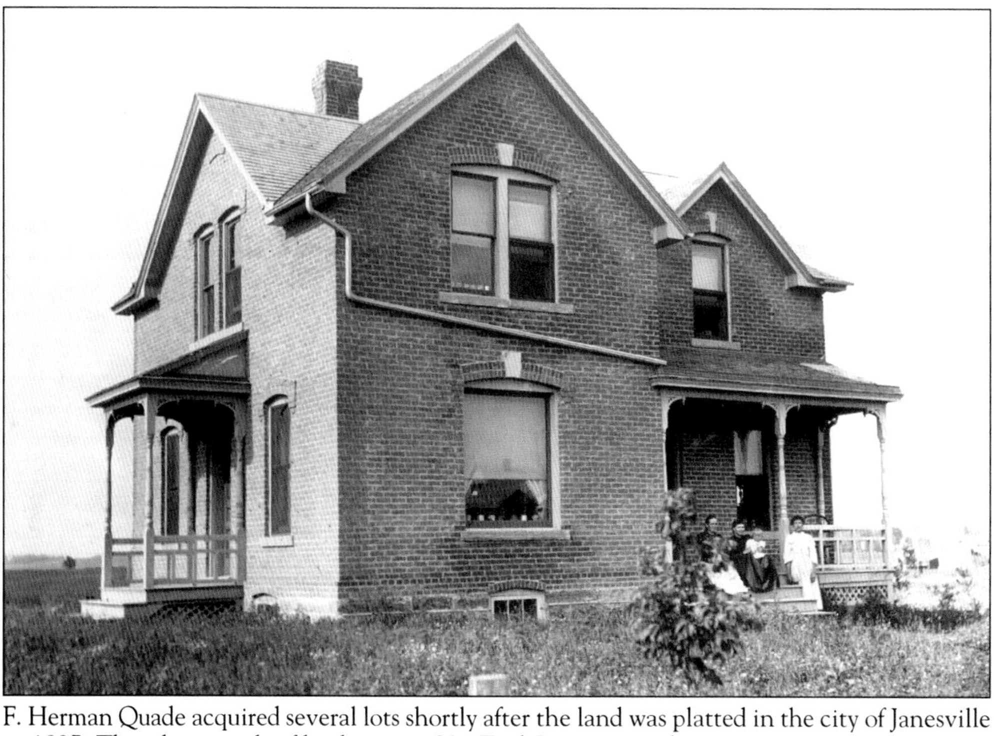

F. Herman Quade acquired several lots shortly after the land was platted in the city of Janesville in 1897. This photograph of his home at 301 Teal Street was taken in 1900.

The Fred Laudert residence is said to be the first house built in New Richland. The home was built by Buncho in July of 1877 as a saloon. After eight months, it was sold to James Murphy who converted it to a residence. One year later, he sold it to M. Murphy who rented it out for a few years and then sold it to Fred Laudert.

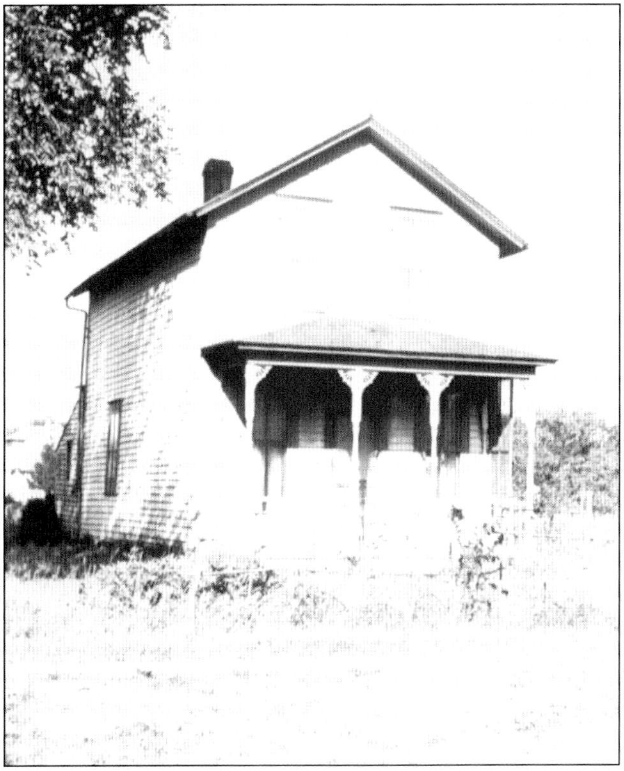

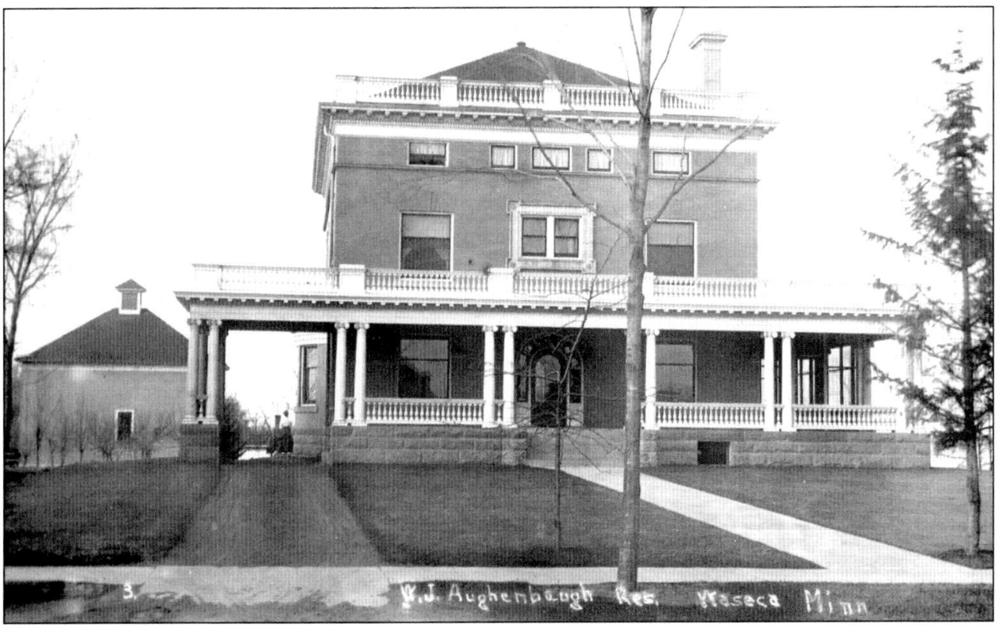

The John Wallace and Carrie (Kocher) Aughenbaugh residence at 831 Third Avenue North East in Waseca is seen here. This house is on the National Register and now serves as the Masonic Lodge. It is a classic example of 19th century Renaissance Revival architecture. The Masons purchased it in 1931 from Daisy Strong, the daughter of the Aughenbaughs, for $5,000. It has been a Masonic Lodge ever since.

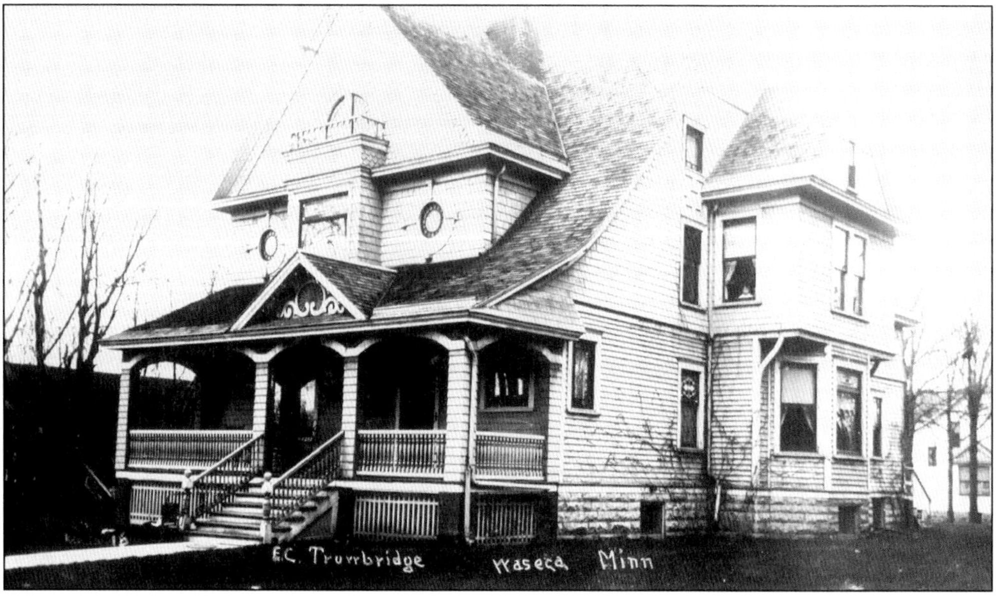

Pictured here is the Ira C. Trowbridge residence at 106 Fourth Avenue North East in Waseca. Ira was the most prominent figure in the early history of Waseca. He purchased the land Waseca now stands on in 1866. In 1867 he brought his wife, Judith (Church) Trowbridge, and family for permanent settlement. This home was built facing the county courthouse on North State Street and was later turned 90 degrees to its present location.

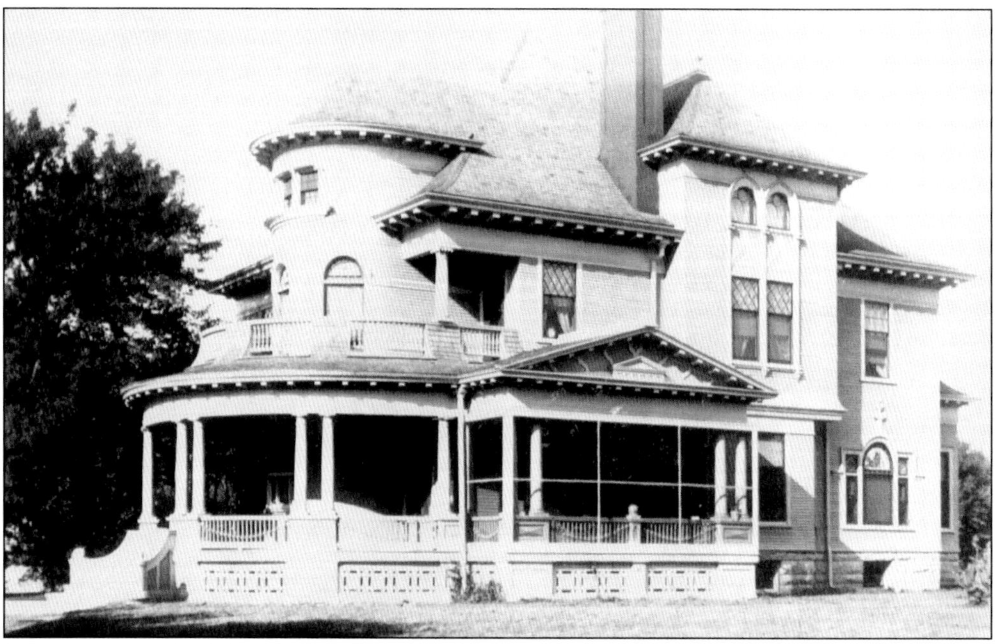

Shown here is the Edward A. Everett residence at 206 Ninth Street North East in Waseca. E.A. Everett was the son of William Everett, the first merchant in Waseca. E.A. took over his father's partnership in the EACO Mill. He first married Antoinette (Miller) and after her death in 1909, married her sister Regene (Miller) in 1916. This house was destroyed in 1958 to follow the conditions of his will.

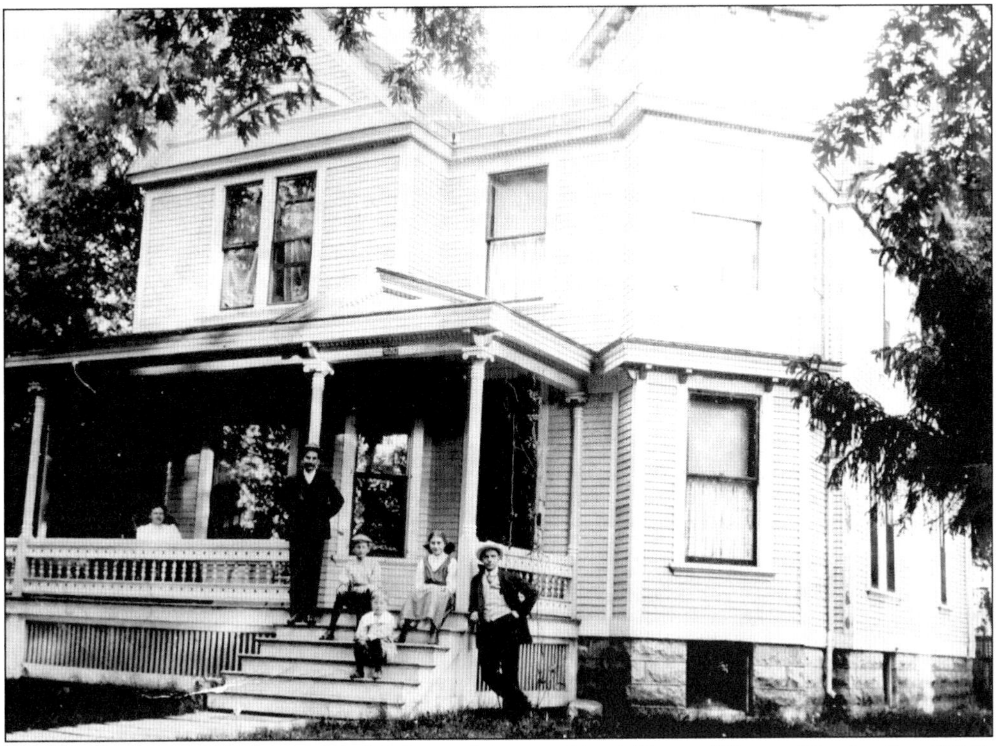

The W.R. Wolf house is located at 522 Second Avenue North East in Waseca. The family of W.R. Wolf, a Waseca merchant and businessman, lived in this house up to 2001 when it was sold out of the family. It is uncertain who built this Queen Anne-style home, but the family theory is that it was a man who came to Waseca to work on the railroad. It was built around 1895, and is the best example of its style in the city of Waseca.

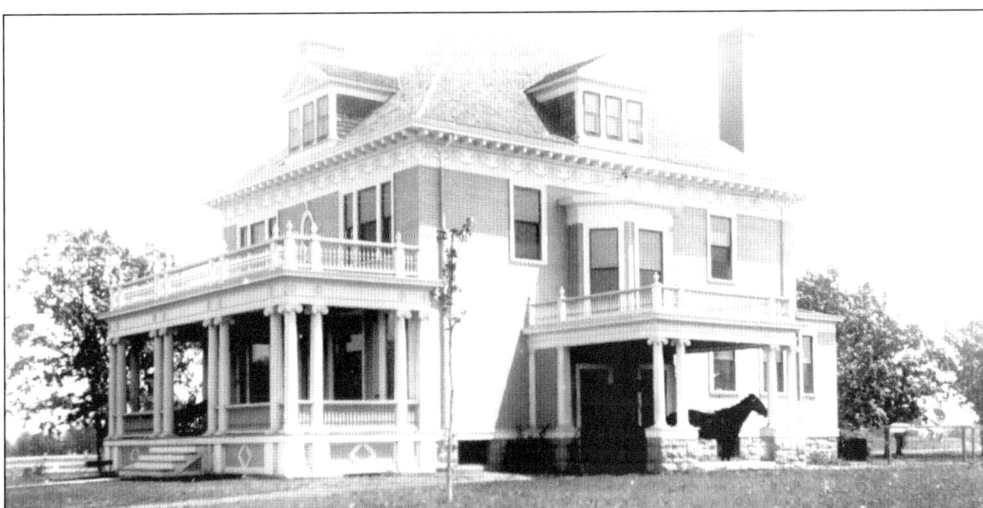

Pictured here is the Charles and Josephine (Preston) Leuthold home located at 824 Elm Avenue East in Waseca. Charles was one of five Leuthold brothers who owned and operated fifteen stores in the state of Minnesota. Charles was born in Kasson in 1868 and came to Waseca in 1888. He married Josephine Preston in 1894 and raised three daughters and one son.

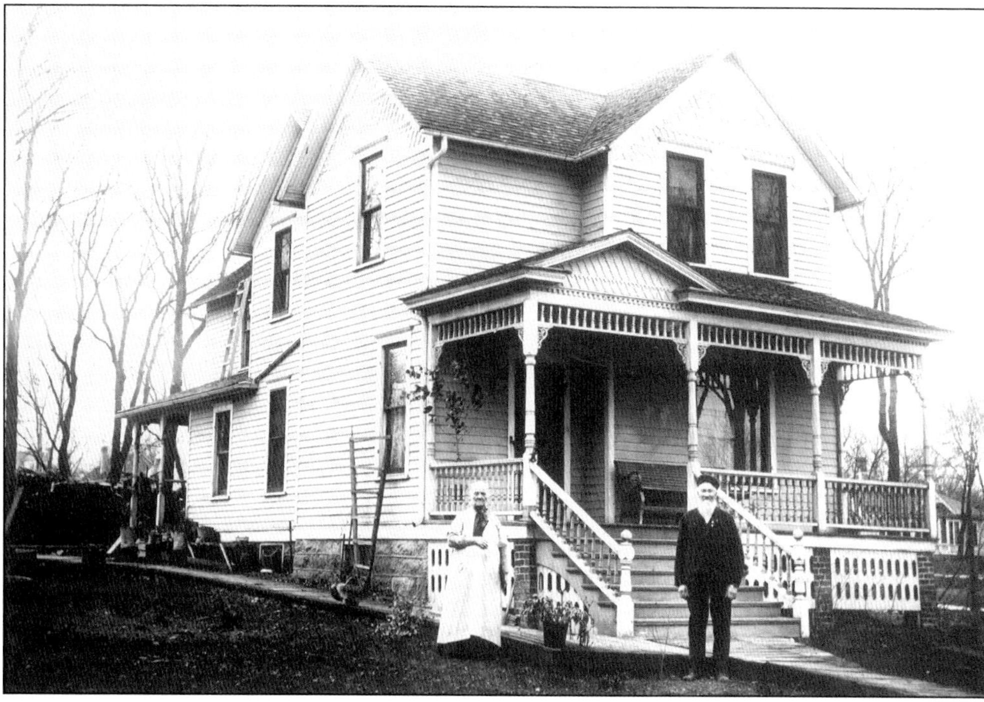

In 1856 August Minske came to Iosco Township in a prairie schooner. He married Caroline Schultz and lived in Iosco until 1898 when they moved to Waseca. August Minske served in the 1st Minnesota Battalion Infantry, Army of the Potomac, during the Civil War. Here he is pictured with his wife, Caroline, in front of their home at 511 Third Street North East in Waseca.

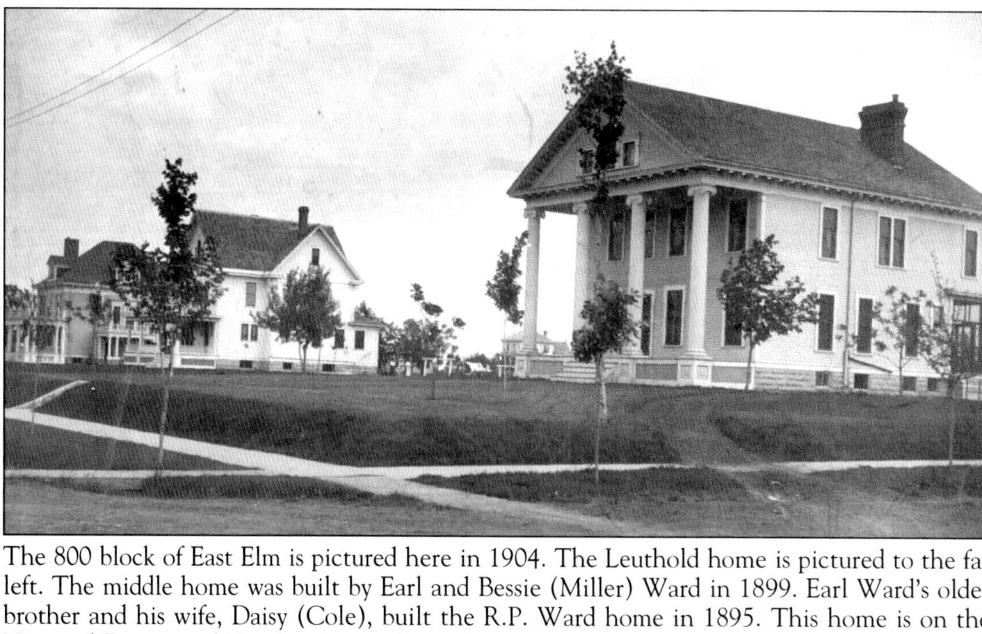

The 800 block of East Elm is pictured here in 1904. The Leuthold home is pictured to the far left. The middle home was built by Earl and Bessie (Miller) Ward in 1899. Earl Ward's older brother and his wife, Daisy (Cole), built the R.P. Ward home in 1895. This home is on the National Register of Historic Sites. The architect, E.S. Stebbins, also designed the Kenwood house in Minneapolis, which was used by Mary Tyler Moore in her TV series.

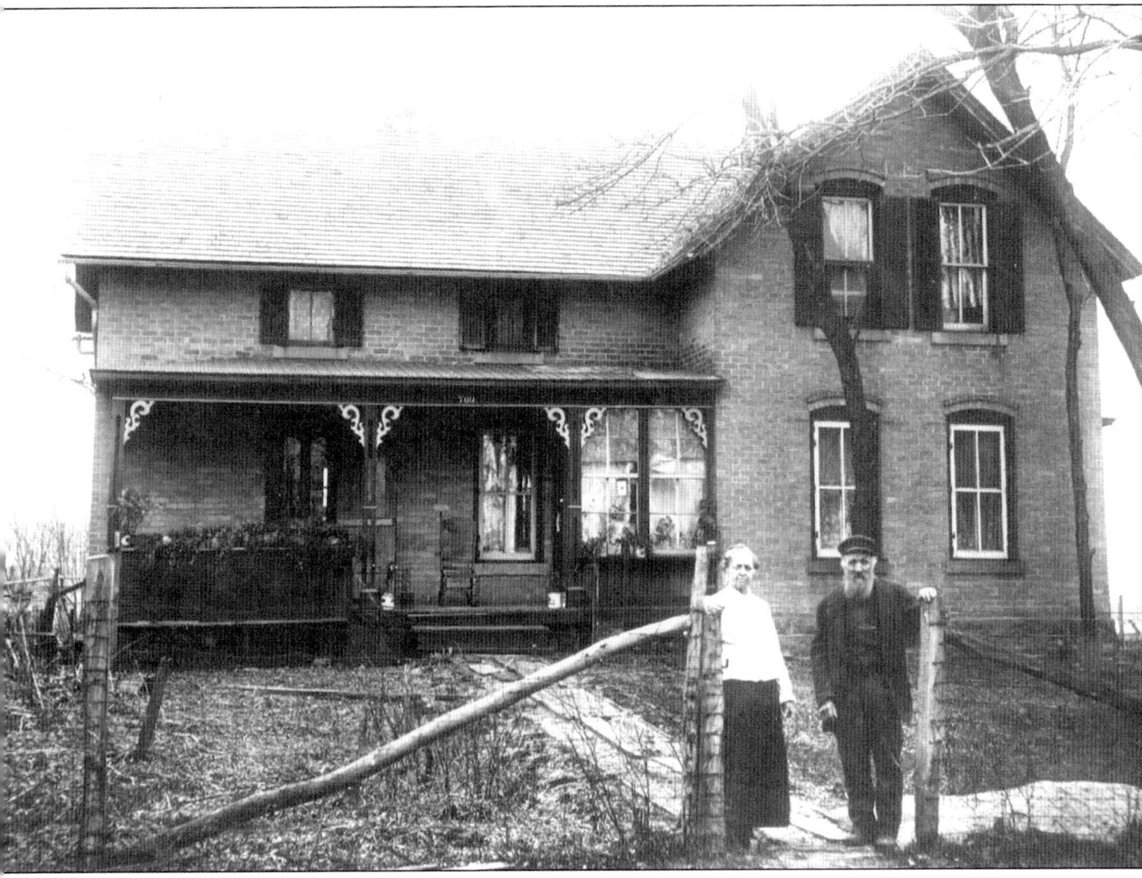

Gust and Mary A. (Bishman) Krassin home at 931 Third Street South West in Waseca is pictured. The Krassin home was built in the spring of 1889. Gust and Mary are pictured on the west side of their home in 1910.

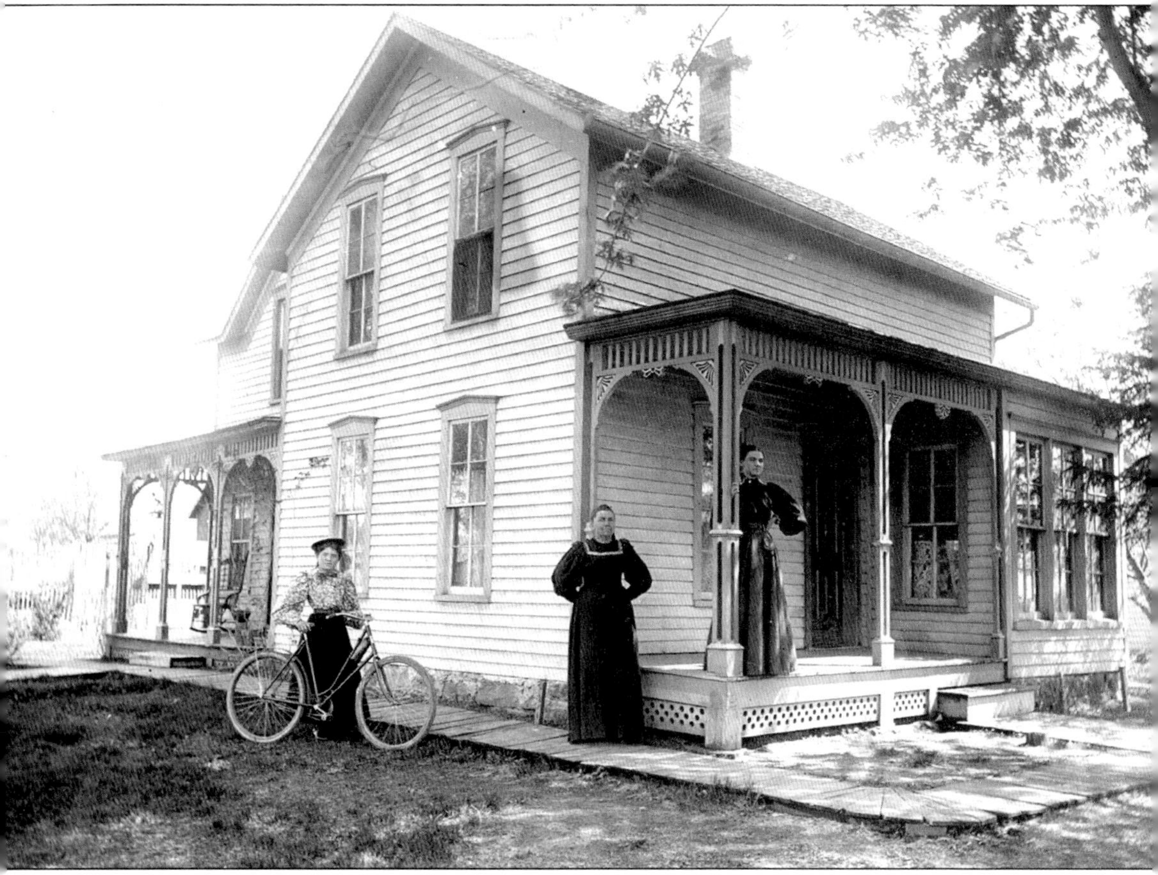

Amanda, Mrs. John Lund, and Della are pictured in August 1897 at their home on Fourth Avenue and Seventh Street South East in Waseca. John Lund was a repairman at the Chicago & Northwestern Railroad carshop in Waseca.

Six

Schools and Churches

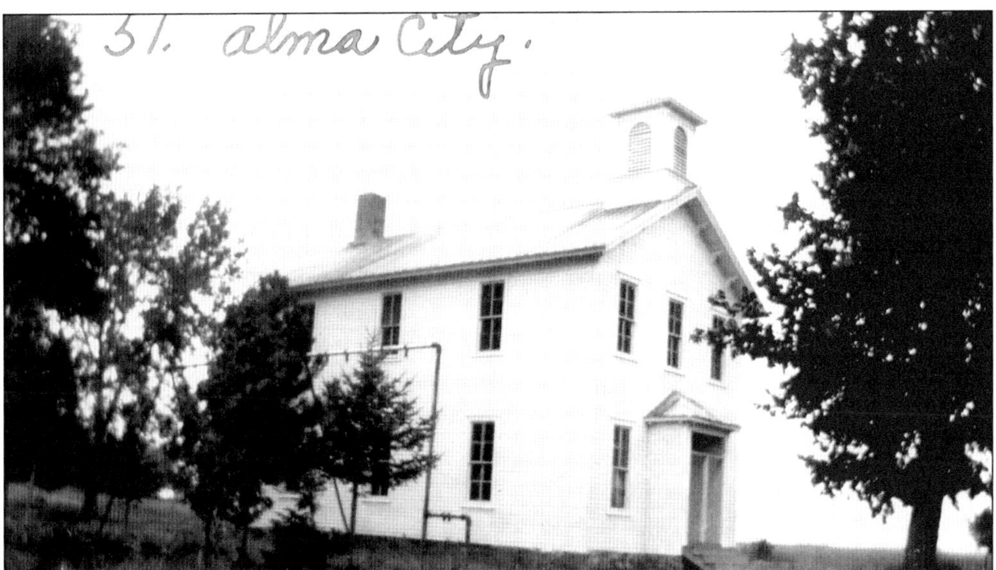

Alma City's two-story schoolhouse is seen here in 1928. After consolidation began in this district in 1954, this building was sold to Charles Folden who used it for a hog house.

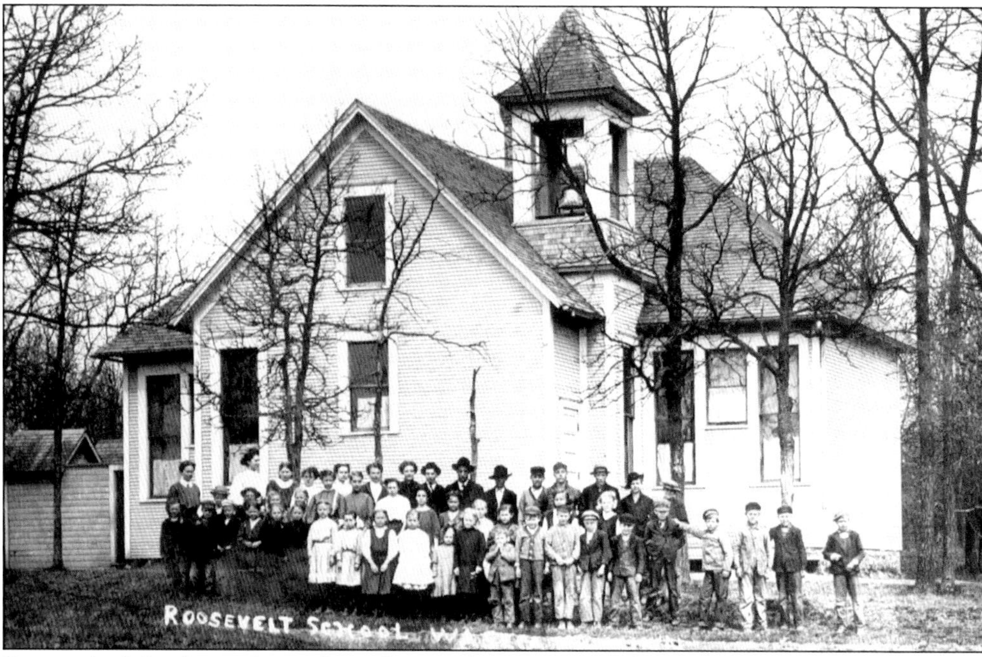

Roosevelt School was located in the northeast corner of section 19 in Blooming Grove Township. This photograph was taken in 1910. A new state labor law passed in 1909 stated that children could not be excused to stay home and work. If parents wanted children excused for work, they had to get a certificate from the superintendent.

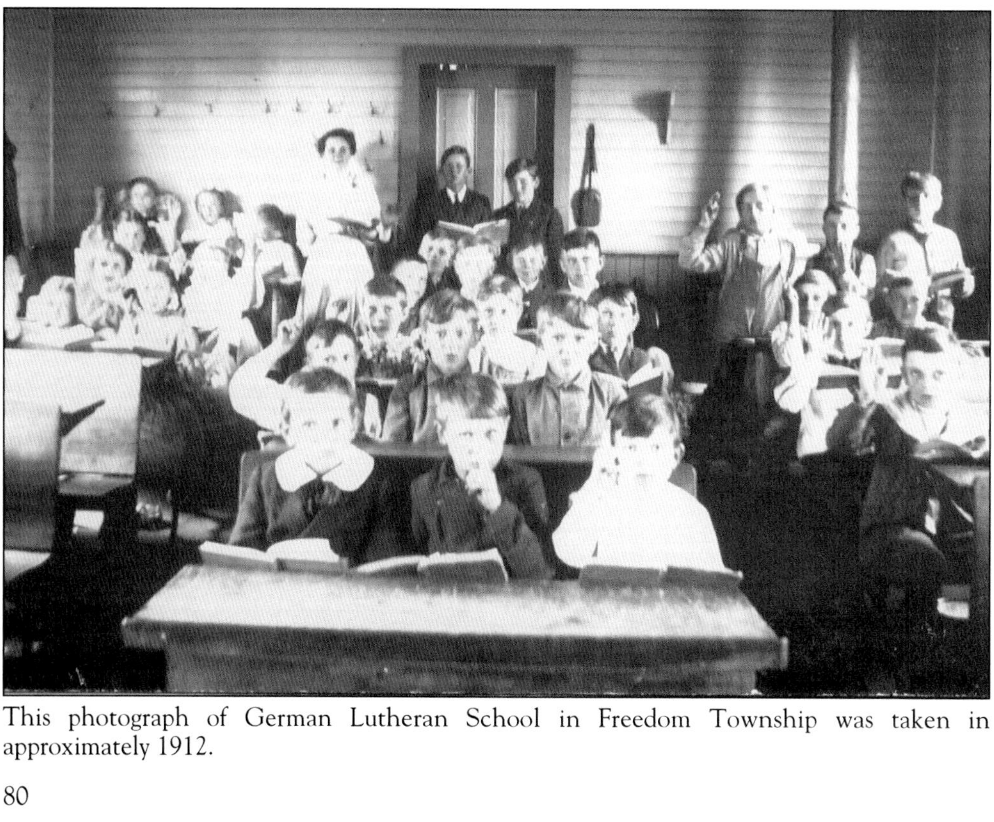

This photograph of German Lutheran School in Freedom Township was taken in approximately 1912.

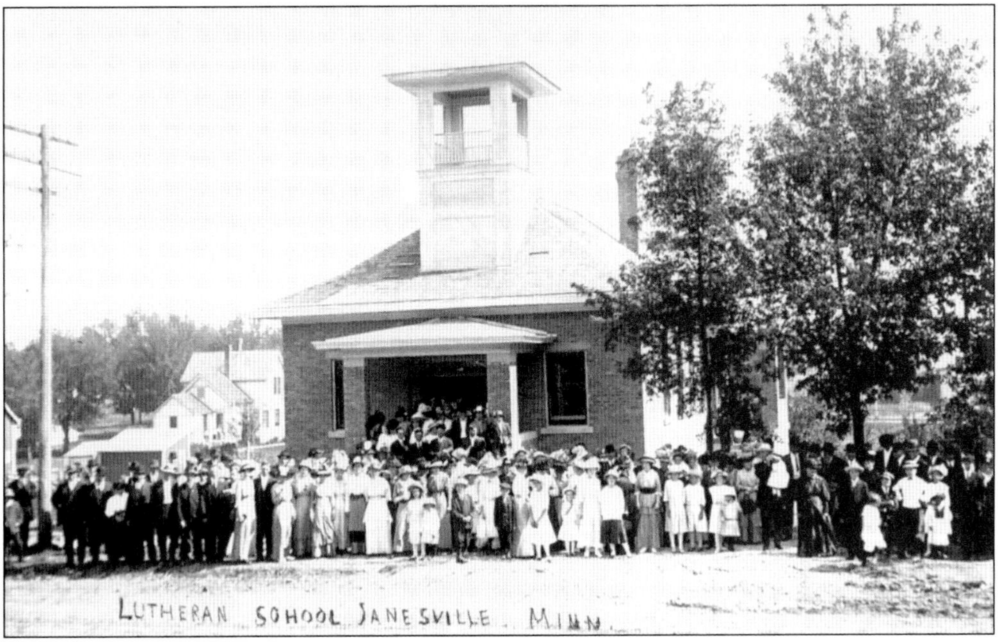

The Janesville Lutheran School is seen here in approximately 1906.

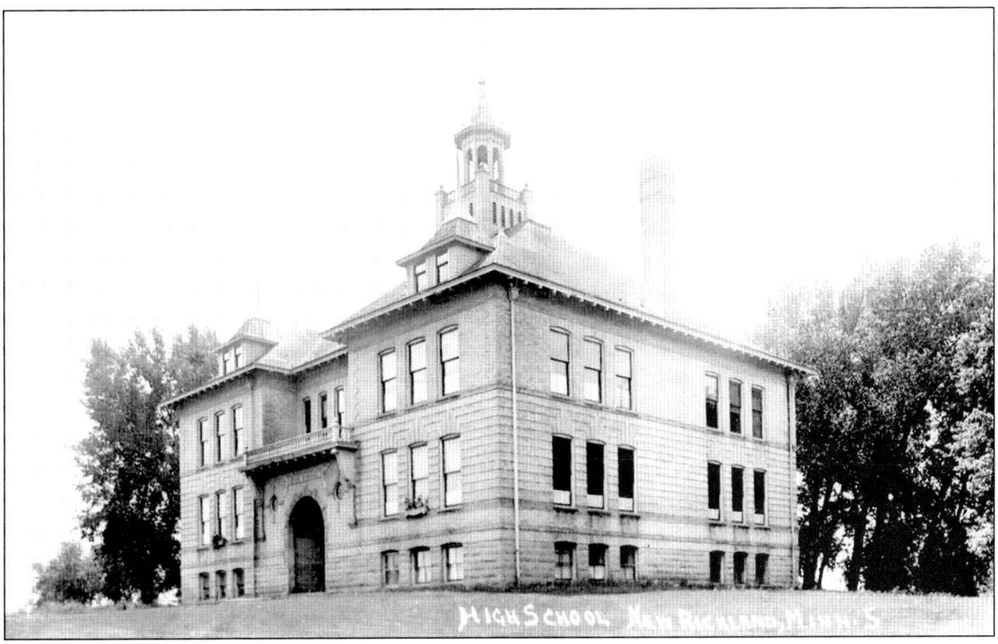

The New Richland High School was erected in 1900 at a cost of $15,000. The old school was moved and used for a poultry house.

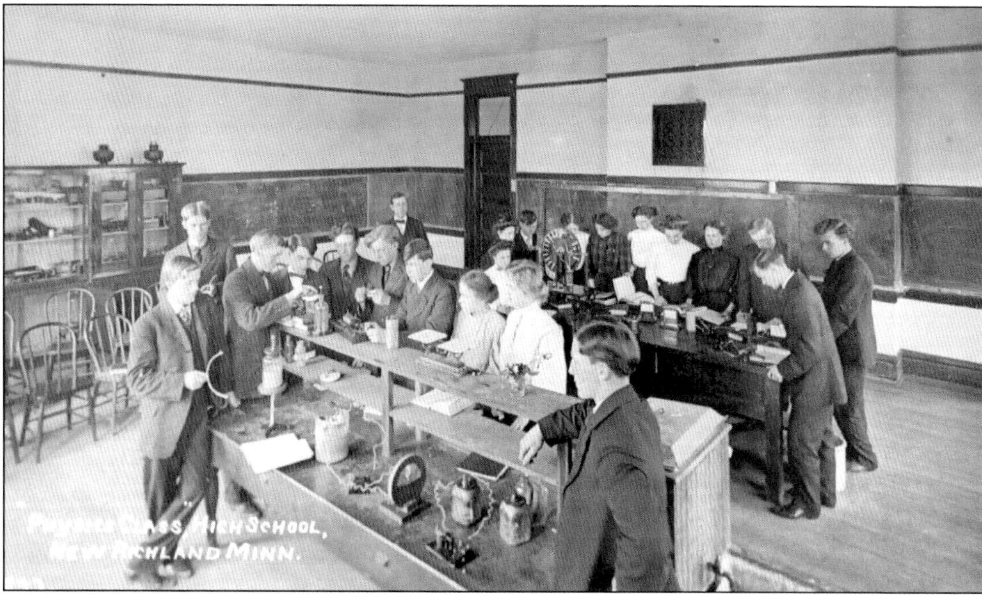

Seen here is the laboratory and physics class of New Richland High School in 1912.

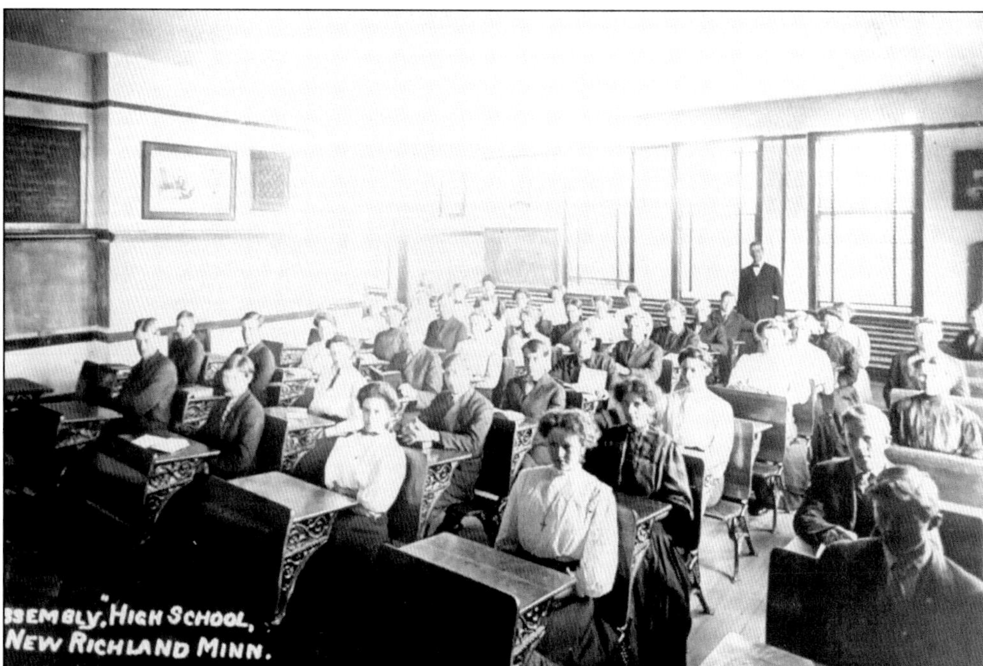

An assembly held at the New Richland High School is captured in this 1909 photograph.

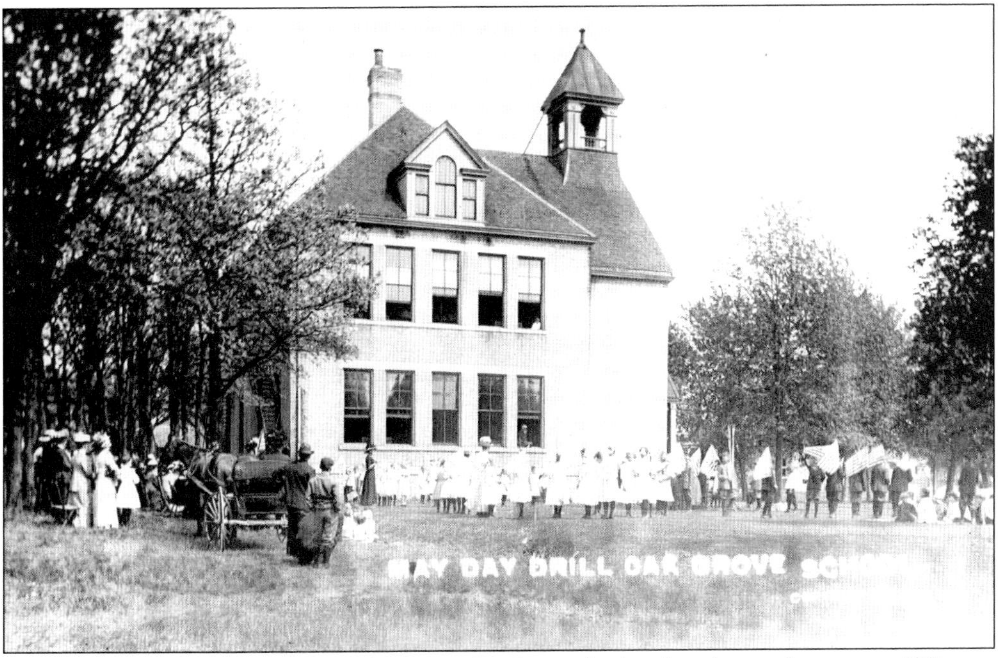

The Oak Grove School was opened in 1894. Students who lived in the northern part of Waseca went to school at Oak Grove. It was located in the southeast corner in what is now Trowbridge Park. In 1931 conditions of the school forced it to close.

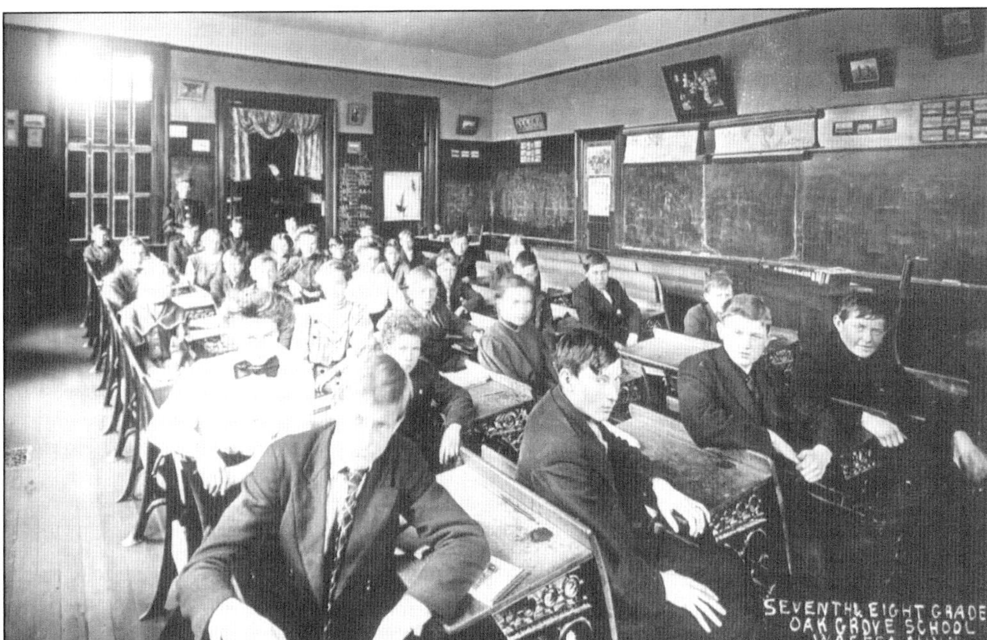

Teacher Hannah Hawkes poses with her seventh- and eighth-grade class at Oak Grove in 1908.

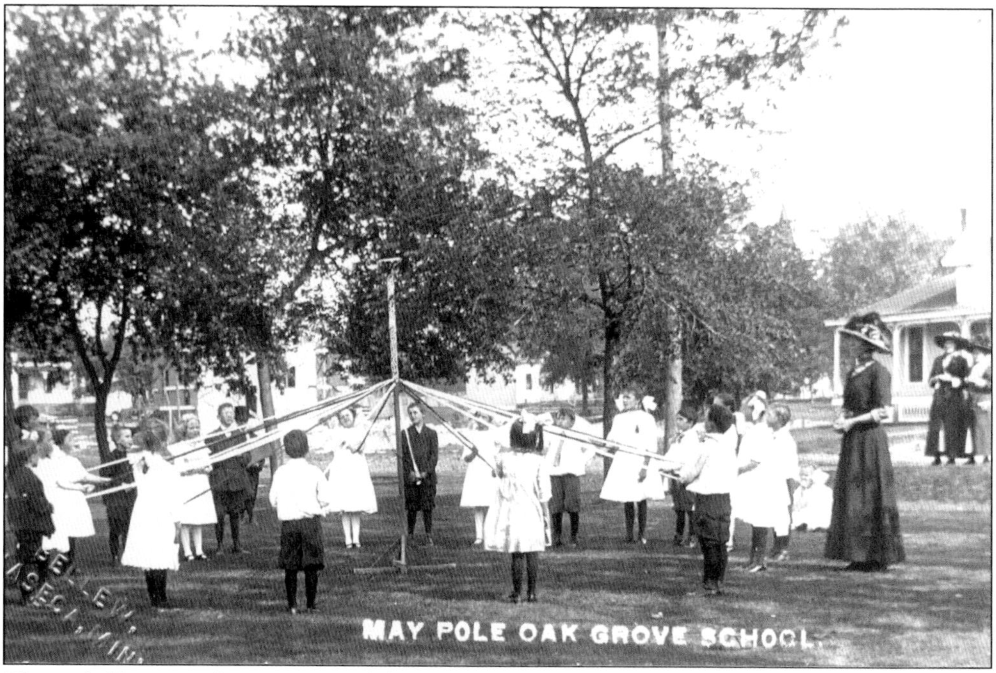

These children are dancing around the May Pole at Oak Grove School. Streamers of colored ribbon were attached to the top of the pole. Each child would hold a streamer and dance in a circle going over the next students, and then under the next student, and then back over the next student. This would weave a colorful design on the pole. It was done to celebrate May Day (first day of May).

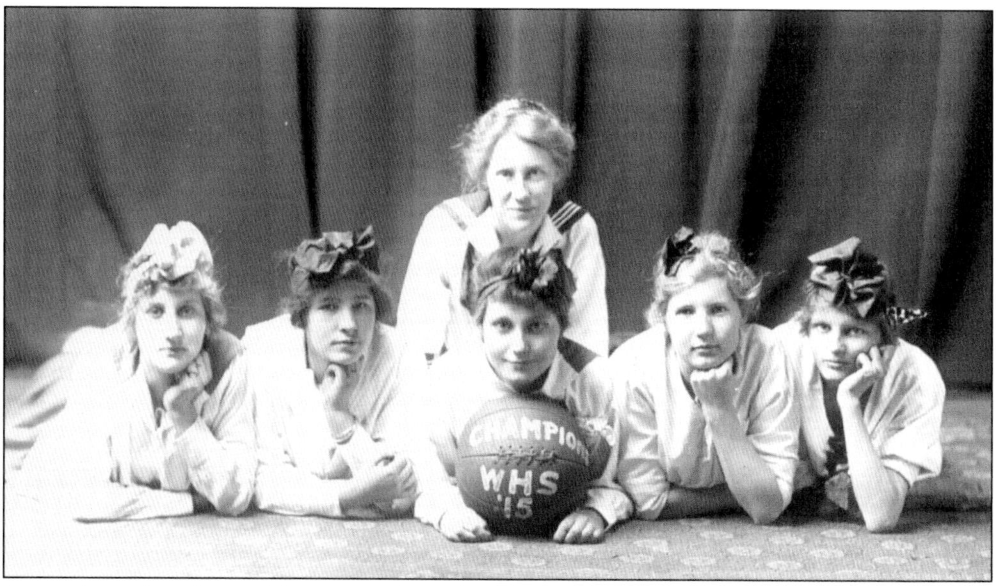

Pictured are the Waseca High School 1915 Girls Basketball Team Champions. It is recalled by Hulda McCarthy that the following girls were on the team: Mary Dalton, Dorothy DeBar, Dorothy Leuthold, Hazel Lust, and Adeline Roesler.

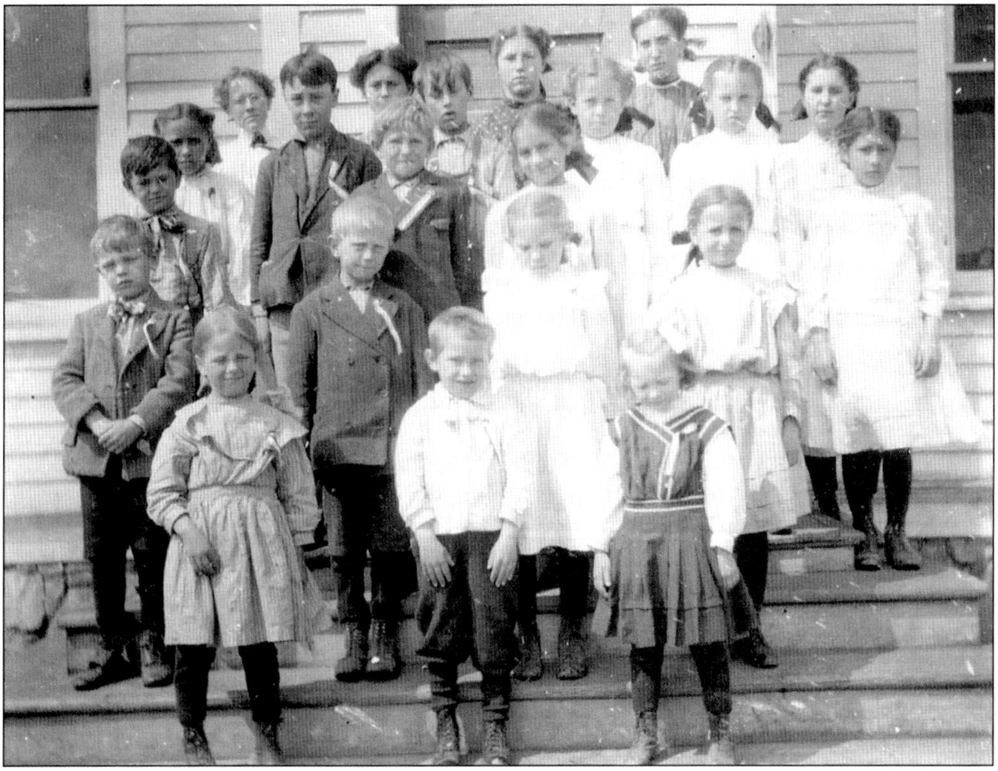

The Boys and Girls Agriculture Club of District 18 in Wilton is pictured here in 1909, from left to right, as follows: (front row) Irene Ewest; (second row) Chester Gehring, Lawrence Ewest, Iva Grunwald, and Alice Bartels; (third row) Arthur Bartels, Ben Ewest, Della Gedosch, and Elsie Grunwald; (fourth row) Clarissa Grunwald, Eva Roesler, Bennie Lechner, Vera Turnacliff, and Esther Gehring; (fifth row) Emma Klug, Alpha Roesler, Lydia Ewest, and teacher, Miss Effie Drum.

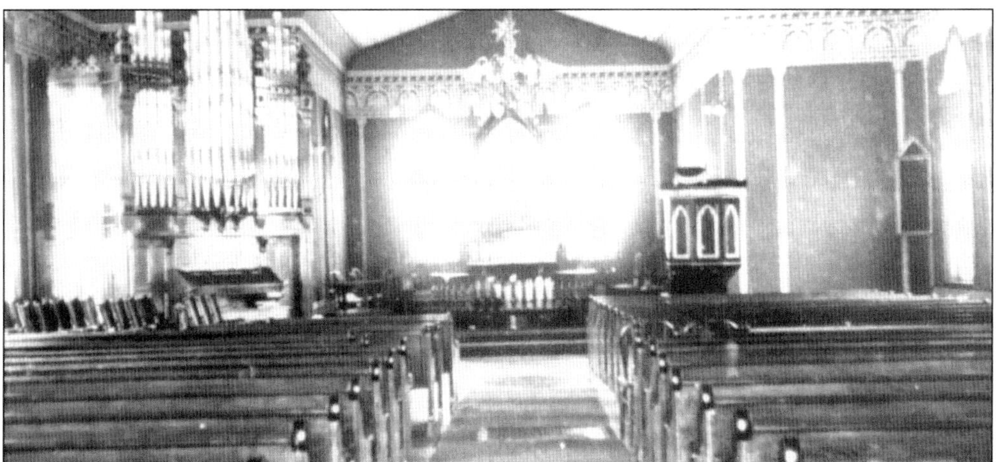

Norwegian settlers on the southern edge of the Vista community organized the LeSueur River Lutheran Church in 1861. The first church was built of logs in 1862. In 1875 a second church was built on the same site. This photograph shows the interior of the 1875 church.

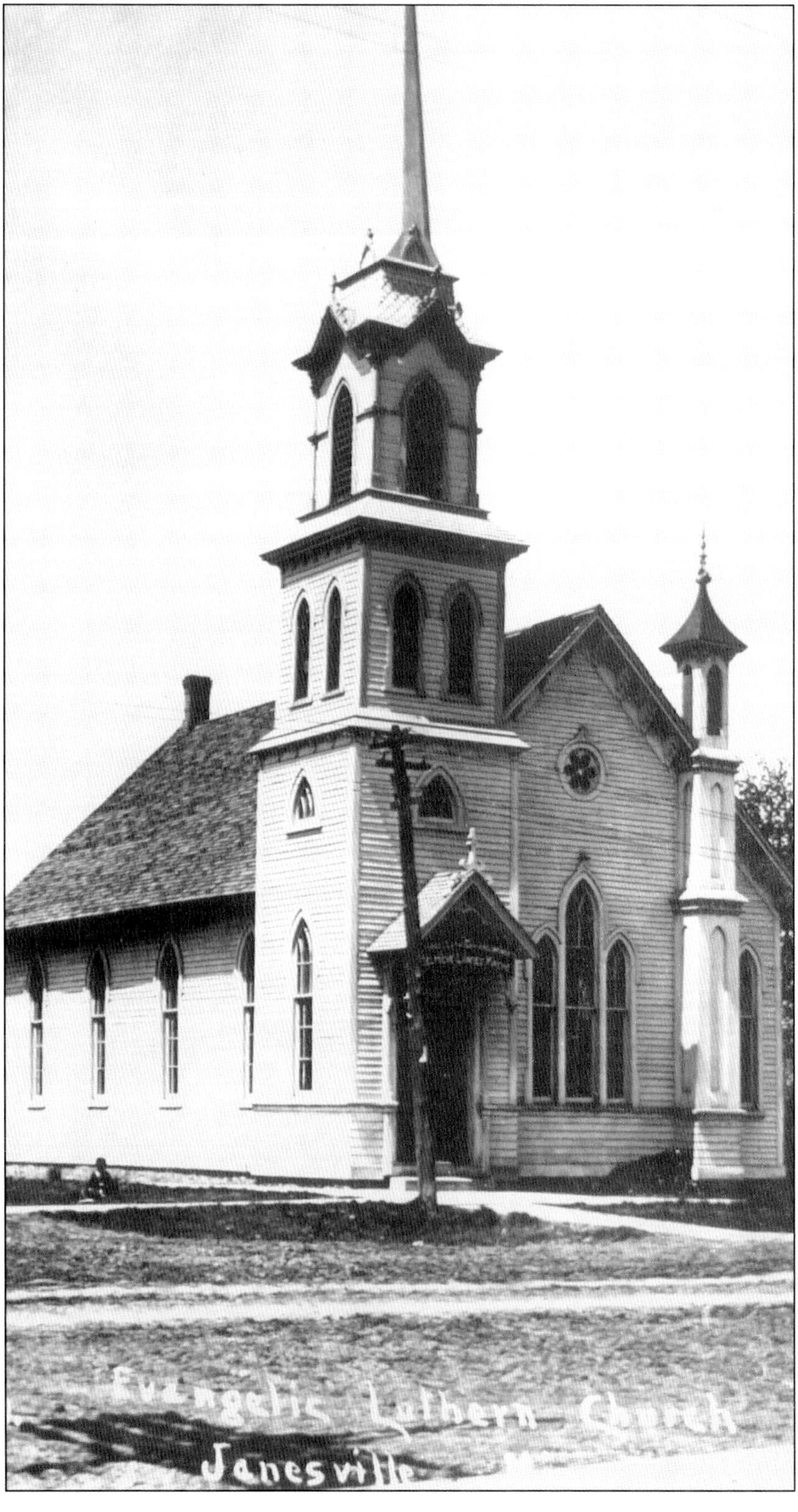

The first church building in the village of Janesville was erected on the corner of Third and Main by the Free Will Baptist Society in 1870, and was used as their place of worship until they disbanded in 1896. A group of Lutherans of the Iowa Synod organized under the name of Evangelical Lutheran and took over the building until they disbanded in the 1920s. In 1928 it was sold, torn down, and rebuilt as a residence.

The first M.E. Church in Janesville was begun in 1885. Eventually it became a Lutheran Church. Since 1965 it has been Faith Lutheran Church.

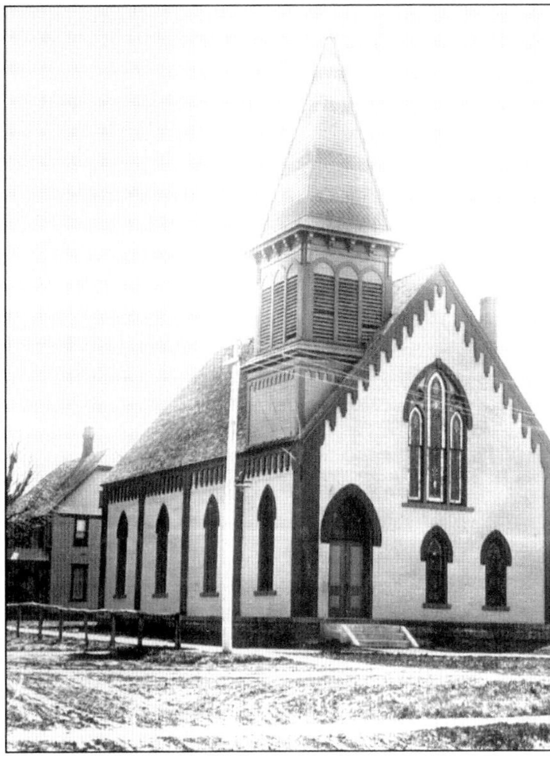

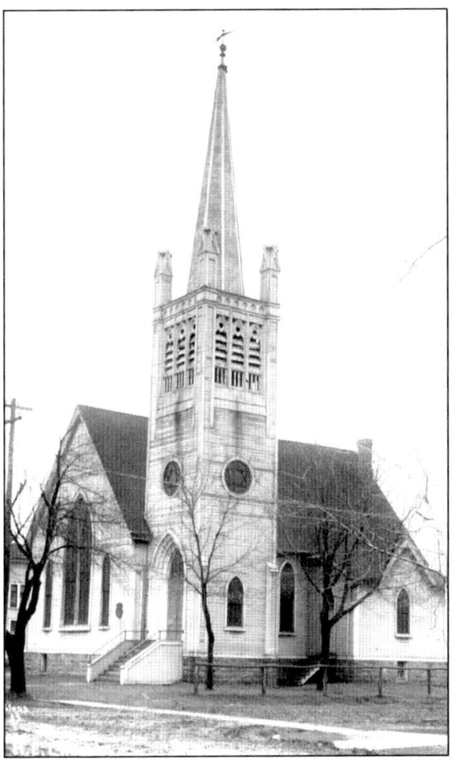

The English Methodist Church was built in 1875 on the west side of what is now Waseca Central Intermediate School. It burned to the ground in 1879. It is told that they would ring the bells in this church on Sunday morning, disrupting the sleep of William G. Ward who lived a half-block away. It was Mr. Ward's practice to sit up half the night on Saturday reading and drinking port. One Sunday morning, he stormed into the church in his underwear and told the congregation he would pay them $100 for each block they would move the church. When the church burned to the ground in 1879, the people of the church re-built it on the corner of Second Avenue and Fourth Street NE. Mr. Ward was billed $300 for the move, which was correct if you figured it was moved one block to the east and then around the block back a block. William G. had to admit it was true, they had moved the church, but the problem was it ended up right across the street from his house. The church now houses the historical society museum.

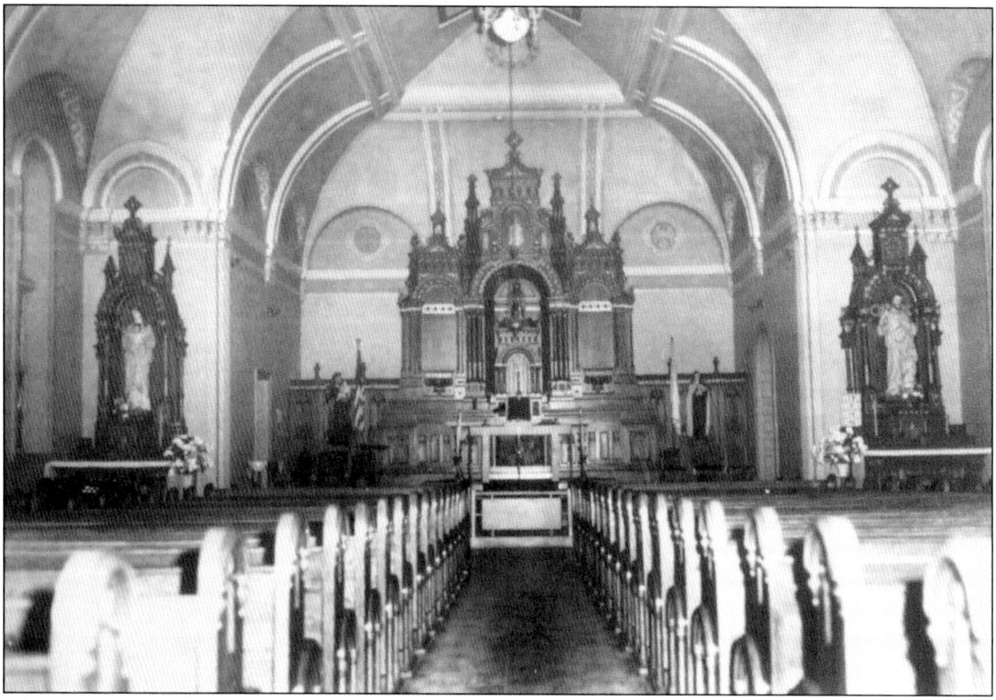

The Roman Catholic families of Waseca County were gathering in the township of St. Mary as early as 1856. The Waseca families met in 1869 at the home of Thomas White to discuss building a church in Waseca. The framing of the new church was begun in 1874. The present church replaced the first Sacred Heart Catholic CHurch in 1899. Above is the original interior of the church.

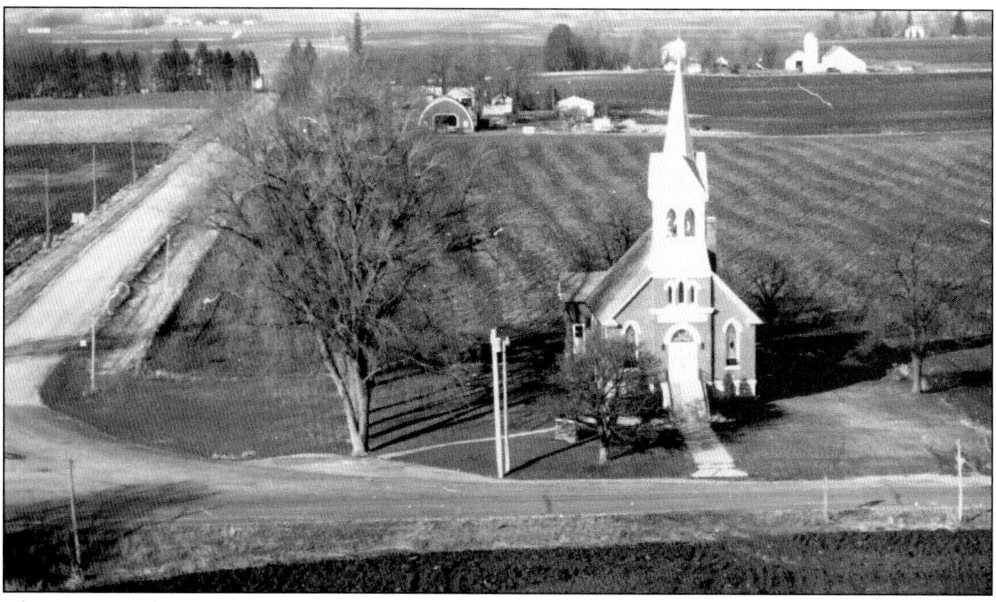

The Vista Lutheran Church, the first Swedish church in the county, was established in Vista in 1858. A church building went up in 1868, a new church was built in 1908, and their first services in English were held in 1922.

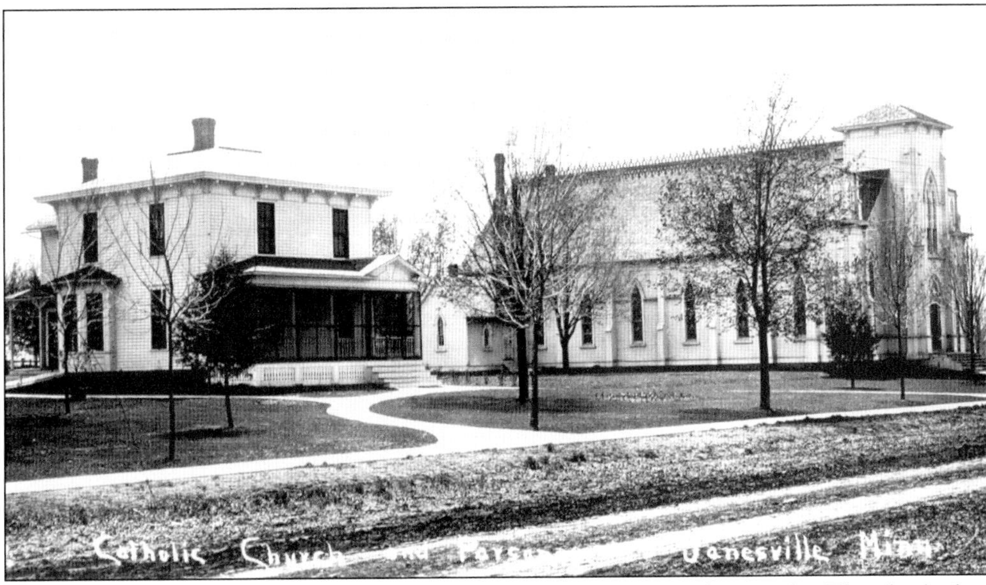

The Roman Catholics in the village of Janesville organized as early as 1854. They built their first church in 1876.

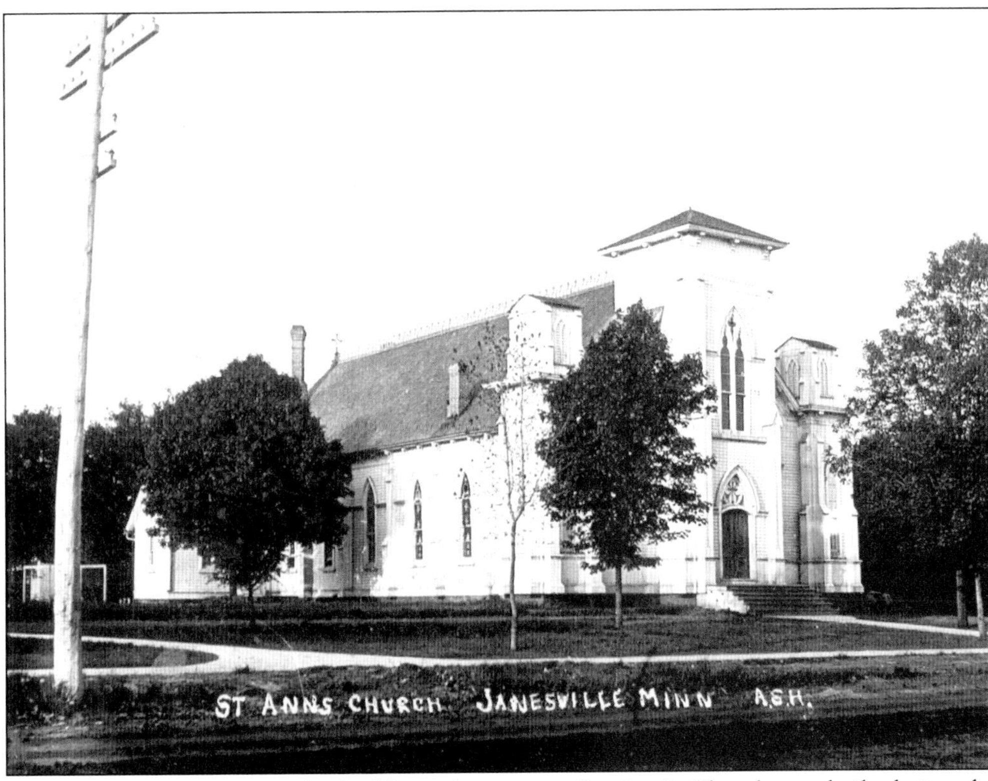

When the parish outgrew the building, the present St. Ann's Church was built during the pastorate of Father Stephan Condron, who served from 1917 to 1927.

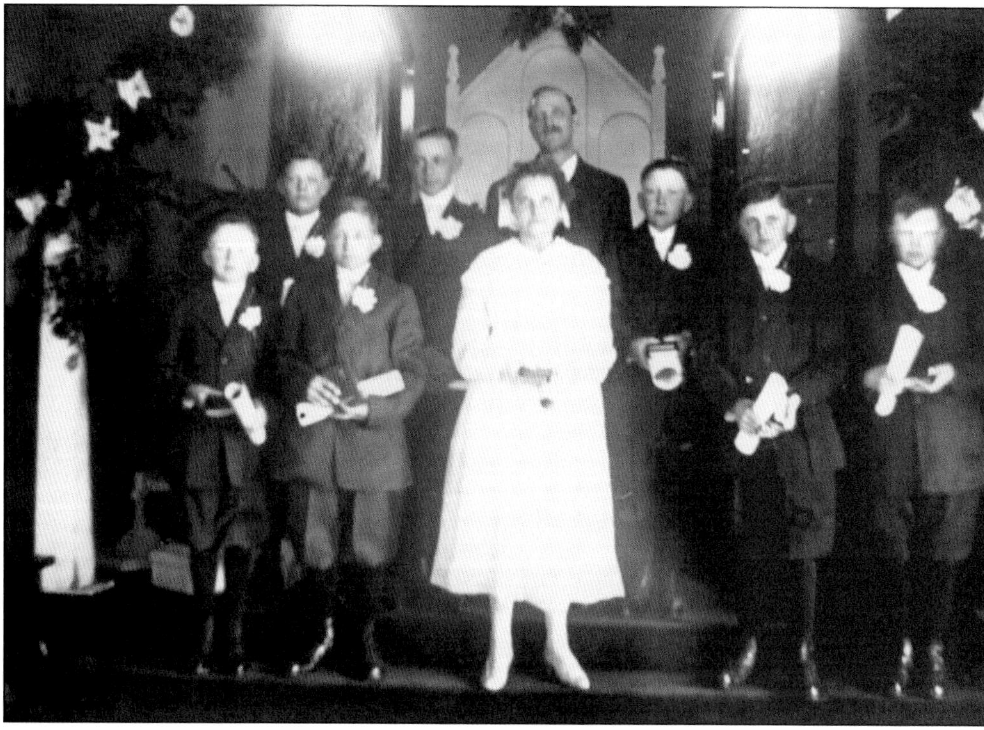

Pictured is a confirmation class at the German Lutheran Church in Freedom Township between 1918 and 1920.

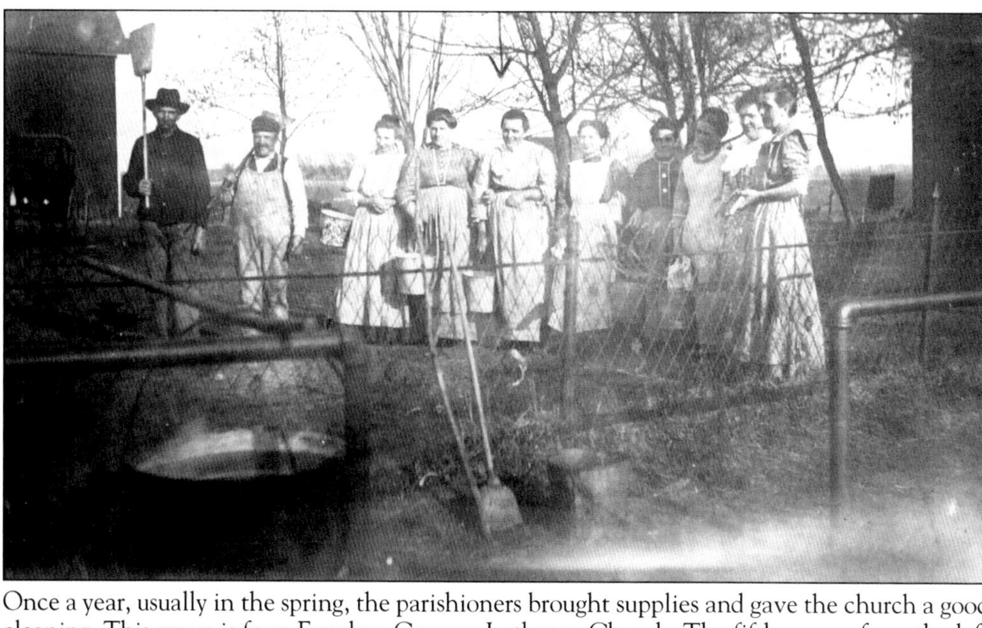

Once a year, usually in the spring, the parishioners brought supplies and gave the church a good cleaning. This group is from Freedom German Lutheran Church. The fifth person from the left has been identified as Ida Mueller Grawunder.

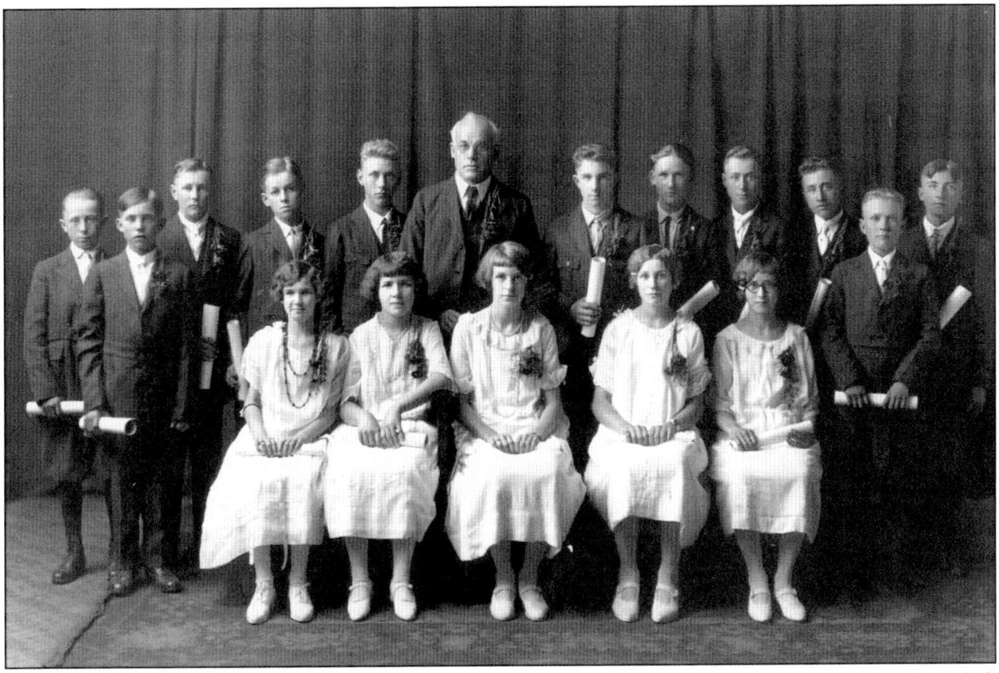

The Trinity Lutheran Church of Wilton's 1924 confirmation class is pictured here, from left to right, as follows: Alfred Kampen, Ewald Kruger, Erwin Wobschall, unknown, Ewald Poplow, Rea Herbst, Lewis Wobschall, Harold Fete, Raymond Brats, Walter Suemnick, Harold Brats, Clarence Tetzloff, Marjorie Wobschall, Alma Klinger, Clara Bauman, Melinda Wobschall, and Florence Bartz.

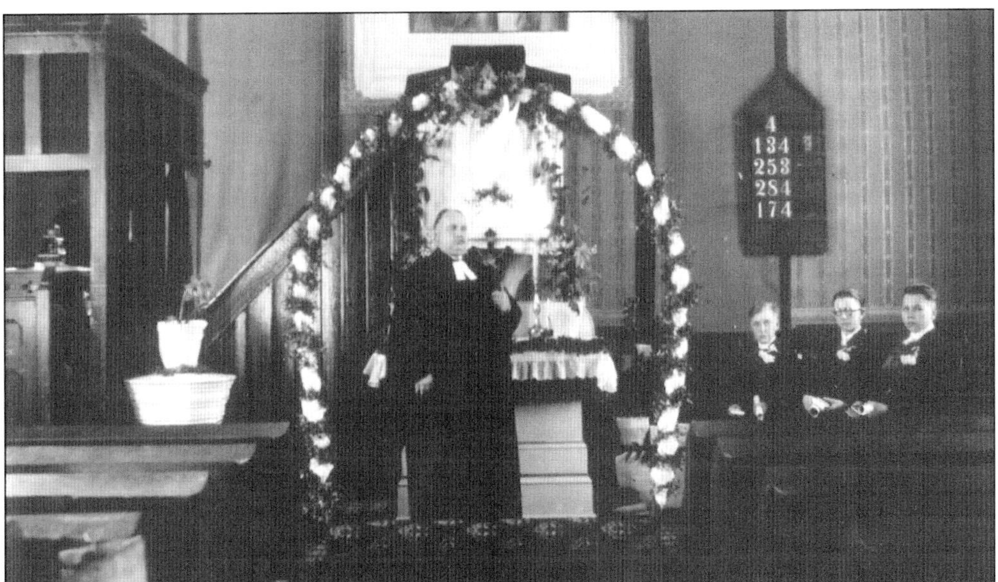

Freedom German Lutheran Church was originally built on the property of Christian Lau and later moved to its present site, which was given by August Bode. The 1918 confirmation class is seen here.

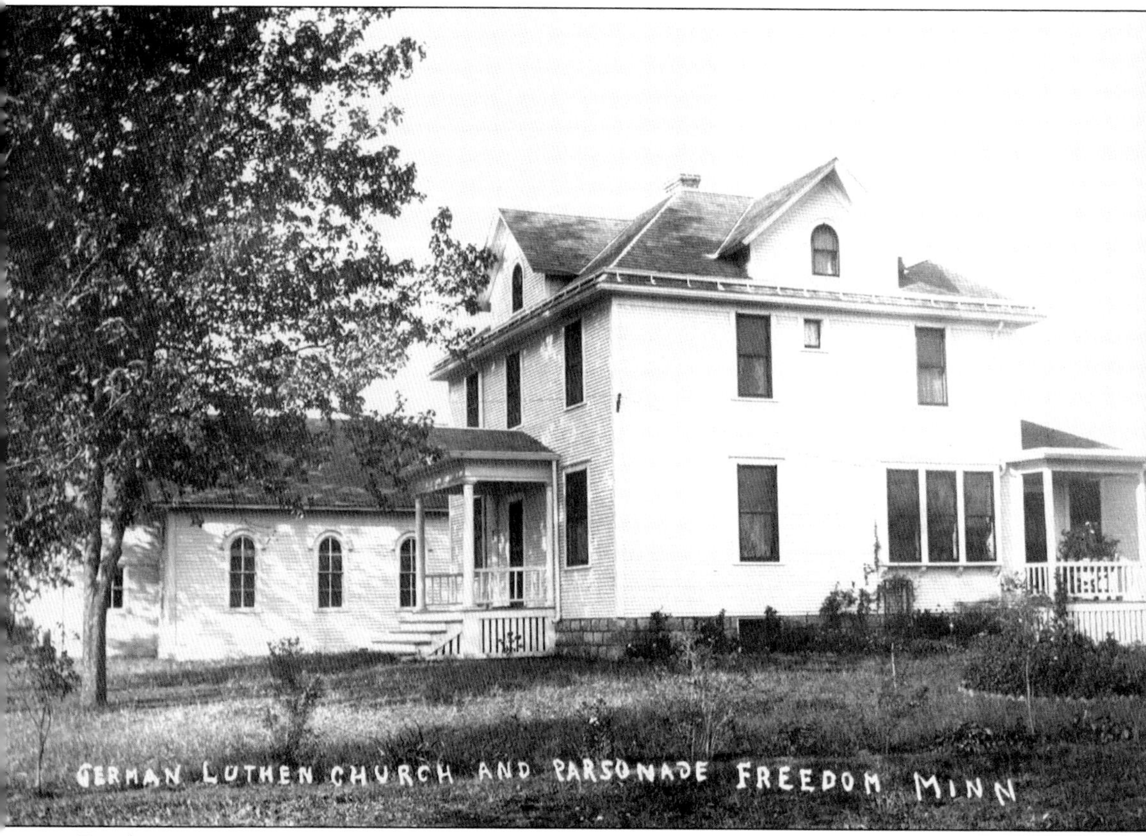

Freedom German Lutheran Church parsonage was built in 1884 in Freedom Township, and a school adjoining was built in 1885. A tower and chancel were added in 1892, and the bell was purchased in 1896.

Seven

GOVERNMENT

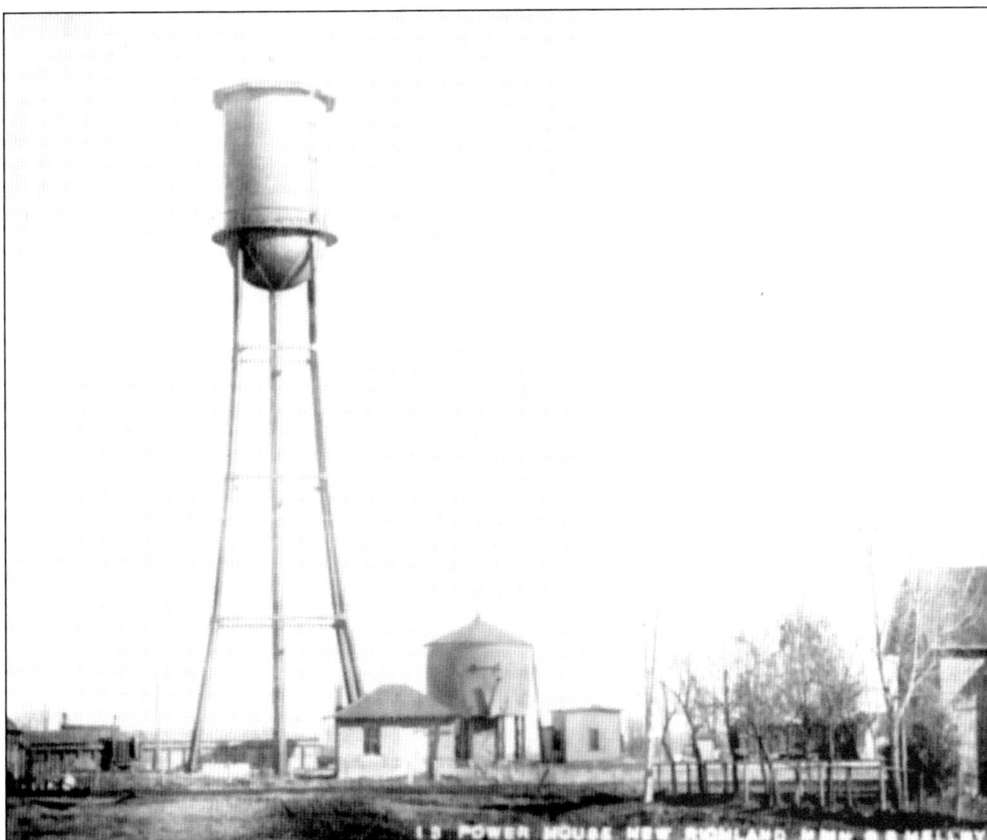

Pictured is the power plant in New Richland in approximately 1900. New Richland signed a 3-year contract to light the city streets. The lights were turned on December 19, 1899.

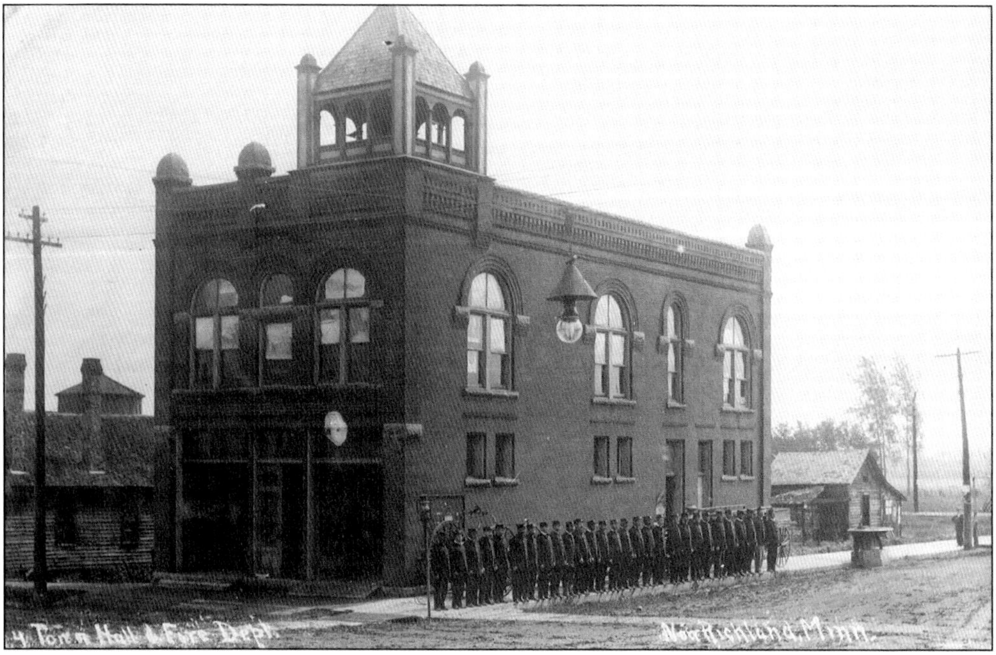

The New Richland Town Hall and Fire Department is seen in 1910, with the volunteers in full dress. In May of 1896 the New Richland City Council voted to build a 27-by-65-foot two-story building. It was to be built on a corner lot in the village and it would cost $3,500. The building would be used as a town hall but would also store the fire truck on the ground floor.

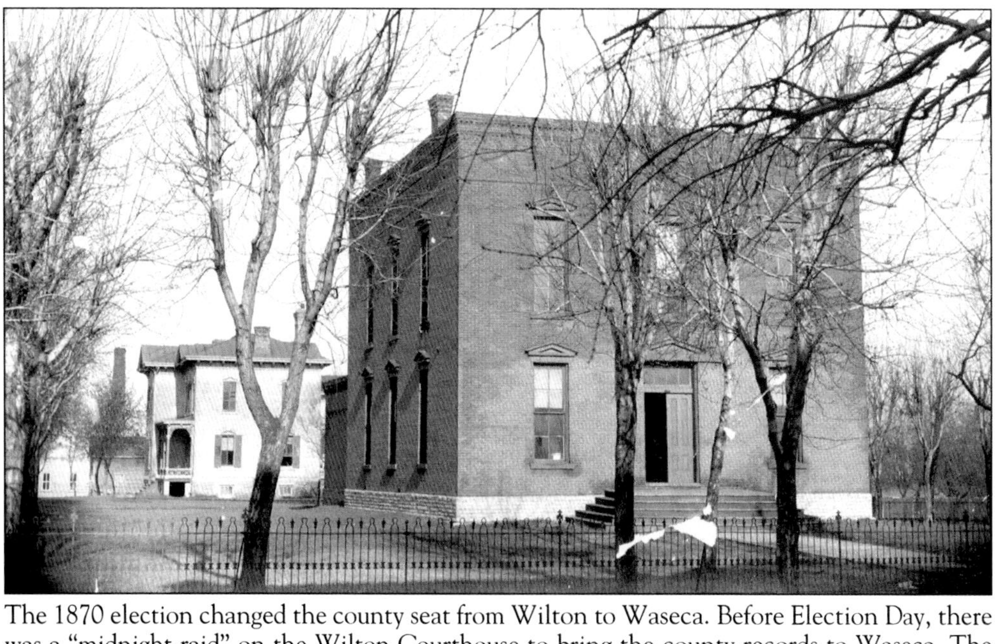

The 1870 election changed the county seat from Wilton to Waseca. Before Election Day, there was a "midnight raid" on the Wilton Courthouse to bring the county records to Waseca. The residence (left rear) eventually became the county jail.

By 1895 newspaper articles were being written about the deplorable condition of the 1870 Waseca County Courthouse. The county commissioners responded by authorizing construction of a new $50,000 plus edifice, completed in 1897 on the same site.

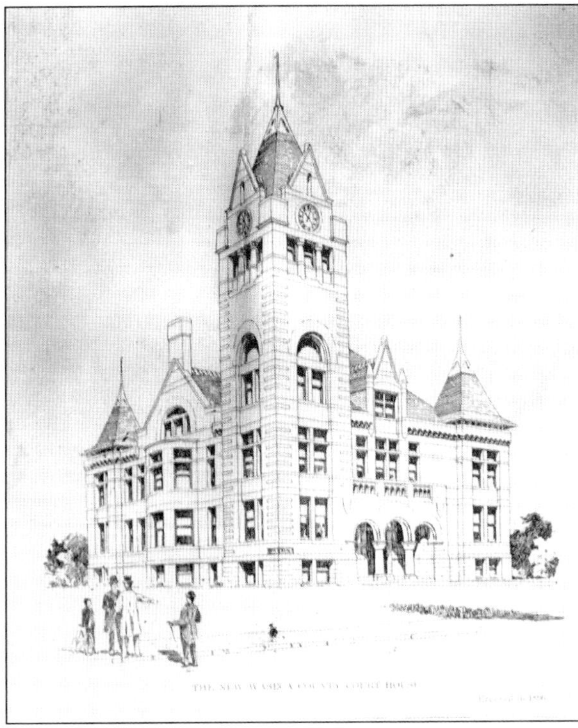

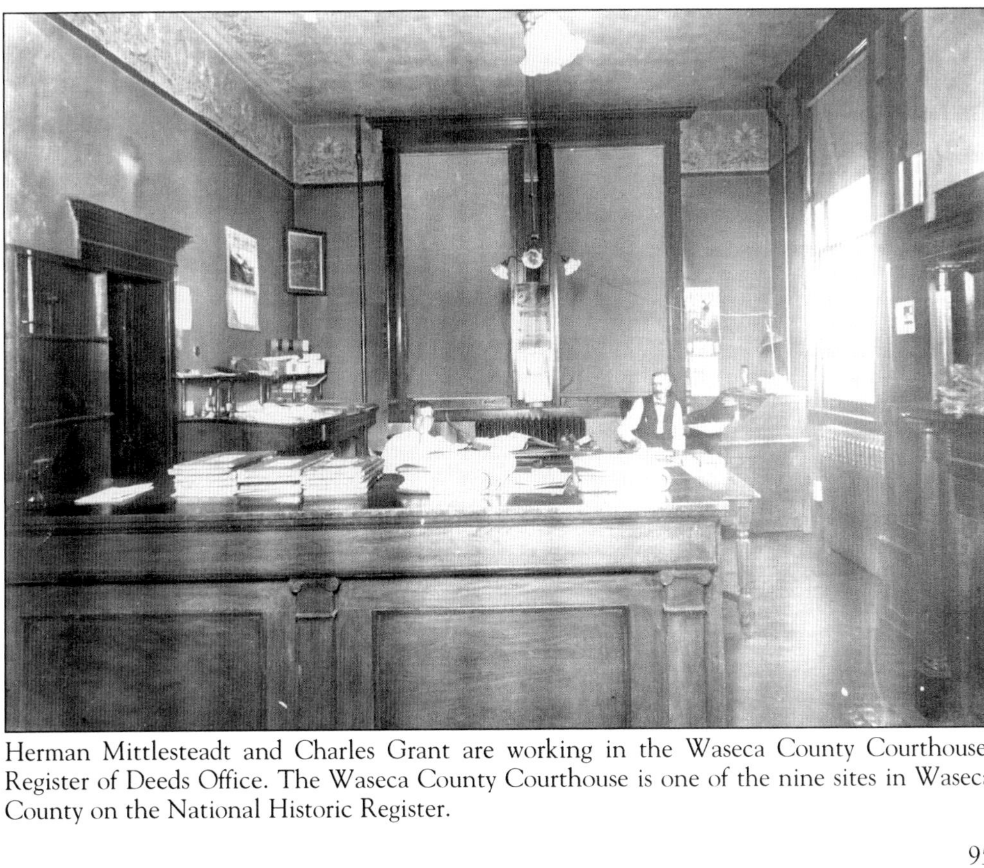

Herman Mittlesteadt and Charles Grant are working in the Waseca County Courthouse, Register of Deeds Office. The Waseca County Courthouse is one of the nine sites in Waseca County on the National Historic Register.

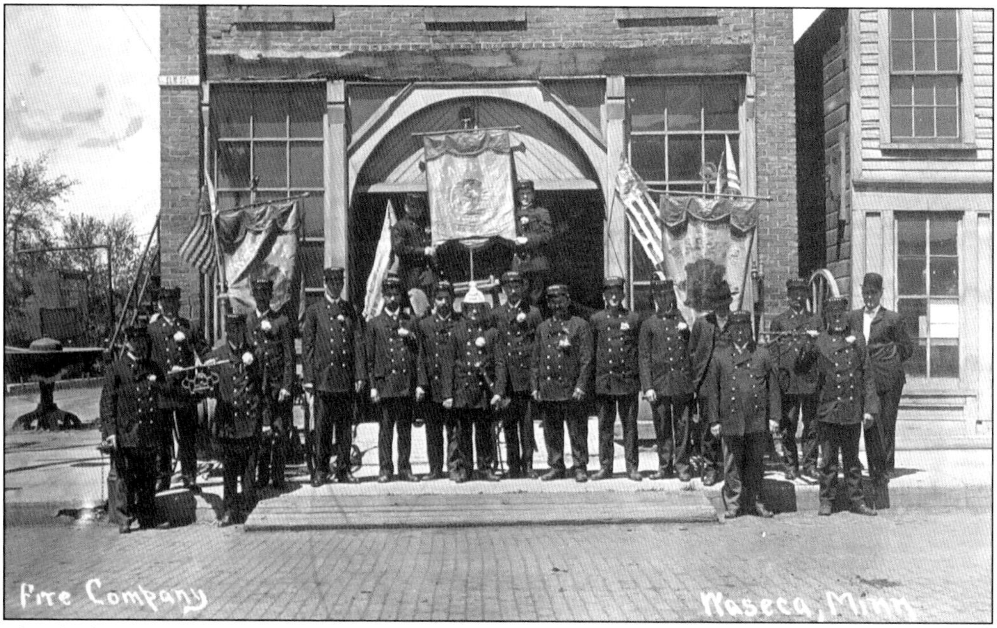

The firehouse also served as the old city hall. It was located on the corner of First and Elm North West. Frank Hoffman was named the first fire warden in 1868. Four ladders varying in height from 16 to 30 feet were purchased at a cost of $14. Members of the first company were Jesse Reese, John Lortis, Peter Coles, E. Morrison, H.V. Davis, Sumner Wood, Charles Platt, C. Ebbinhouser, John Roland, Allan Goodspeed, S. Swenson, M.D. Collester, Fred Clayton, Gus Staak, C.M. Oster, C. Christopherson, Ellsworth Goodspeed, E.B. Collester, George W. Smith, J.M. Robertson, J.W. Aughenbaugh, Thomas Breen, William Schlicht, Wenzel Krueger, A.J. Lohren, J.A. Lilly, William Miller, and John F. Murphy.

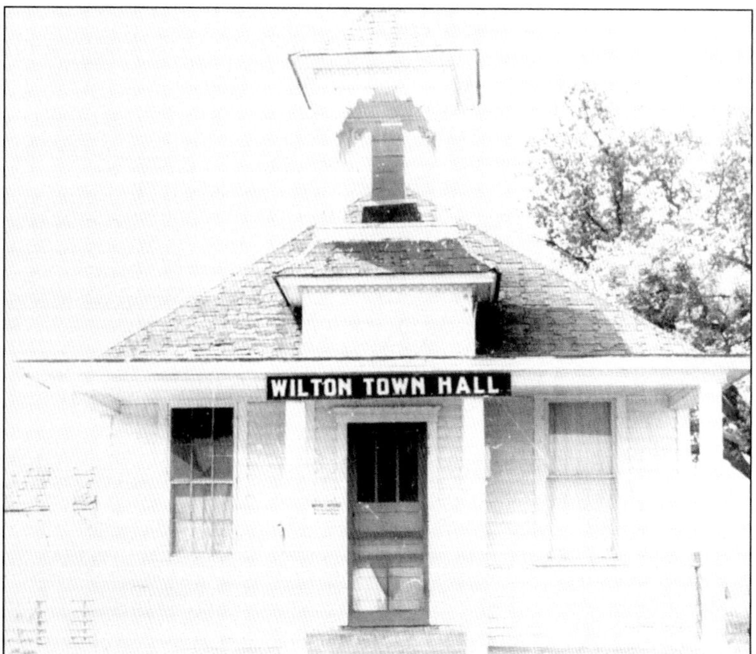

School district 18 was organized in the late 1850s. The original building was replaced and this building was used as a school until 1956, when district 18 consolidated with district 829. In the fall of 1959, the town hall was located at Silver Lake. The old district 18 schoolhouse was purchased and remodeled. It presently serves as a very spacious town hall.

Eight

VETERANS

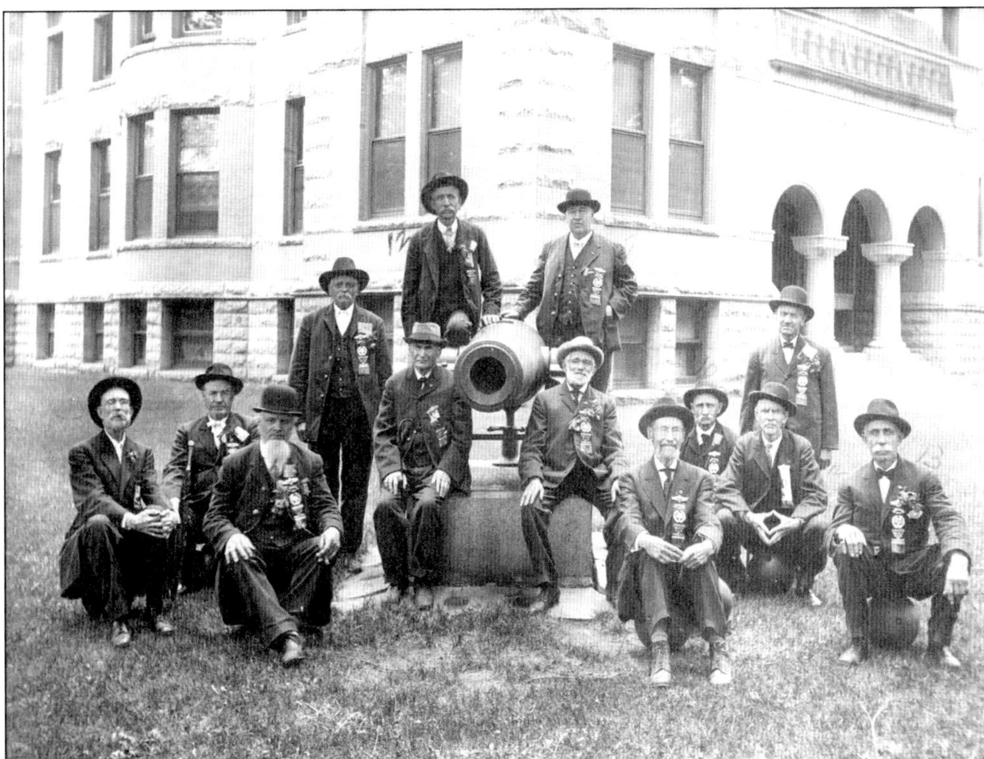

This 1905 photograph is of 13 members of the Grand Army of the Republic (GAR) of Civil War Veterans. Seated, from left to right, are George A. Smith (Co. A, 8th ME Infantry), James H. Murphy (10th WI Battery), Sam Prail /Prechel (Co. E, 26th WI Infantry), Daniel Koechel (Co. D, 4th WI H.A.), Henry Geist (Co. C, 4th WI Calvary), Samuel Frost Wyman (Co. I, 3rd MN Infantry), Nels Johnson (Co., A, 11th WI Infantry), William Hoover (Co. G., 5th MN Infantry), and A.F. Wolcott (Co.K, 1st MN H.A.). Standing, left to right, are Joseph Young (Co. A, 96th IL Infantry), L.C. Wheelock (Co. F, 95th IL Infantry) Harry A. Read (Co. F, 28th IA Infantry), and D.J. Dodge (Co. C, 2nd MN Cavalry).

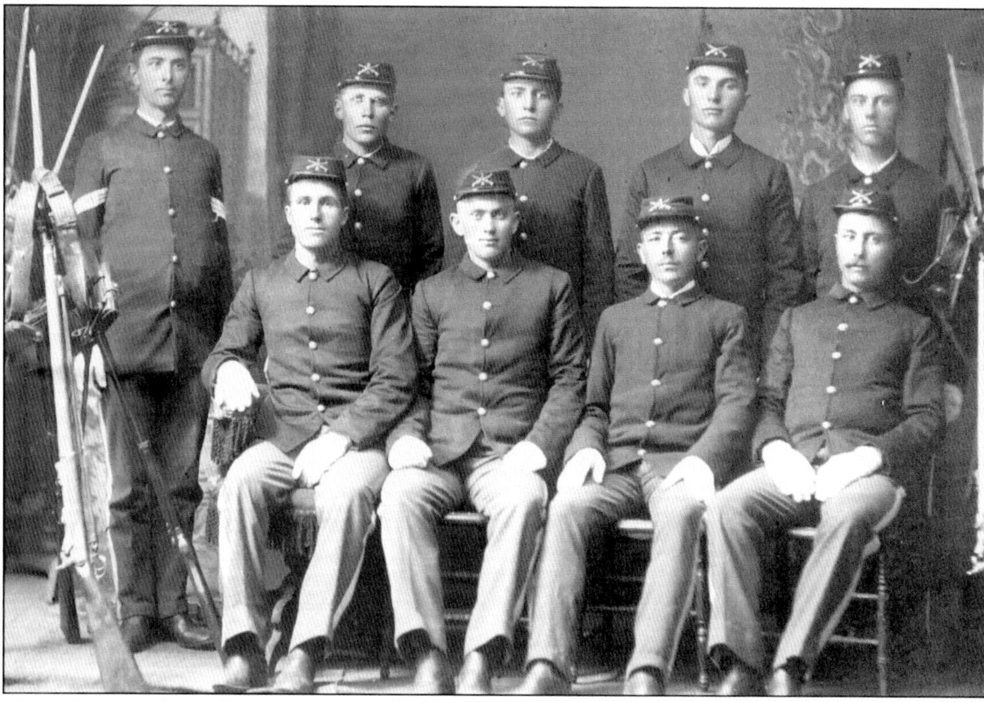

The "Freedom Squad" was Freedom Township's contribution to the Spanish-American War. They are Milo Hodgkins, George Wallace, Ed Deyling, Everett Griffith, Rola Davidson, Andrew Sandsmark, John Farrish, and Smith Hodgkins.

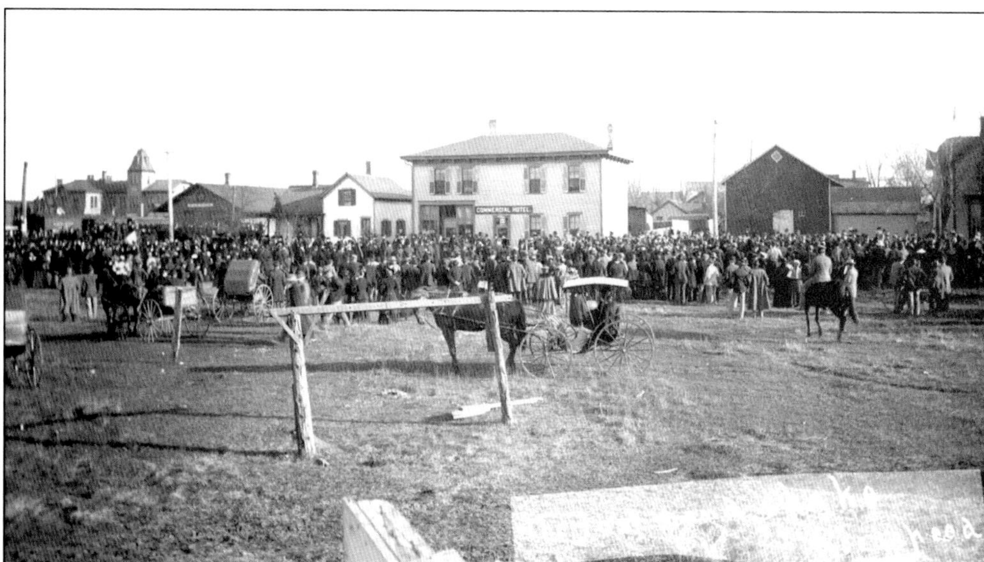

Co. K, 12th MN Volunteers, are leaving for St. Paul to serve in the Spanish-American War in 1898. This scene shows relatives and friends gathering to say good-bye. The boys are leaving from the M.&St.L Depot. Sacred Heart School is visible in the background.

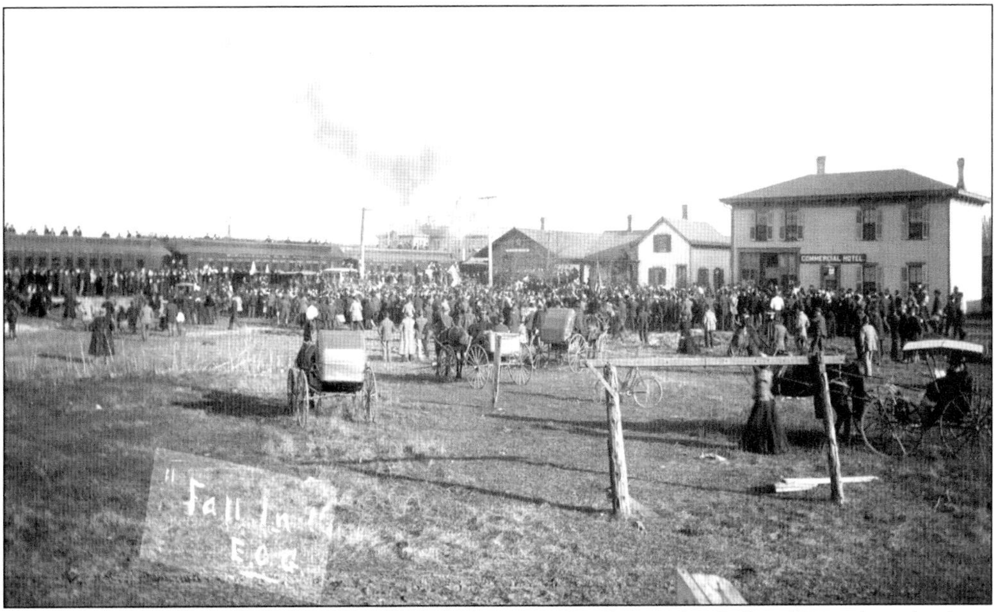

"Fall in" the train has arrived and the soldiers are loading. The Billiard Hotel is the long two-story building. The depot is in the center of the photograph.

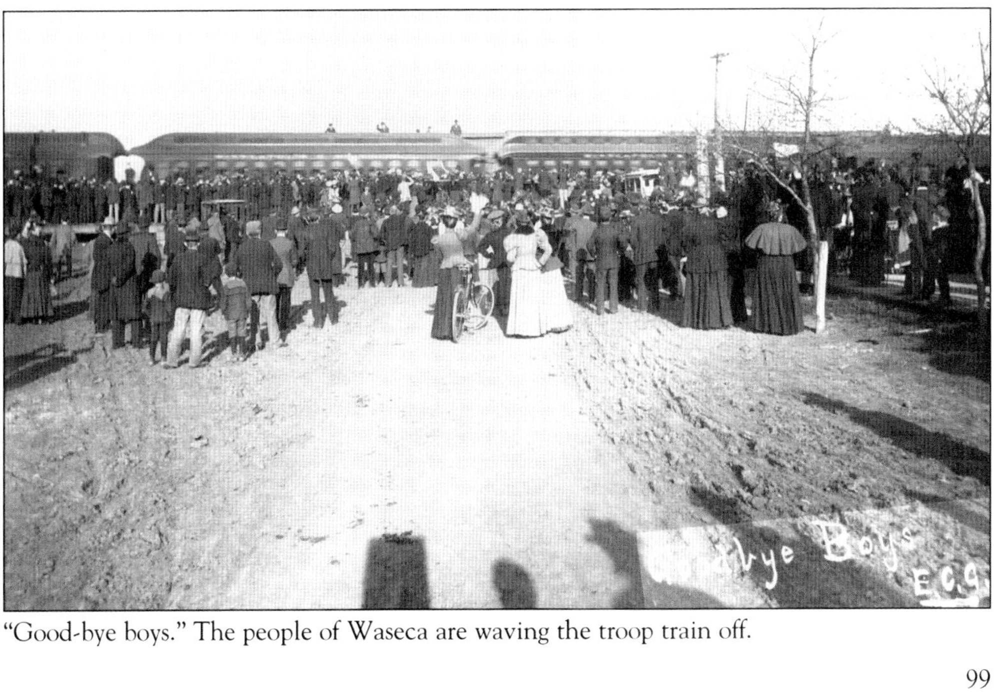

"Good-bye boys." The people of Waseca are waving the troop train off.

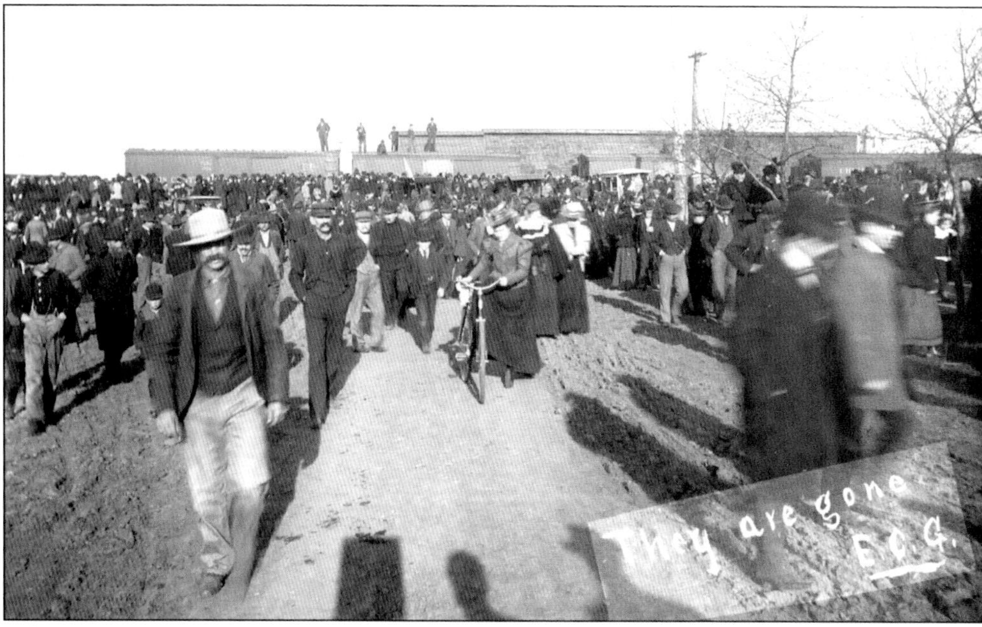

"They are gone." The train has pulled out and citizens are starting to walk away.

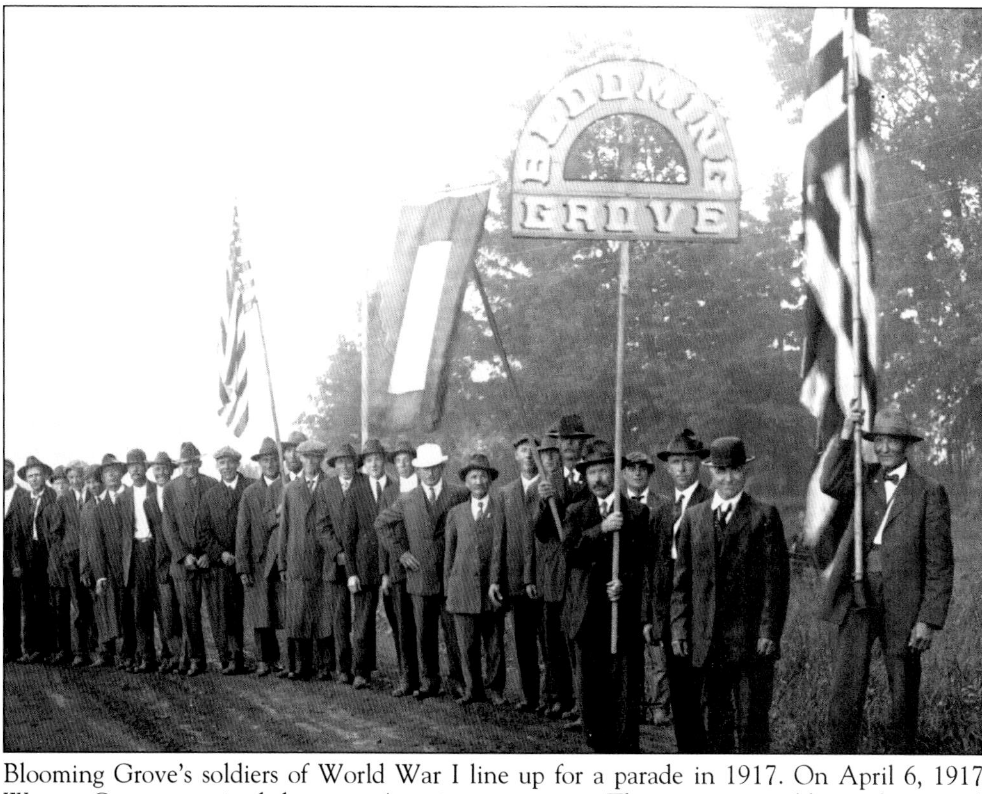

Blooming Grove's soldiers of World War I line up for a parade in 1917. On April 6, 1917, Waseca County received the news America was at war. The country would join forces with France, England, Belgium, and Italy for the cause of liberty. Over 700 men from Waseca County signed up. Twenty-one men lost their lives.

Nine

ORGANIZATIONS

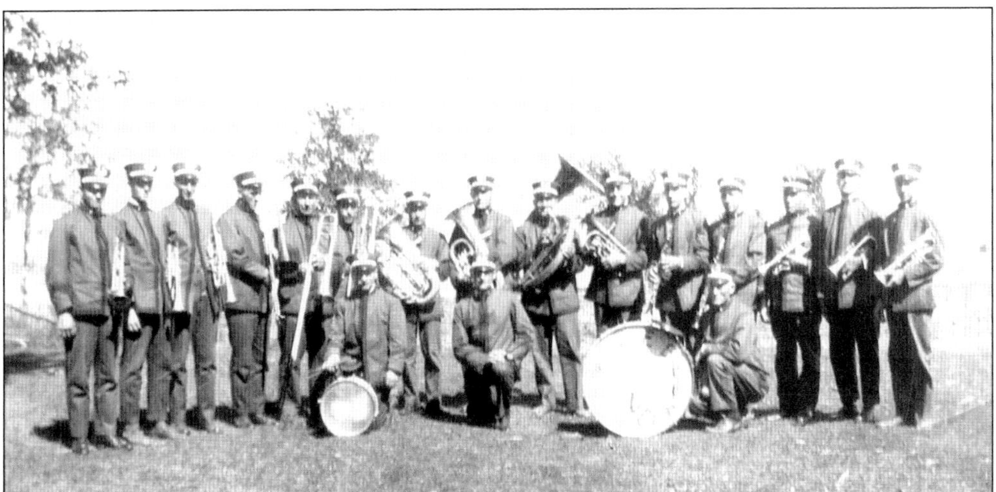

The Freedom Band, according to a notation on the back of this photograph, was a "group associated with the Immanuel Lutheran Church of Freedom Township." The drum has simply "Freedom Band" printed on it. They are partially identified as Carl Manthe (sixth from left), Otto Kiewatt, Mr. Lau, Reinhold, Art, Alfred, and Ernst Marquardt.

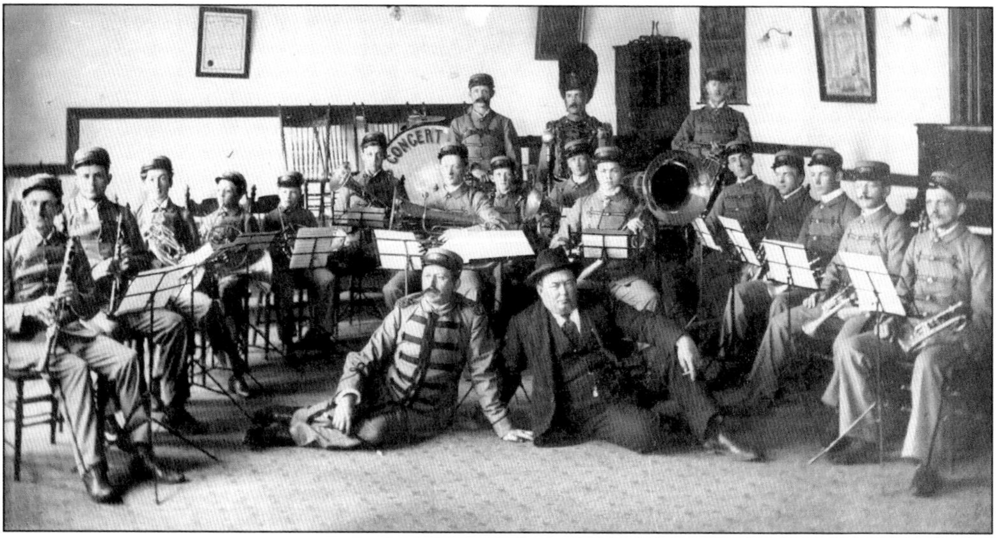

The Janesville Concert Band posed on August 17, 1898, in a practice hall; wearing band uniforms and sitting in a semi-circle for band practice, from left to right, are Burr Davidson, Joe Amberg, Ed Finley, Walter Hollmichel, Kenneth Miner, Ed Hollmichel, Arthur Miner, Al Nyquist, Archie Cordry, Harry Miner, Mr. Sloan, Bert Ives, Seth Dodge, Frank Miner, and George Faltermeyer. Standing in back are Powell Ayars, Joe Goodrich, and Joe Davidson. Seated at left in front on floor is band leader, Mr. Herman; and at right is Dr. Martin Taylor, who started the Janesville Concert Band, also known as Taylor's Concert Band.

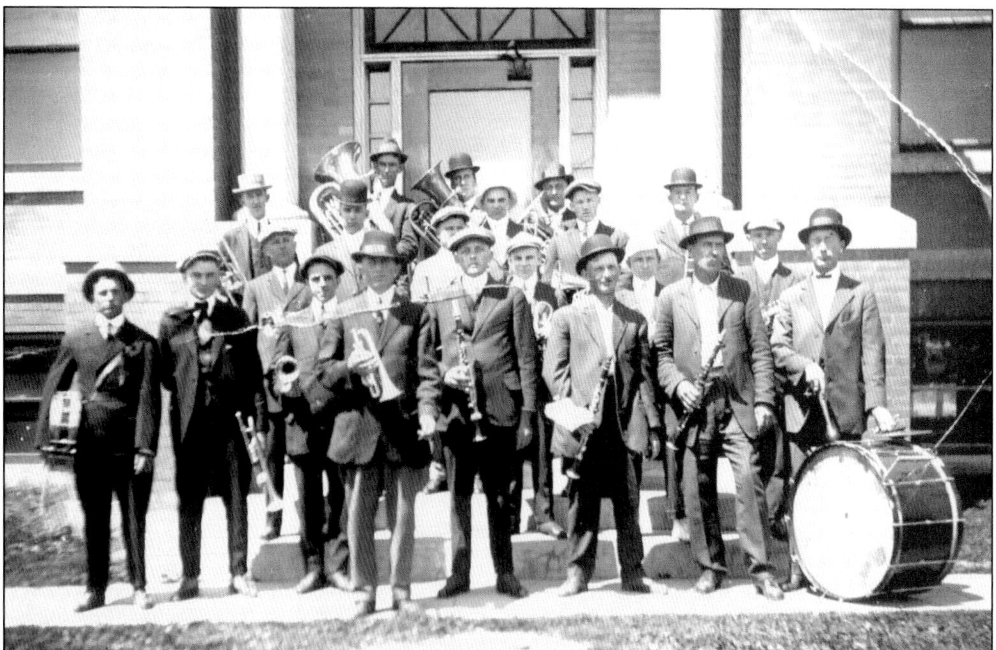

The Janesville Concert Band poses in front of the Janesville Public Library in 1918. The library is one of the nine National Historic Register sites in Waseca County. It is a classic example of a Carnegie Library with very few changes to its interior or exterior.

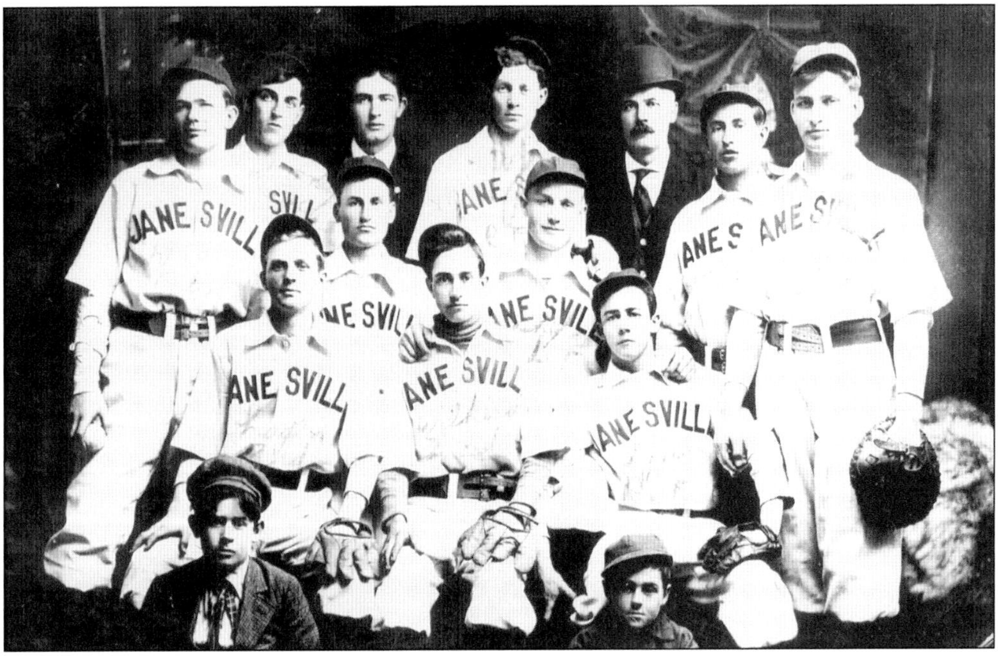

The Janesville baseball team has been partially identified as Davis, Jones, Munthy, Arnold, Shepard, Hagen, Wilkison, Shepard, and Lynch.

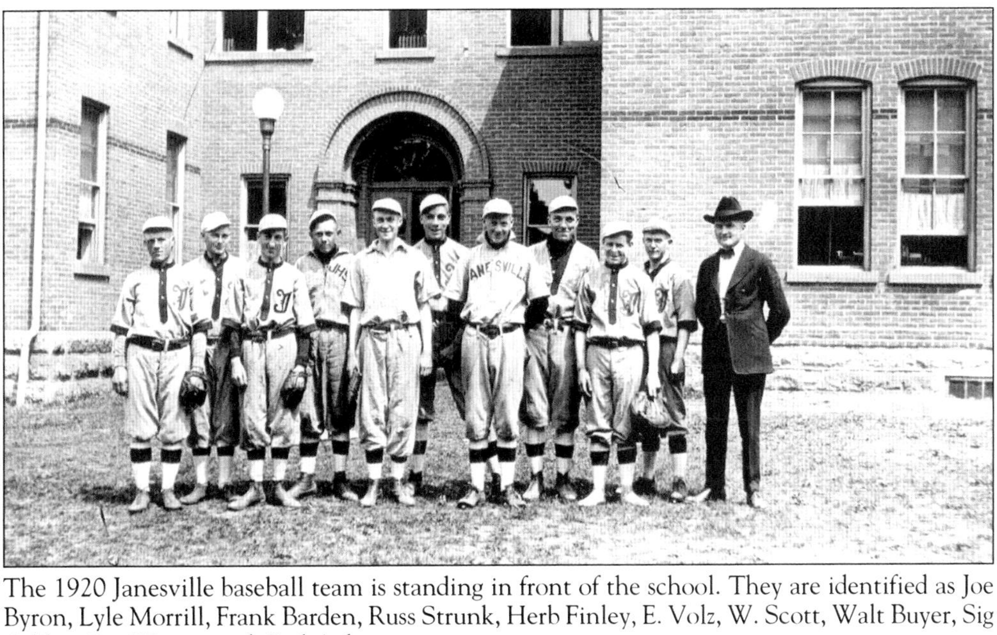

The 1920 Janesville baseball team is standing in front of the school. They are identified as Joe Byron, Lyle Morrill, Frank Barden, Russ Strunk, Herb Finley, E. Volz, W. Scott, Walt Buyer, Sig Gilday, Pip Wagge, and Carl Aaberg.

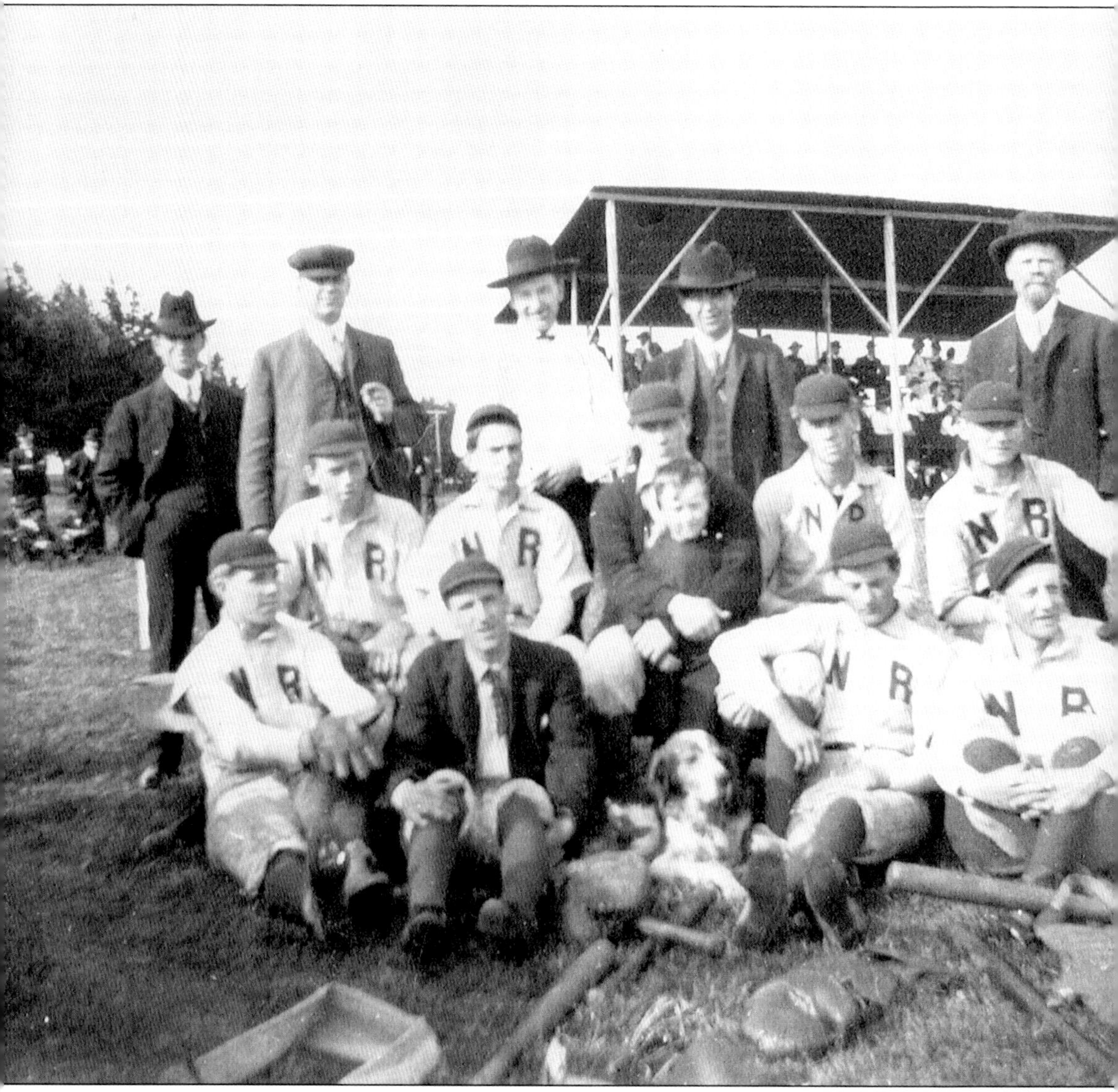

The 1900 New Richland baseball team poses complete with mascot sitting in uniform, ready to play ball. Even the crowd appears to be waiting patiently for the game to start. Emil Schwenke is second from left and Leo Max Klersig is sitting to his left.

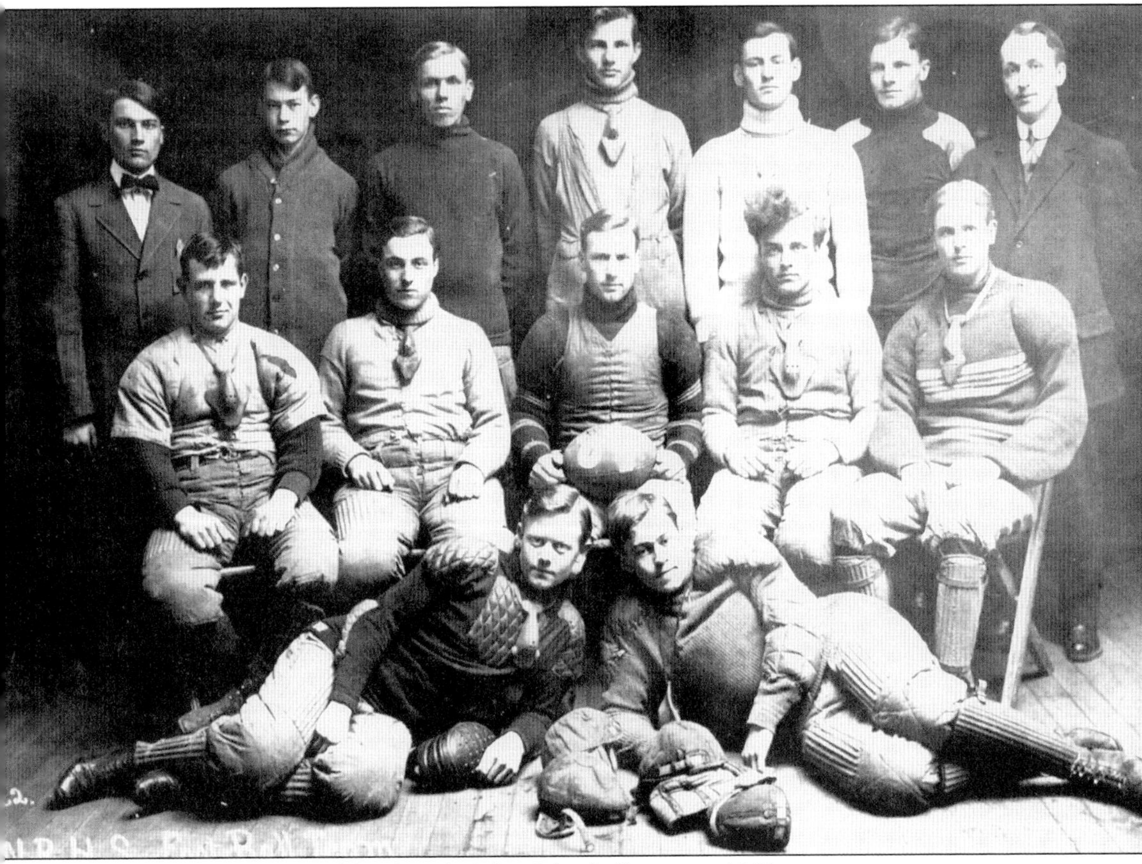

Pictured is the New Richland High School football team in 1909.

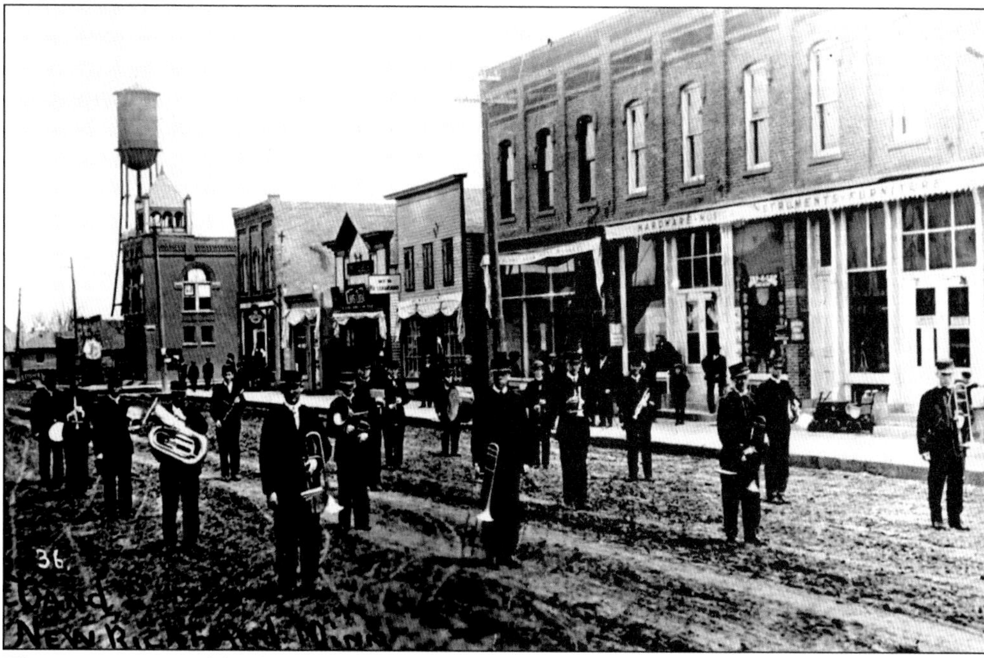

The 1918 New Richland band is in uniform, standing at attention in the dirt street ready to march. In the background is the water tower, electrical lines, New Richland City Hall, New Restaurant, Oien Store, Nitschke Market, and a hardware and furniture store.

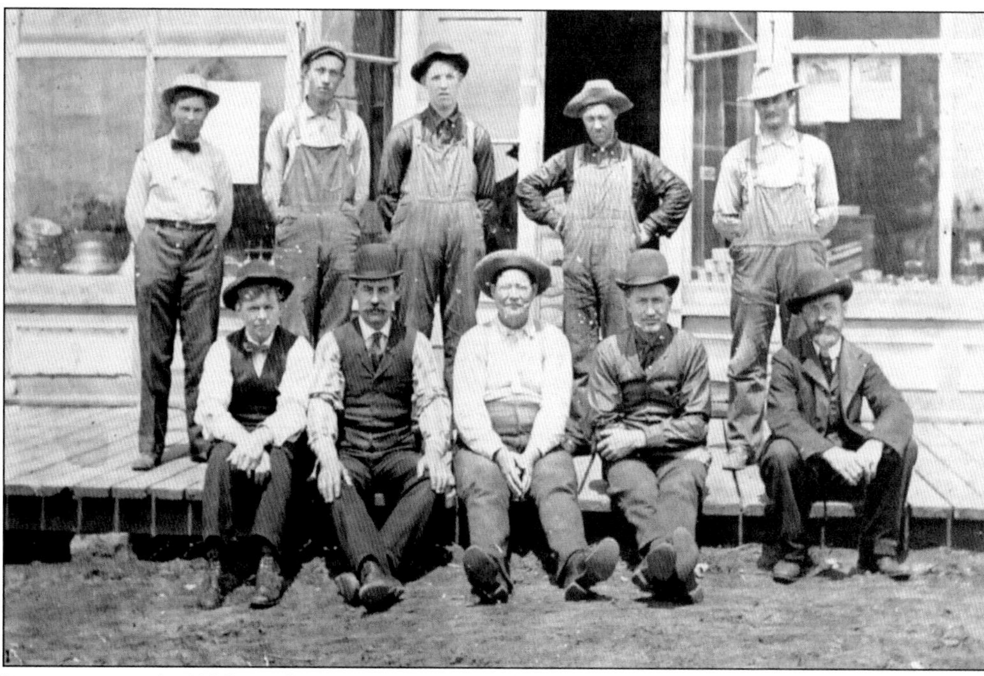

In approximately 1905, an Otisco group poses in front of the Johnson Store. In the middle back row is A.J. Anderson, the buttermaker, and in the front row on the left is Herman Peterson. If one were to guess by the clothing, it could be said that this group is a mixture of "farm boys" and "city slickers." Someone else had other ideas, as the notation written on the front is "Otisco Hobos".

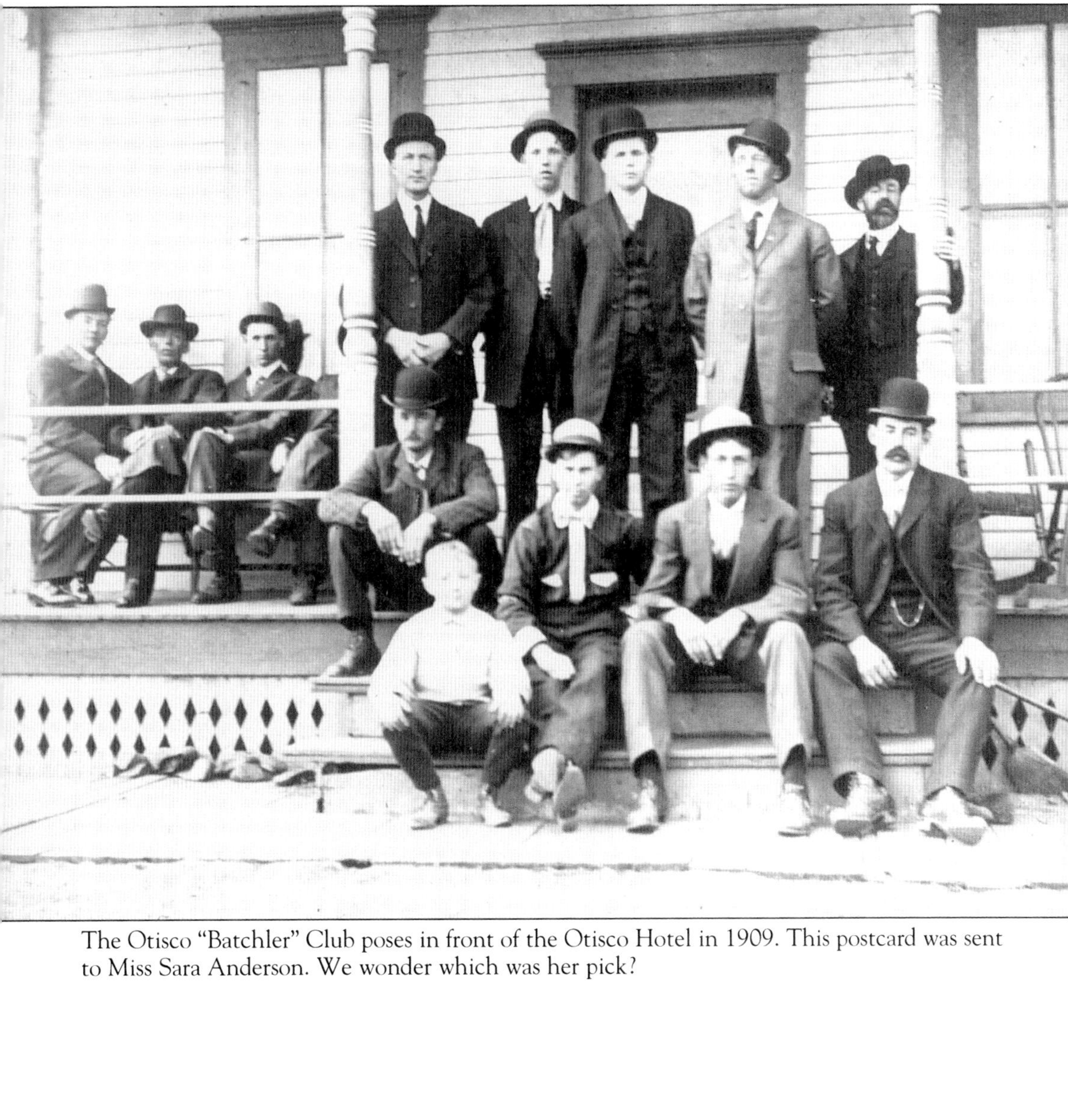

The Otisco "Batchler" Club poses in front of the Otisco Hotel in 1909. This postcard was sent to Miss Sara Anderson. We wonder which was her pick?

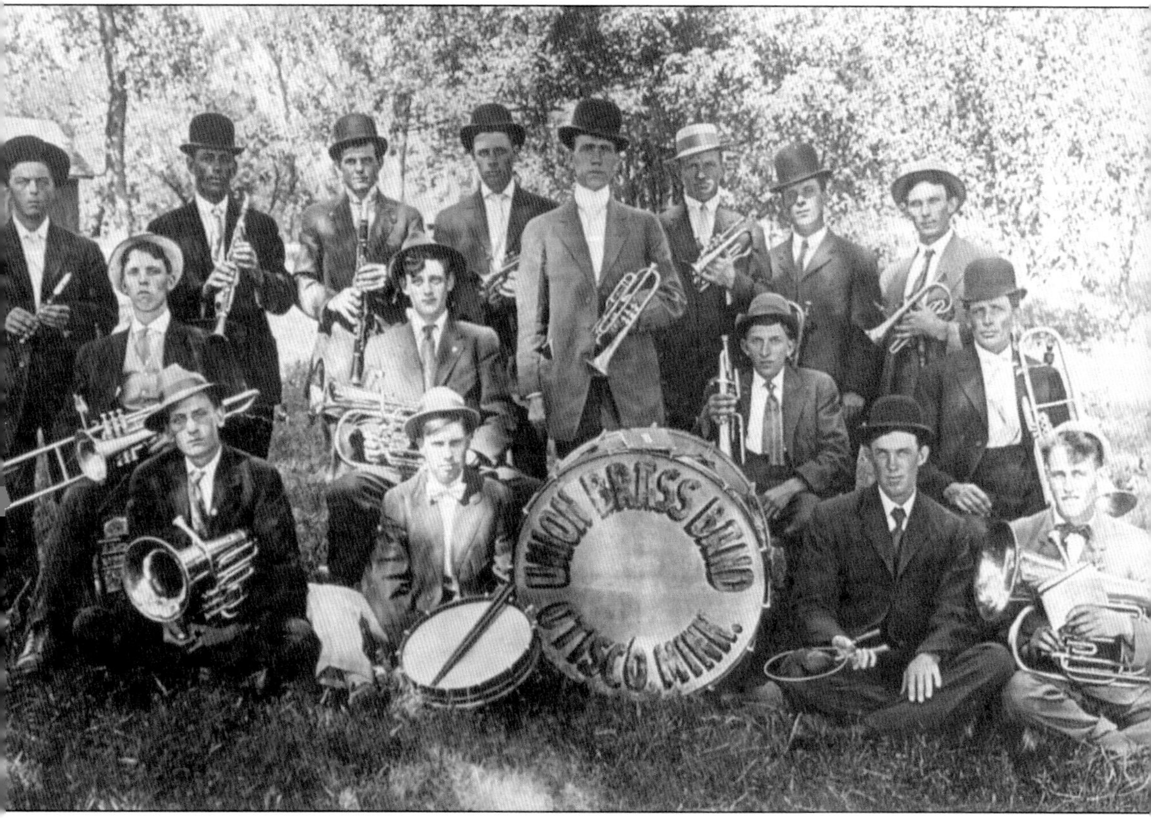

The 1911 Otisco Union Brass Band decked out in their best pose with their instruments.

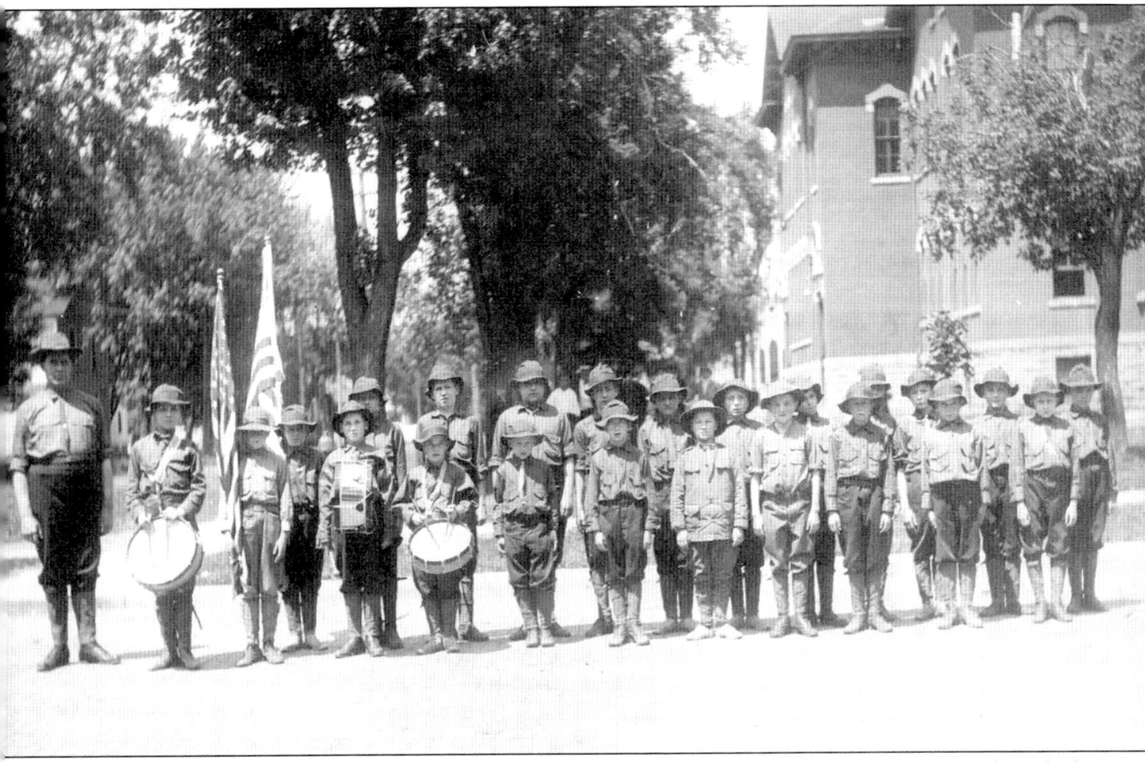

The Waseca Boy Scouts stand in front of the school at parade attention. They are identified as Reverend George Stoew, scoutmaster; Will Cummins, Neil Gore, Gordon Didra, Holland Norton, George Meyers, Jack Leuthold, Allen Wolf, Owen Smith, Ward Watson, Will Carrol, Chester Wyman, Erwin Hertz, Harvey Larson, Oren Roessler, Walter Hertz, Kenneth Lust, Roy Mellinger, Earl Faes, Lowell Lust, Fred Roessler, Stanley, the assistant scoutmaster, Anderson, Roy Meddagh, unknown, unknown, and Jurgen Martinson.

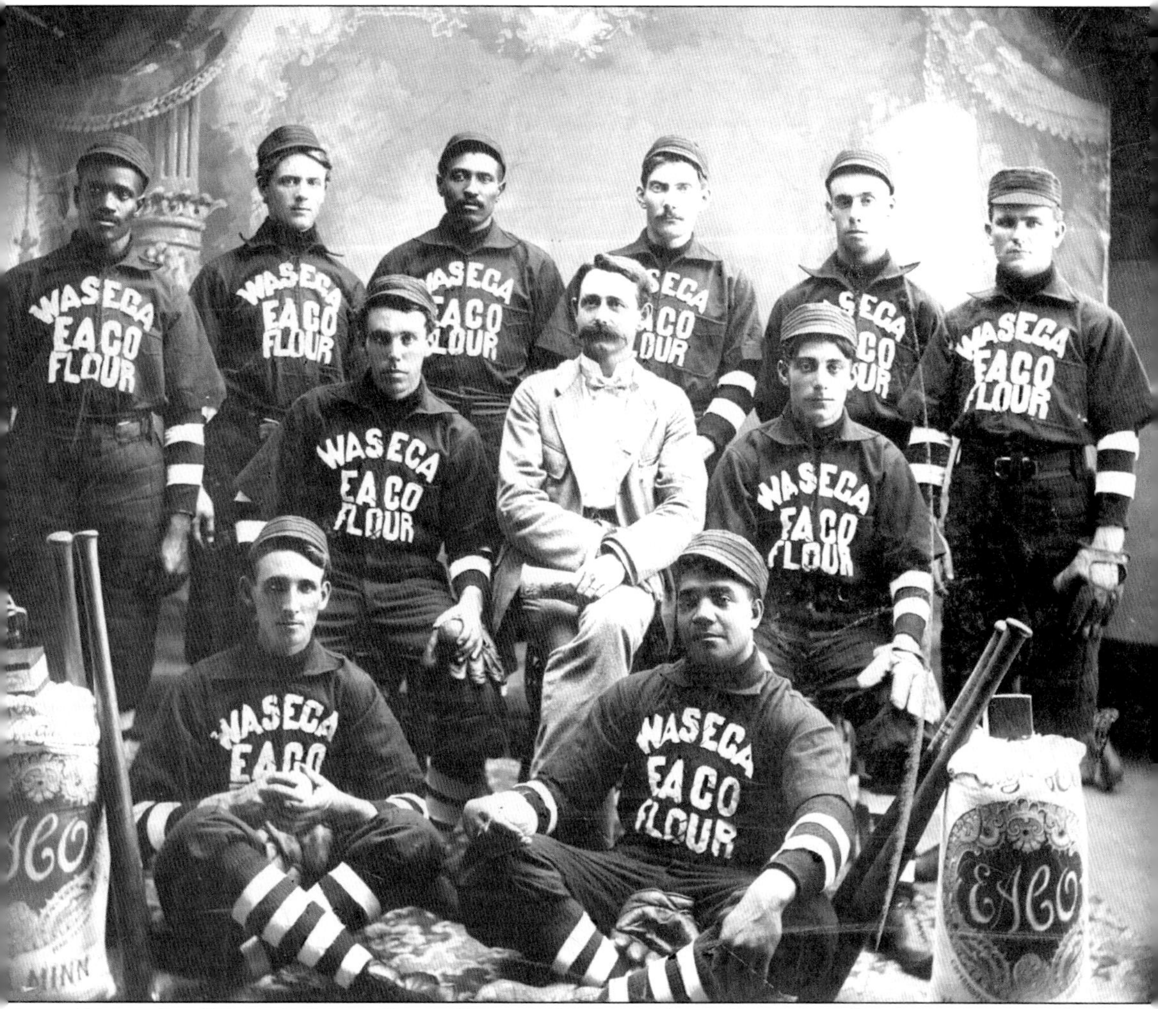

Pictured is Waseca's famous baseball team of 1900 and 1901. In 1900 the EACO team—of which W.J. Armstrong was manager, R.P. Ward, the president, and L.W. Sterling, the treasurer—won the state amateur championship. They played 57 games that season and lost only 15. The team is pictured, from left to right, as follows: (front row) William Brisbane (pitcher), and Ed Woods (pitcher); (middle row) William Foster (center field), W.J. Armstrong (manager), William Veron (second base); (back row) Bob Foote (catcher), Theodore Snyder (right field), Bill Joiner (short stop), C.R. Wattles (first base), S. Foster (left field), and Bob Mackey (third base). They played the best clubs in Minnesota, Iowa, and Wisconsin, and even journeyed to Chicago to play the Flandreau Indians and the Chicago Marquettes. In 1901 the team reached the peak of its fame, winning the amateur titles in Minnesota, Iowa, and South Dakota. Rivalry between Waseca and Litchfield that year made the state championship series the greatest attraction before or since. Owner of the Lexington Park in St. Paul was offered a percentage to stage the game in the park. They refused because they said they couldn't afford to pay the ushers out of what they figured the gate would bring. So Waseca and Litchfield rented the grounds for a flat $50 to the everlasting sorrow of the St. Paul Management. Special trains were run and the game drew over 10,000 people. Waseca won the game by a 9–2 score.

Ten

Recreation and Celebrations

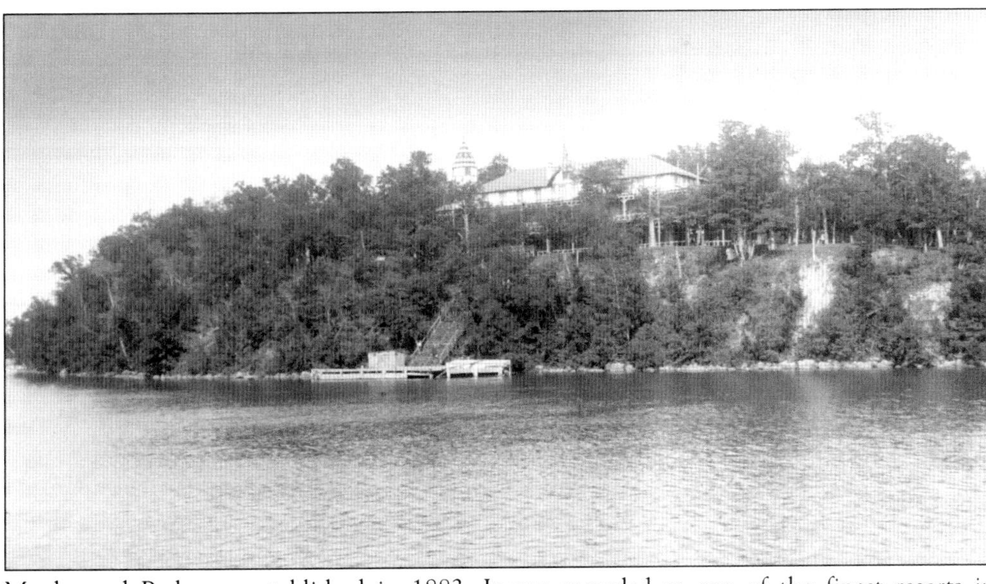

Maplewood Park was established in 1883. It was regarded as one of the finest resorts in Minnesota. From 1883 to 1898, the park was host to a traveling show called "Chautauqua." The Chautauqua movement was named after a lake in upstate New York where the first assembly was held in the 1870s. Many Chautauqua troops toured America from the 1870s through the 1920s.

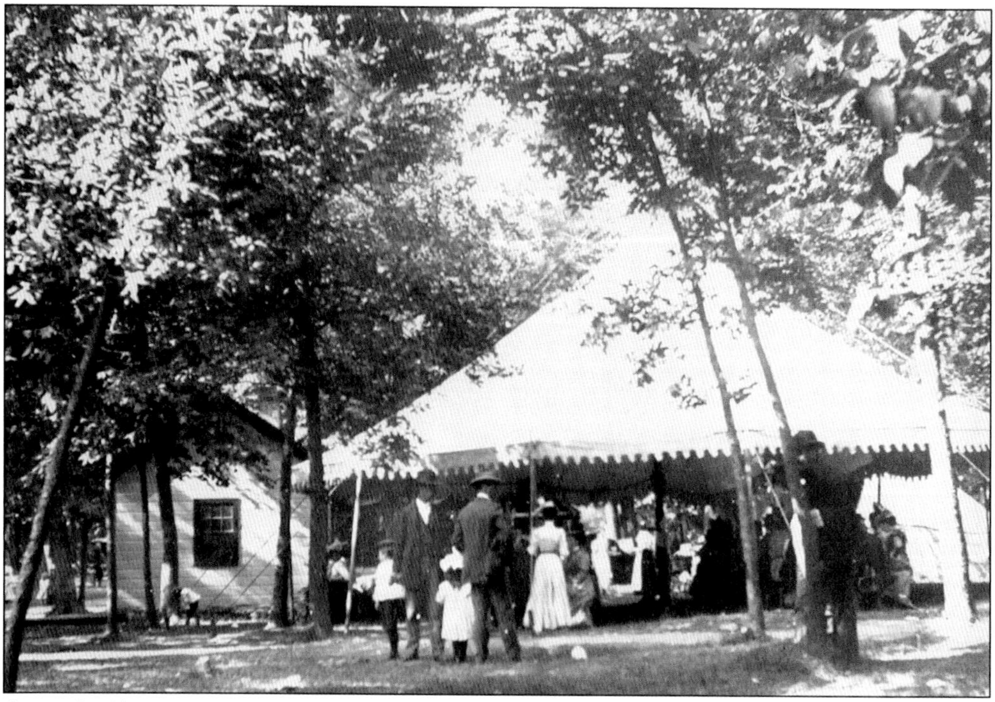

An early Chautauqua assembly is seen here at Maplewood Park. The purpose of the assembly was to bring education, religion, economics, and culture to the people in rural America. Hundreds of people traveled by train to attend these assemblies. Horse-drawn buses could bring as many as 40 passengers to the Maplewood gates.

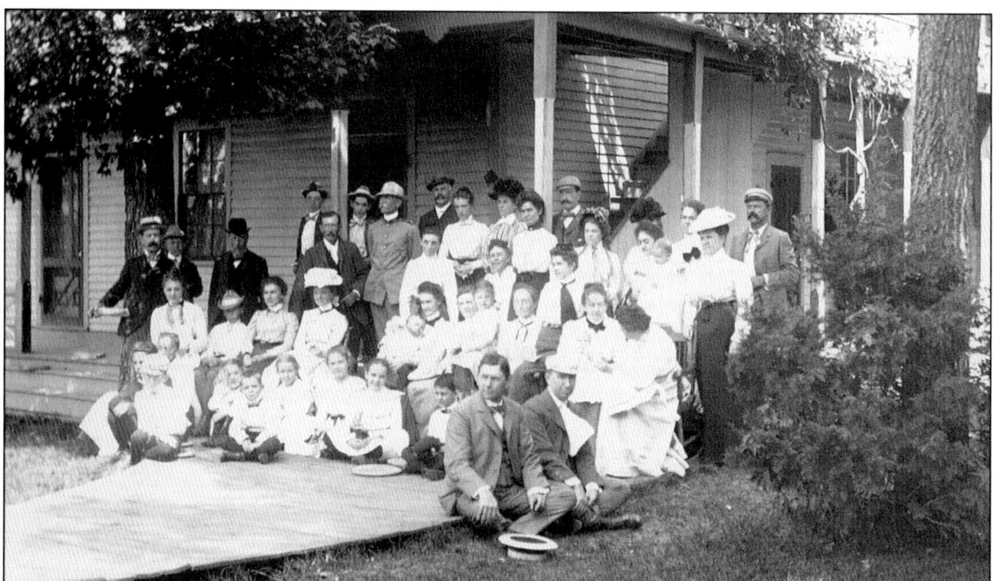

A three-story hotel was built in Maplewood Park in 1883 at a cost of $5,000. The upper levels had 40 rooms for guests. Tent platforms were also available to rent as well as canvas tents and furniture. There was a large auditorium which seated 500 or more, a meeting hall, grocery store, stable and, for recreation, a one-lane bowling alley and a wooden waterslide.

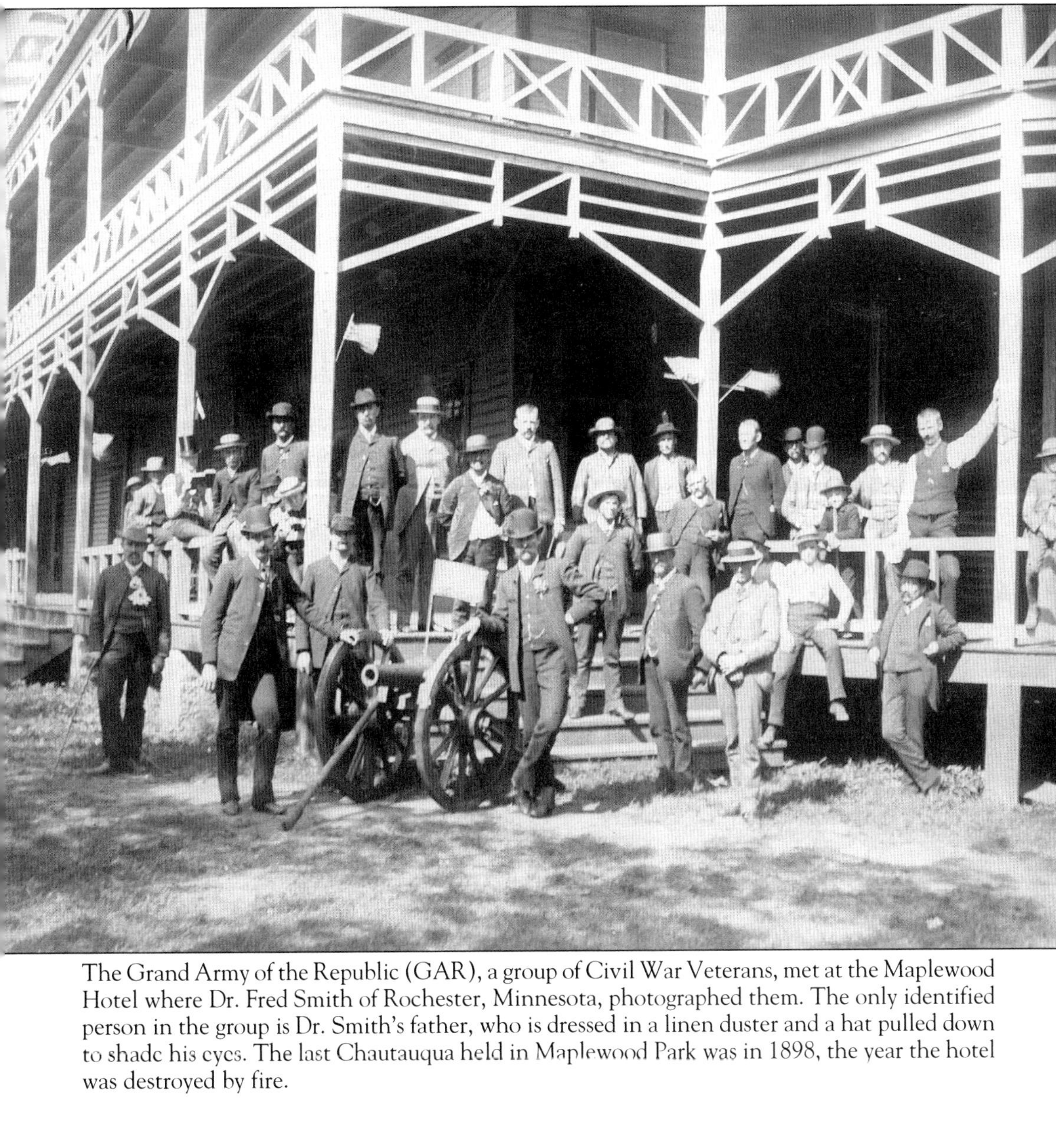

The Grand Army of the Republic (GAR), a group of Civil War Veterans, met at the Maplewood Hotel where Dr. Fred Smith of Rochester, Minnesota, photographed them. The only identified person in the group is Dr. Smith's father, who is dressed in a linen duster and a hat pulled down to shade his eyes. The last Chautauqua held in Maplewood Park was in 1898, the year the hotel was destroyed by fire.

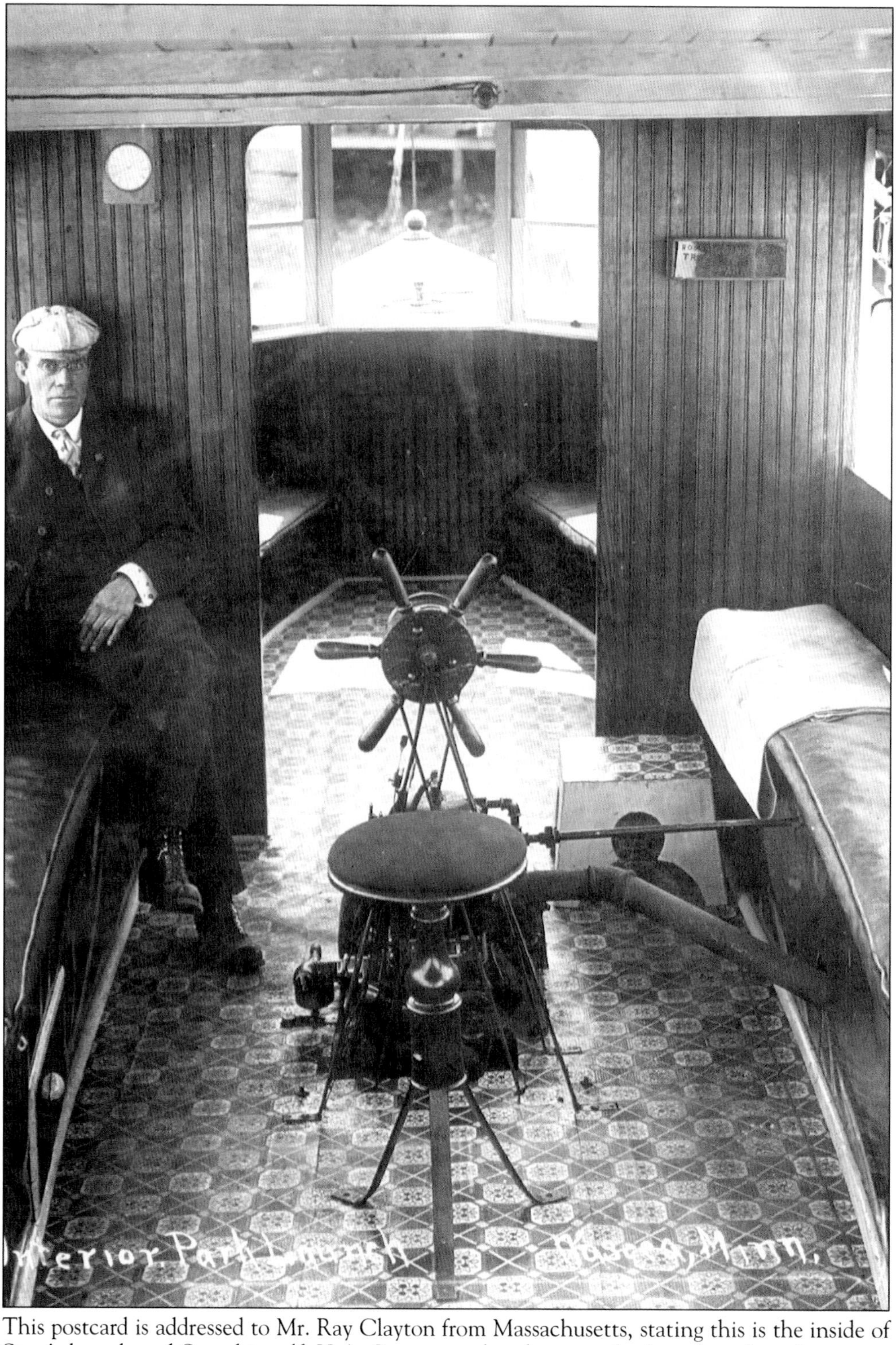

This postcard is addressed to Mr. Ray Clayton from Massachusetts, stating this is the inside of Starr's launch and Starr himself. H.A. Starr owned and operated a boat launch and camping and picnic grounds on the northwestern shore of Clear Lake. It was called North Star Park.

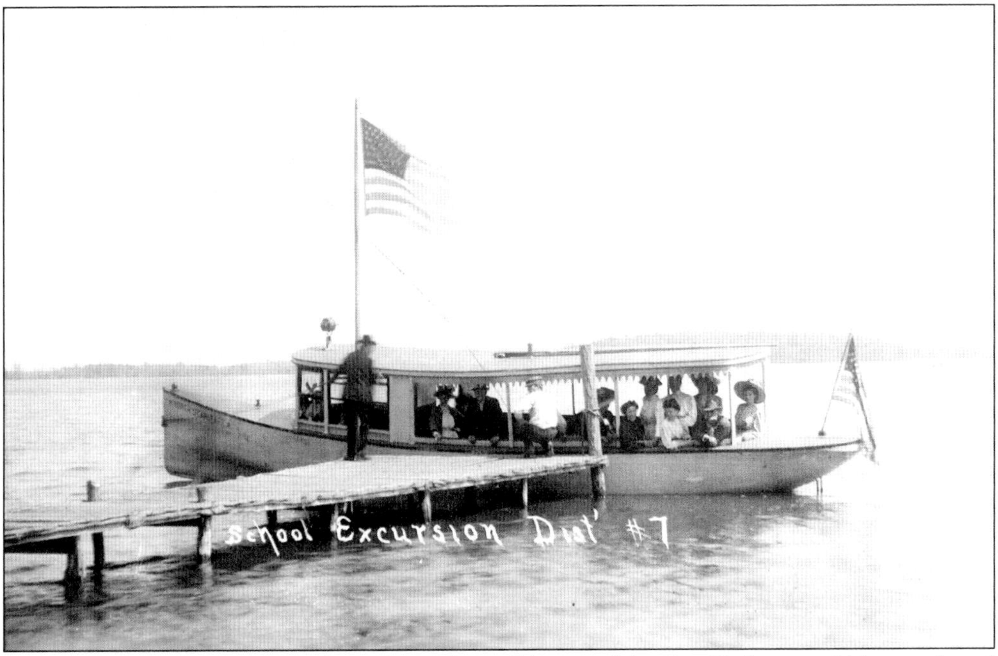

The launches traveled to and from the park at all hours of the day. Tickets could be purchased at Thompson's Boathouse.

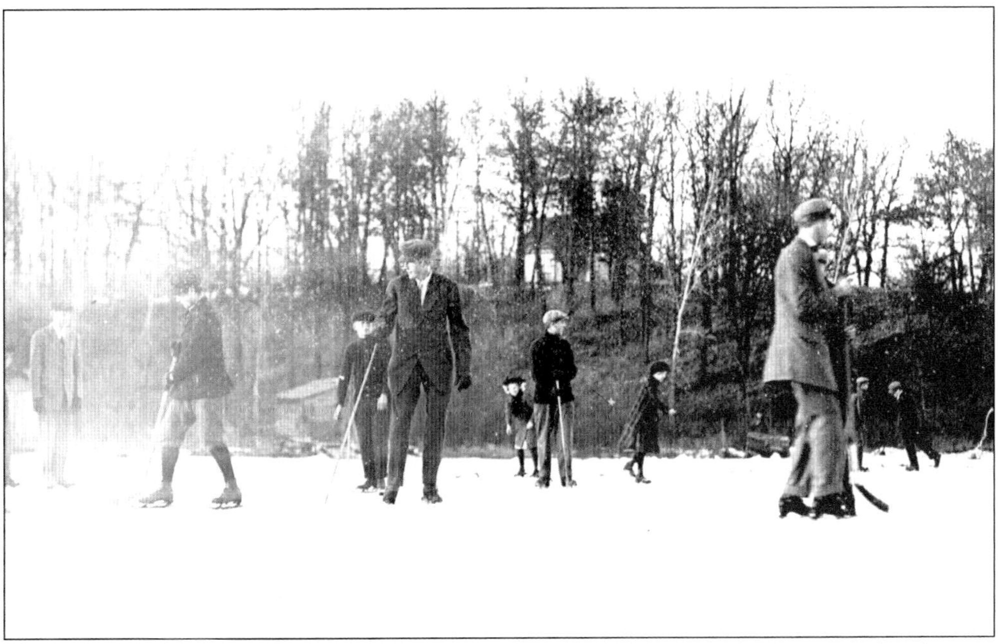

This image of Winter's Point, Clear Lake, is dated 1911. Clear Lake was a popular place in the winter months as well. The lake ice was cleared and lighted at Garret's in 1899. Garret's later to became Thompson's Boathouse. In 1925 music was added for skating. Ice carnivals and masquerades were held. An estimated 500 people attended one masquerade at Garrett's rink on January 18, 1898. Ice boating and sailing was also considered a fashionable amusement in the 1880s.

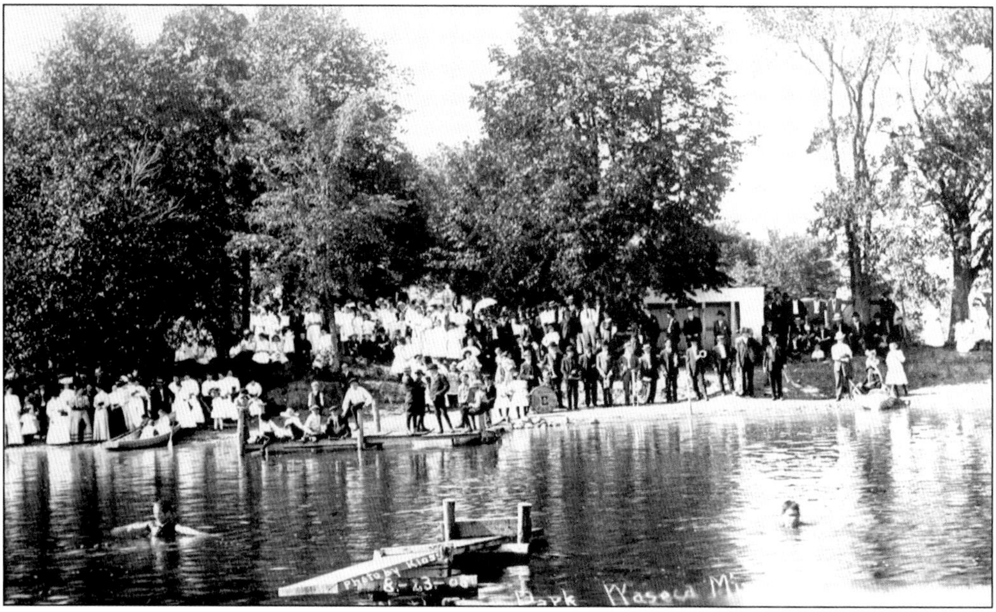

Attendees enjoy themselves at the 1908 M.N.A. and Workman Picnic at North Star Park. In March 1917, H.A. Starr announced plans to build a modern bathhouse—a two-story building with changing booths, sterilizing room, showers, and office. H.A. Starr placed an ad in the *Waseca Journal* on October 30, 1929, announcing the closing of the North Shore Boat Livery: "Notice, on account of poor health I have decided to sell my boats and quit business. Boats are for sale at a bargain."

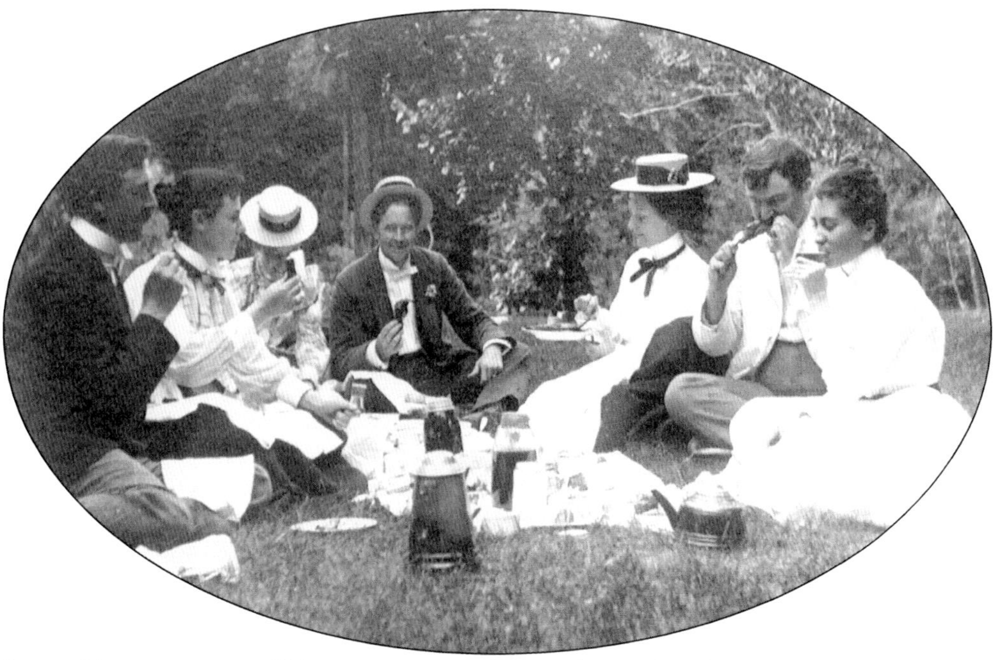

Pictured here is a group of Waseca young people picnicking. The place is unknown, but North Star Park is a likely possibility. Pictured, from left to right, are William and Mrs. Swift, Hetty Everett, Guy W. Everett, unidentified, E.A. Everett, and Nettie Miller (Everett).

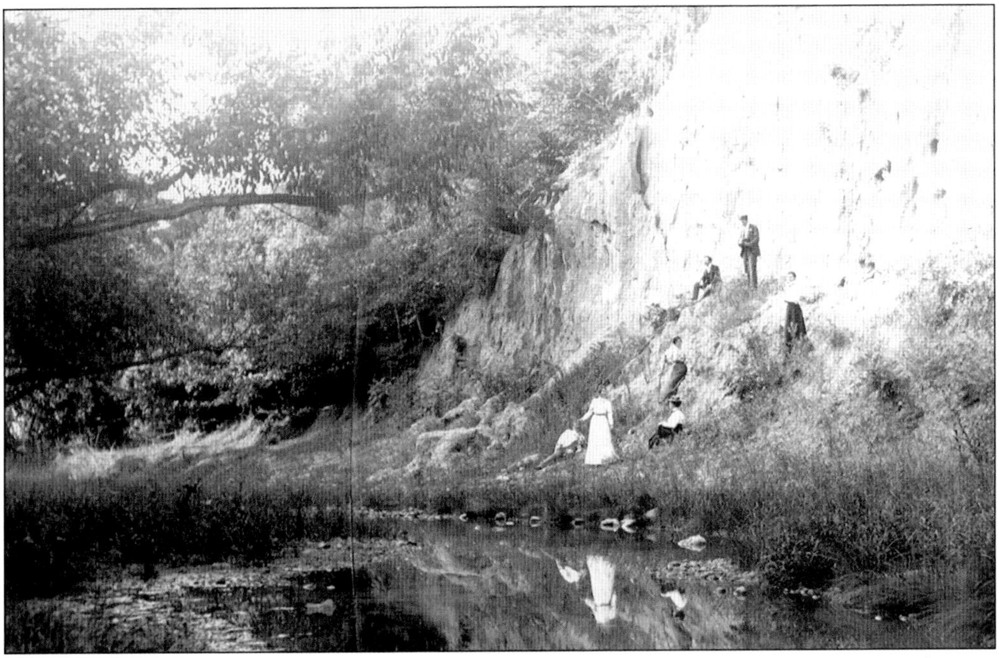

Pictured is a scene along the Little LeSueur River just below a sandy cliff in what is now known as Court House Park. Nettie (Miller) Everett is standing in white dress. Her husband, E.A. Everett, is sitting reclined to her left.

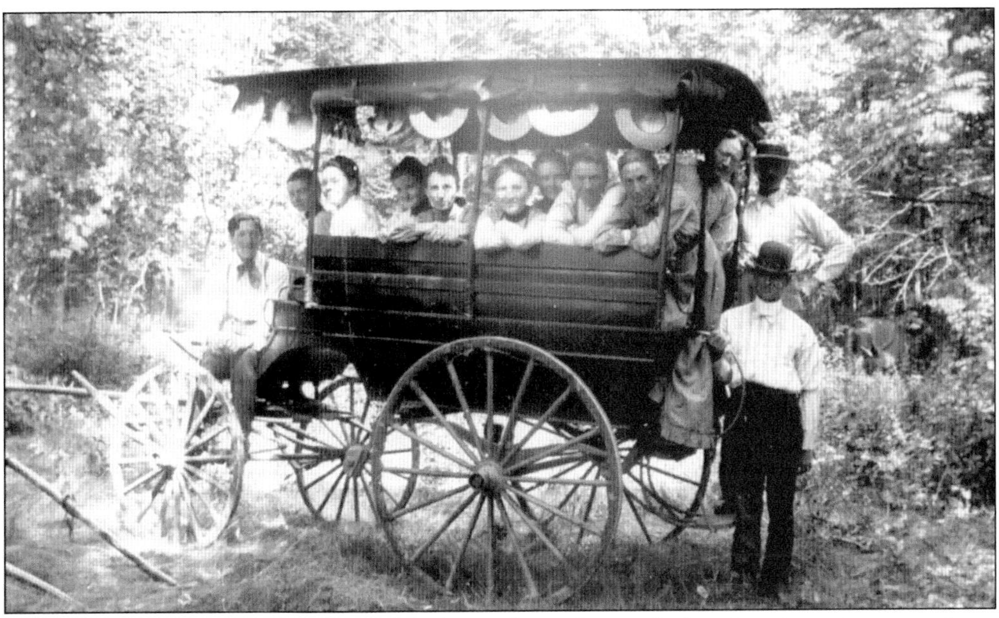

This group of young people pose in their horse-drawn bus with their hats hung in a row above their heads. It is not known where this picnic took place, but it is known they are having a grand time. This photograph came to the collection in Julia Hawks' photo album. She is seated the fourth from left and her sister Hannah Hawks is the first on the right hanging over the side of the bus. More than one rig was used to carry them to their destination, as the tongues of other rigs are visible on the ground to the left.

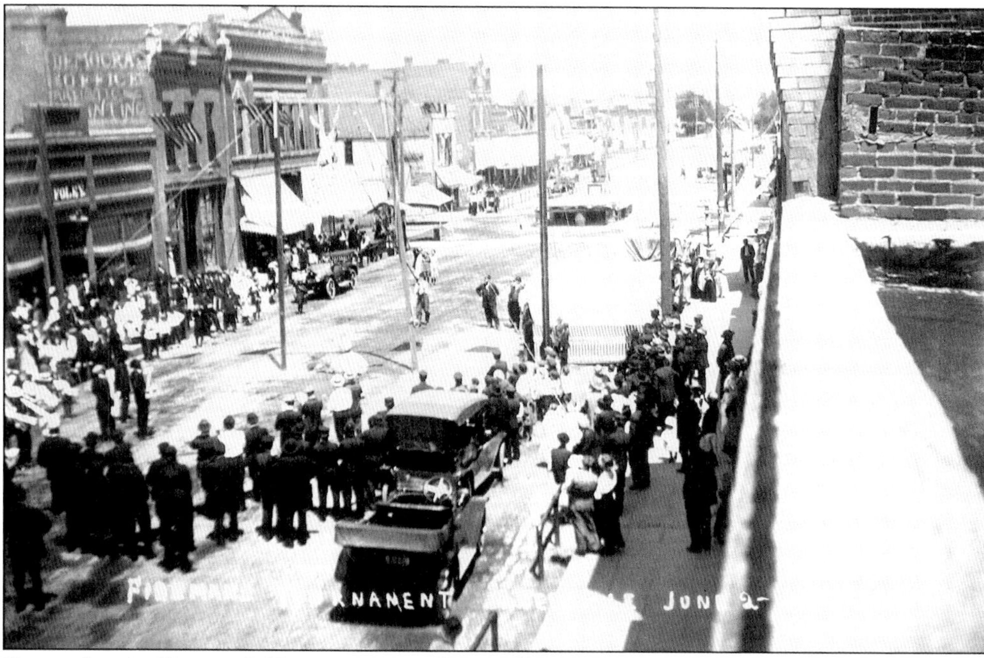

Pictured is the Firemen's Tournament on Janesville's Main Street on June 2, 1914.

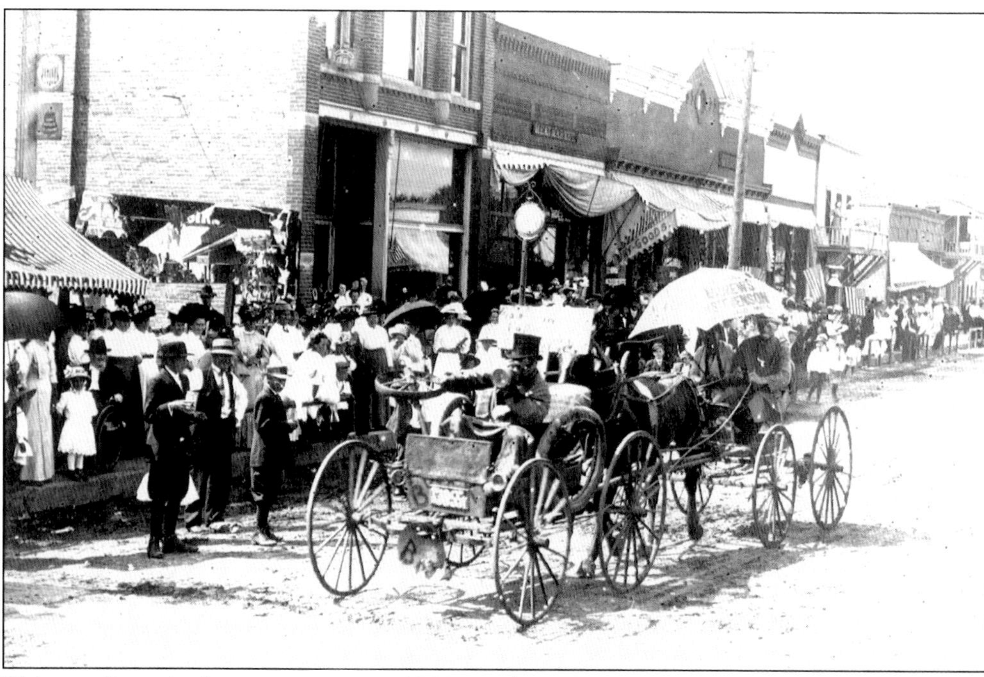

This peculiar vehicle participates in a 1900 parade on Main Street in Janesville.

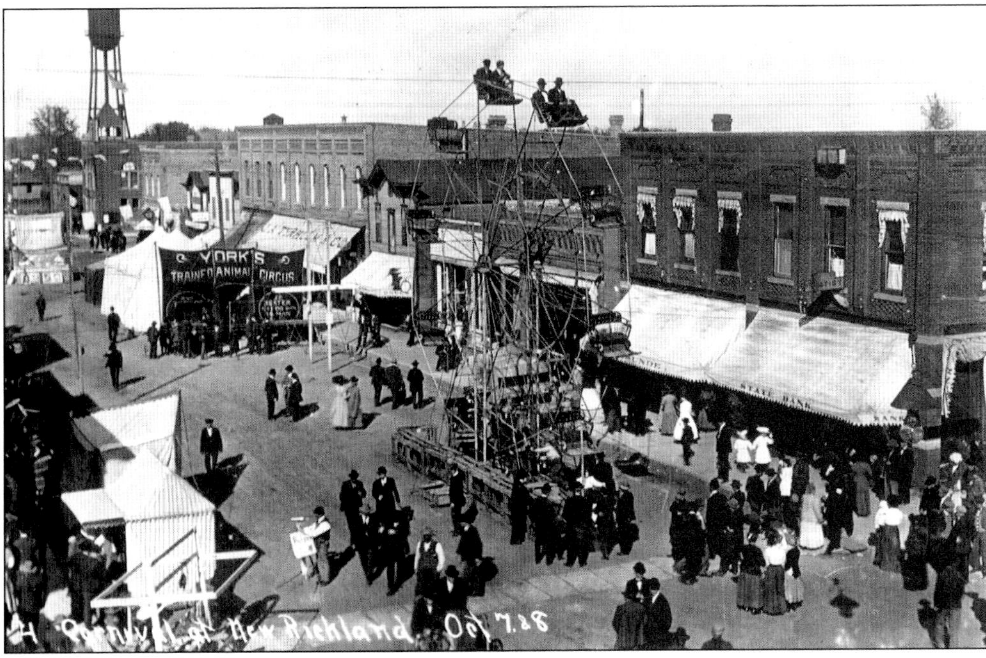

Seen here is a street carnival in New Richland.

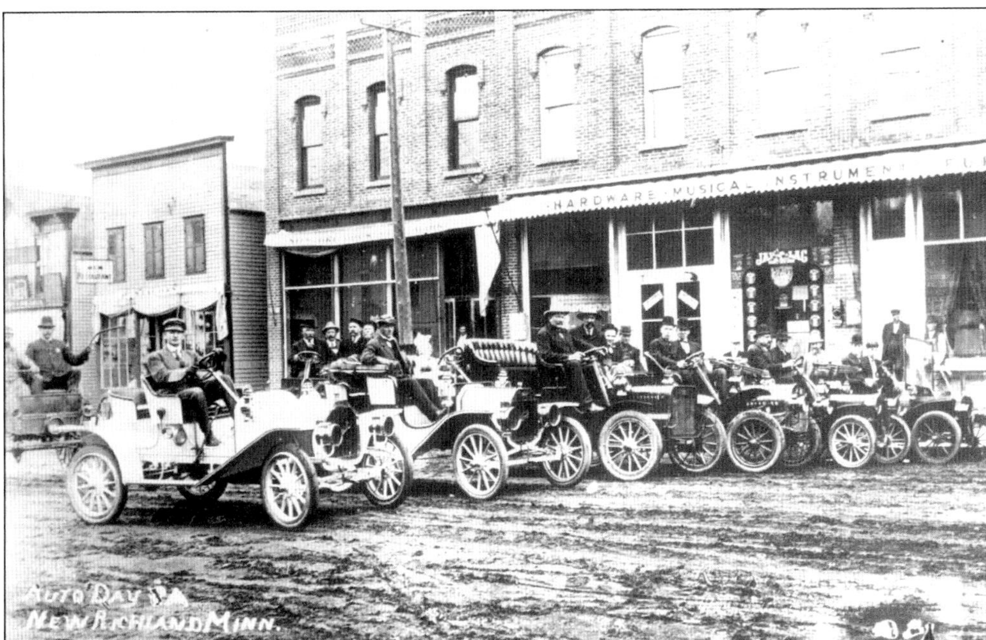

"Hold me Newt" they cried while these fierce demons of the road lined up for a Sunday tour in 1909. New Richland celebrates its Auto Day. Some of the drivers identified are Dr. H.O. Hagen, F.H. Kruger (who purchased the first car in New Richland), Herbert Bestman, and Harold Sunde (with John Christenson as a passenger).

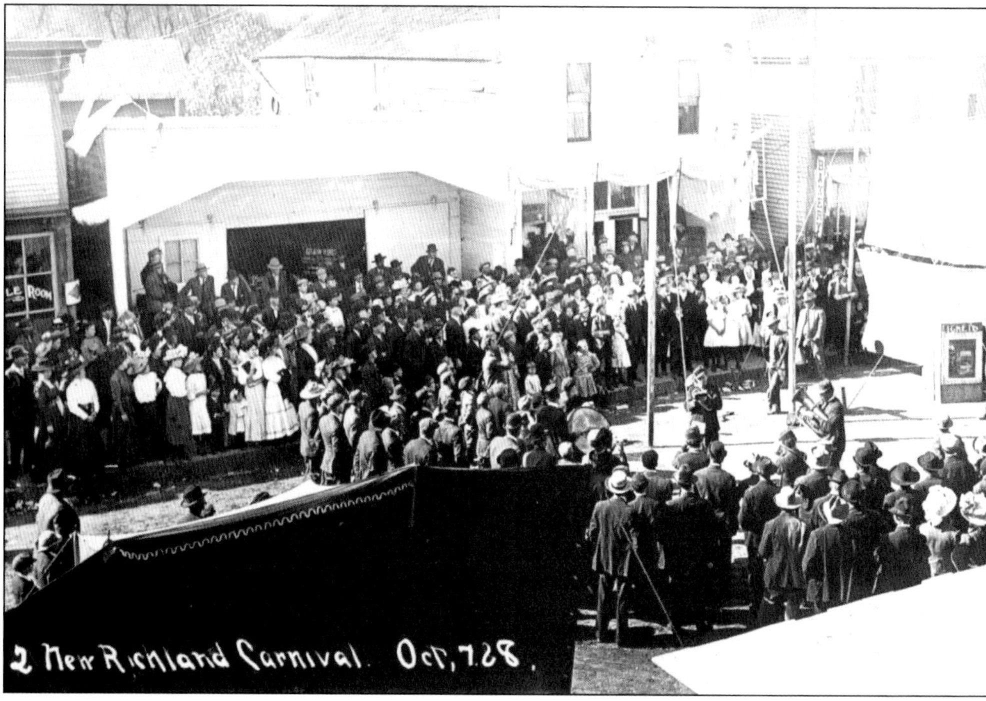

Pictured is the New Richland Street Carnival crowd in 1910.

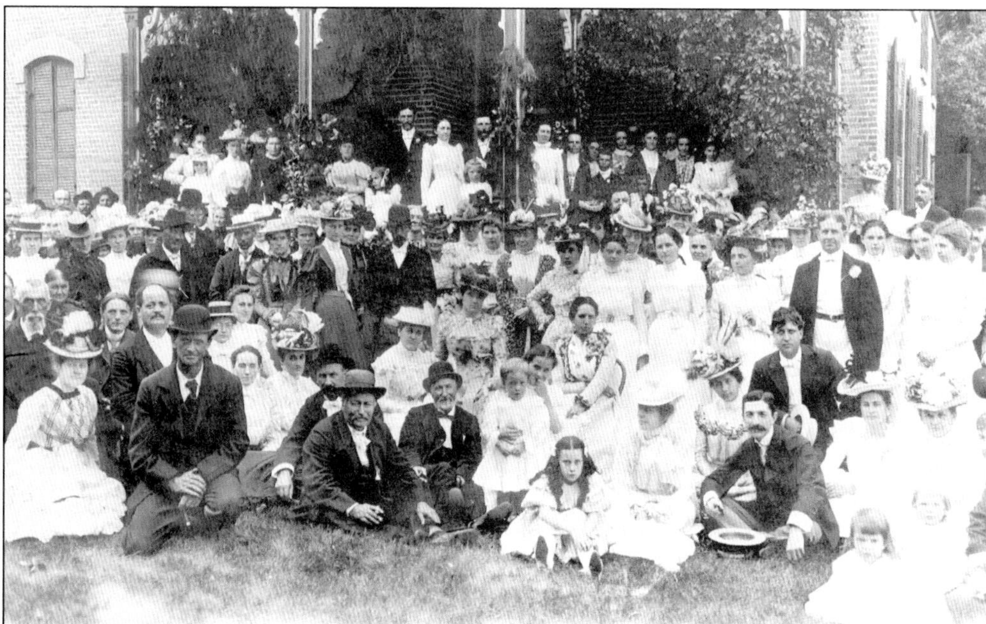
Many friends and family turned out for Nancy Phelps' marriage to Andrew Henderson on August 30, 1899. Andrew died in an accident in his roller mill in Madelia in 1900. Nancy died in California in 1921. Both are buried at Woodville Cemetery in Waseca. They were married in her parents' home on County Road 2, just west of Waseca. The Phelps house was built in 1869 and was on the National Historic Register until it was torn down in the early 1990s.

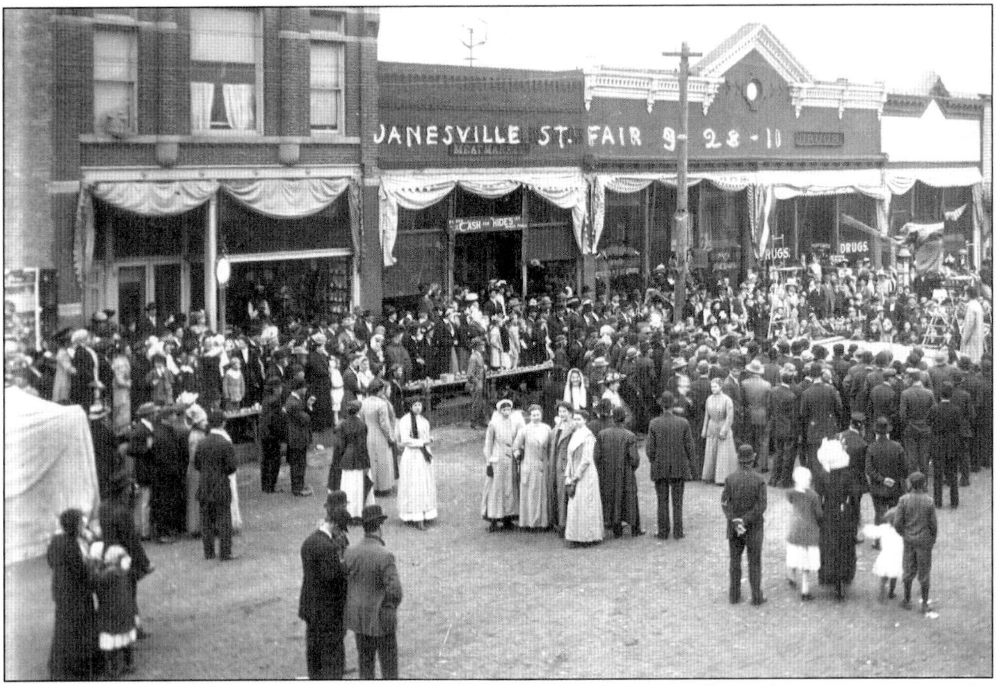

A large crowd has gathered to watch a balancing act being performed on the stage at the Janesville Street Fair on September 28, 1911.

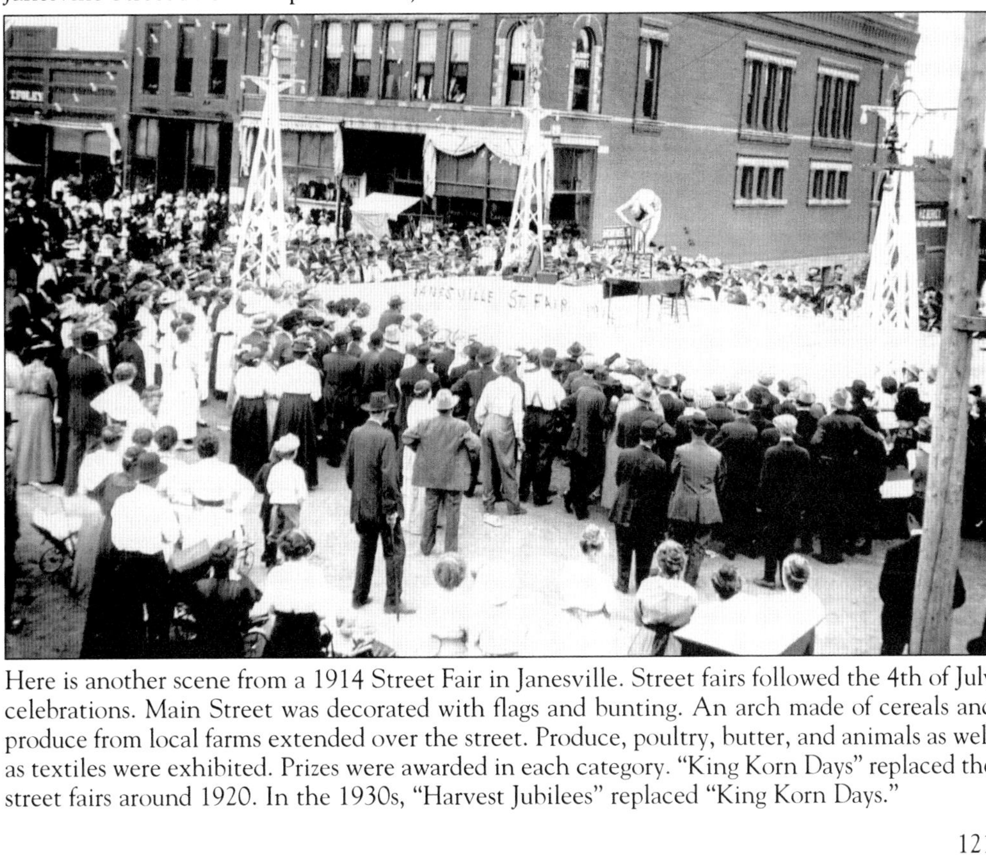

Here is another scene from a 1914 Street Fair in Janesville. Street fairs followed the 4th of July celebrations. Main Street was decorated with flags and bunting. An arch made of cereals and produce from local farms extended over the street. Produce, poultry, butter, and animals as well as textiles were exhibited. Prizes were awarded in each category. "King Korn Days" replaced the street fairs around 1920. In the 1930s, "Harvest Jubilees" replaced "King Korn Days."

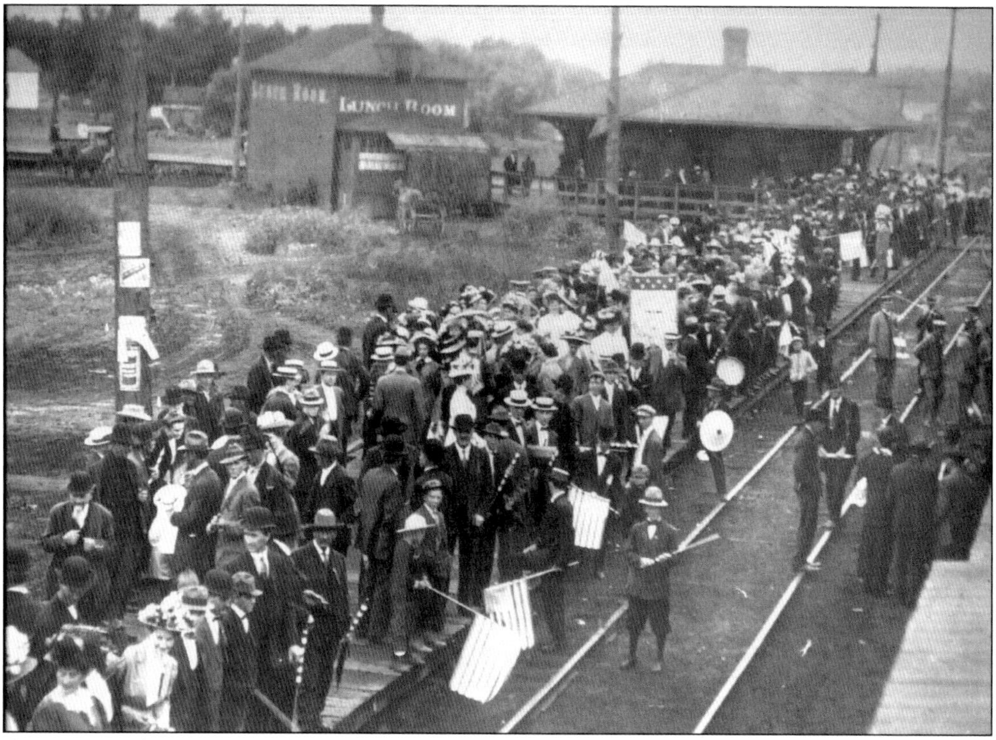

Approximately 1,500 people line the platform in Waseca waiting for the train to the New Richland 1909 Fourth of July Celebration. In the background is the original depot that served both lines. It was built like a "V."

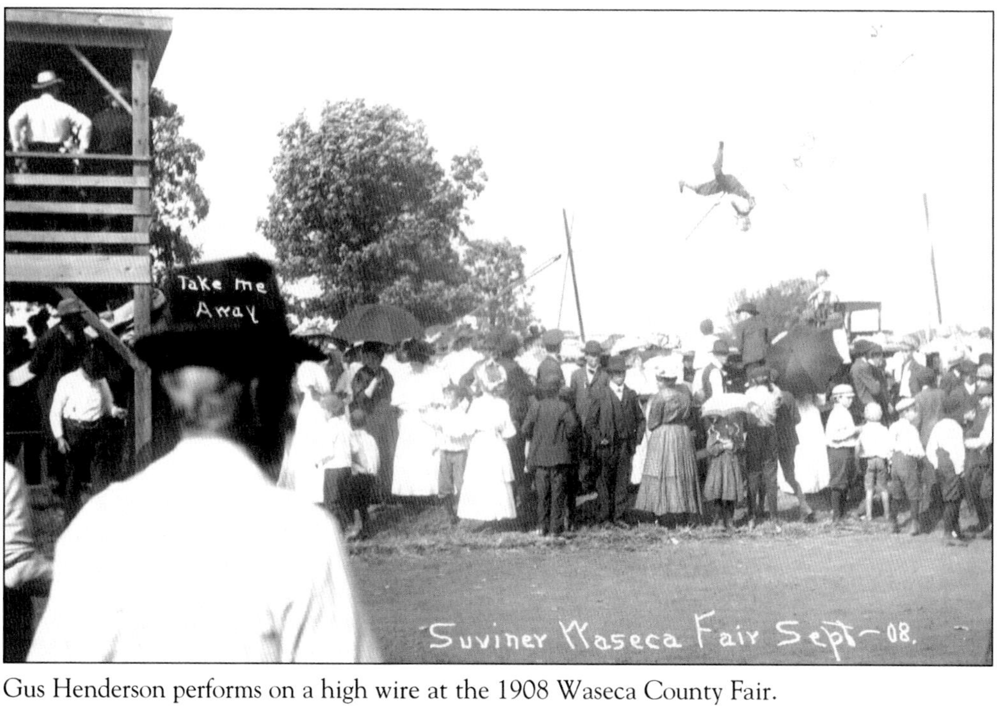

Gus Henderson performs on a high wire at the 1908 Waseca County Fair.

Herman Panzram sits at the Waseca State Fair booth in approximately 1885. Waseca County's best produce is used to impress state fair-goers.

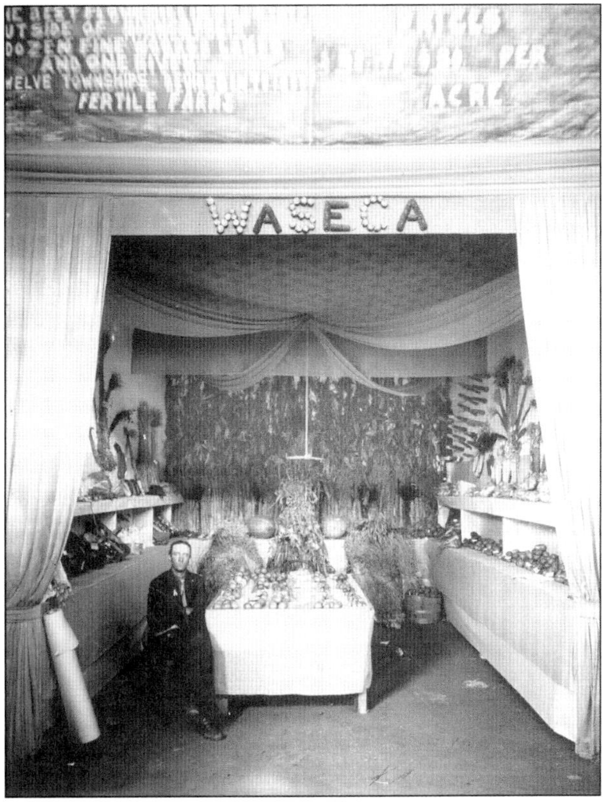

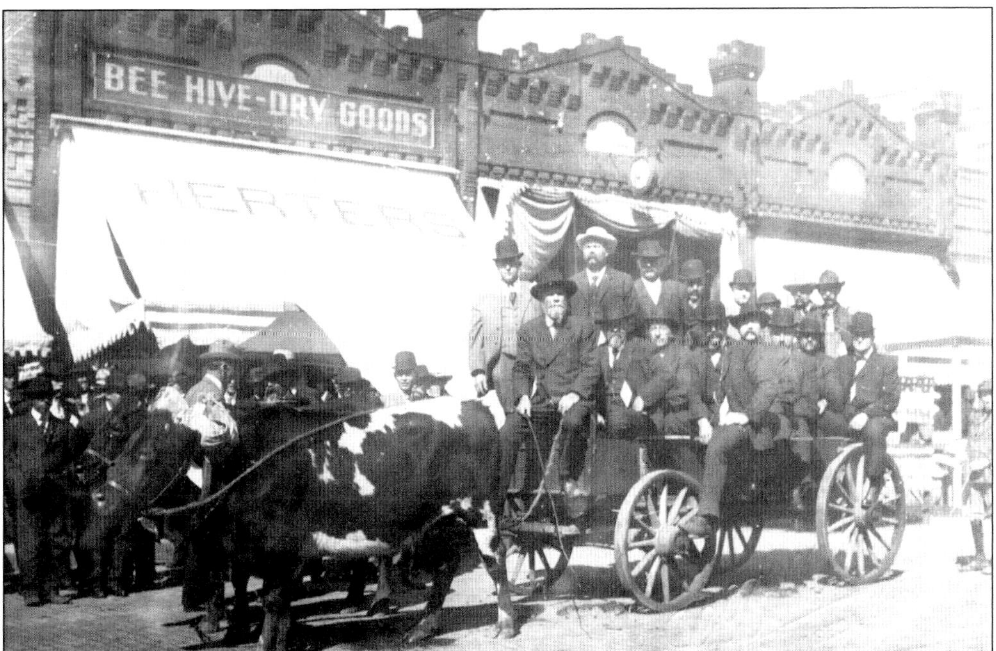

New Richland livestock are pictured in the Waseca County Fair parade in 1909. A parade was put on nightly during the fair to stimulate interest in the fair activities.

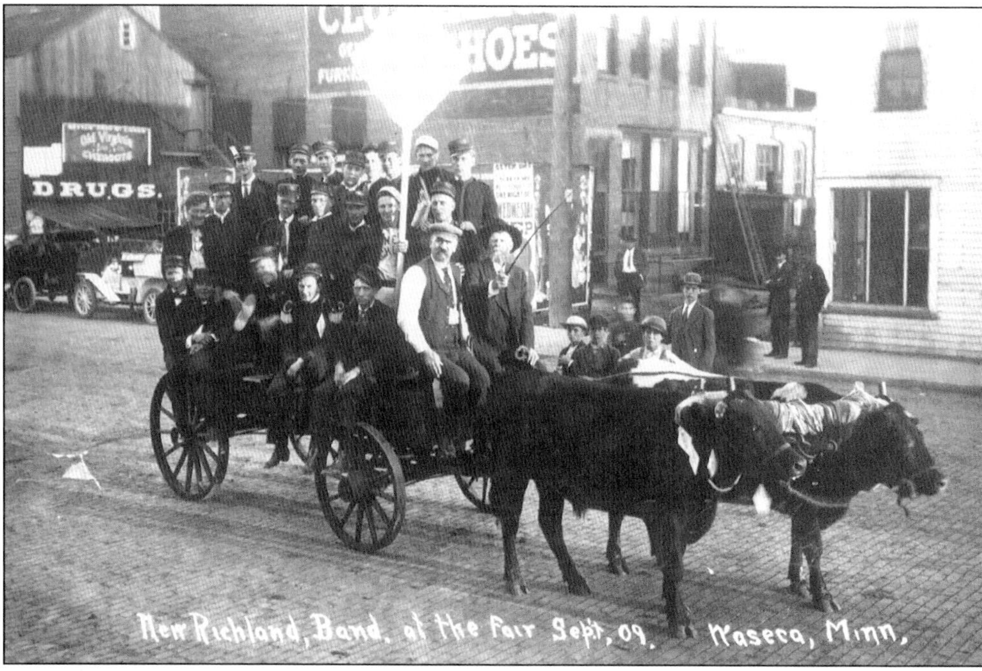

The New Richland Band is seen at the September 1909 Waseca County Fair.

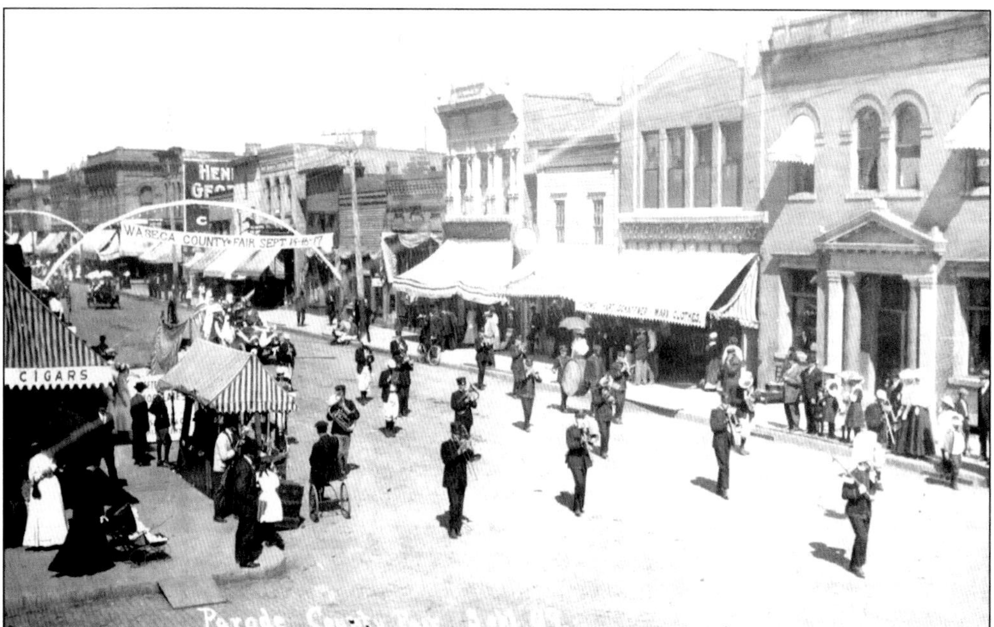

A marching band is seen at the 1909 Waseca County Fair. This would be one of many bands marching nightly to promote the fair. Each day of the fair had a different community spotlighted.

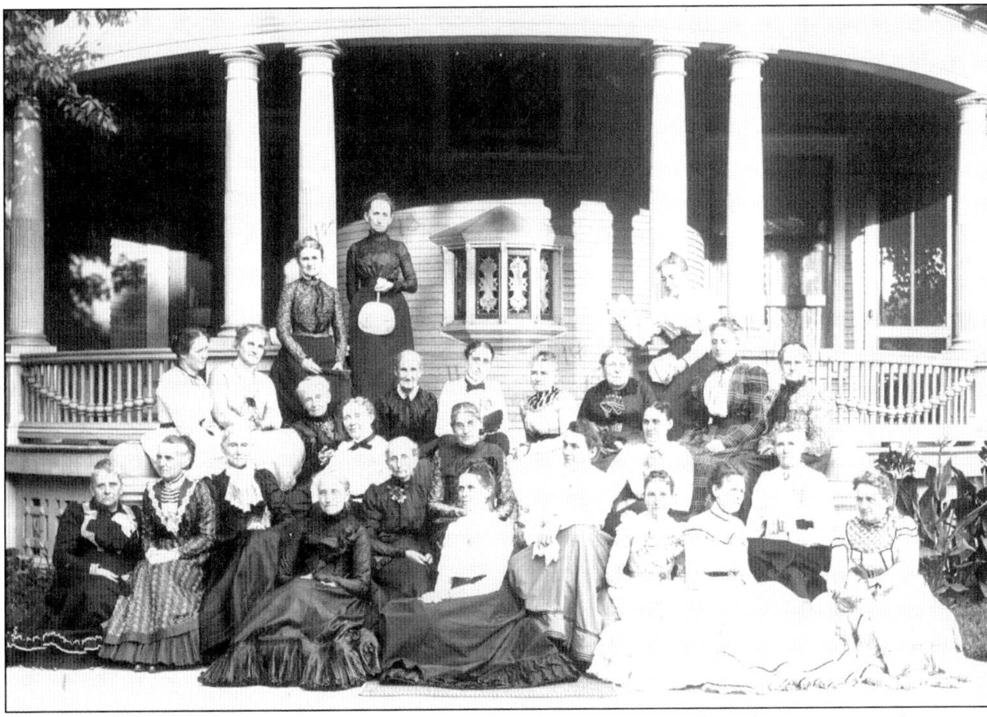

Mrs. Everett's Birthday celebration is captured in this photograph. Those in attendance are Mrs. E.B. Lewis, Mrs. Buckman, Mrs. E.C. Goodspeed, Mrs. P.C. Bailey, Mrs. O.D. Swin, Grandma Whitney, Miss Mary Smith, Mrs. Charles Wright, Mrs. Parm. Norton, Mrs. E.B. Collester, Mrs. W. G. Ward, Grandma Parmelee, Mrs. S. Preston, Mrs. Ranney, Mrs. Simon Smith, Mrs. Brubaker, Mrs. Garland, Nell Young, Mrs. Linsey Wert, Mrs. E.P. Latham, Mrs. Trowbridge, Mrs. Eri Wood, Mrs. William Everett, Mrs. Aughenbaugh, Mrs. Hecht, and Mrs. Rinehart Miller.

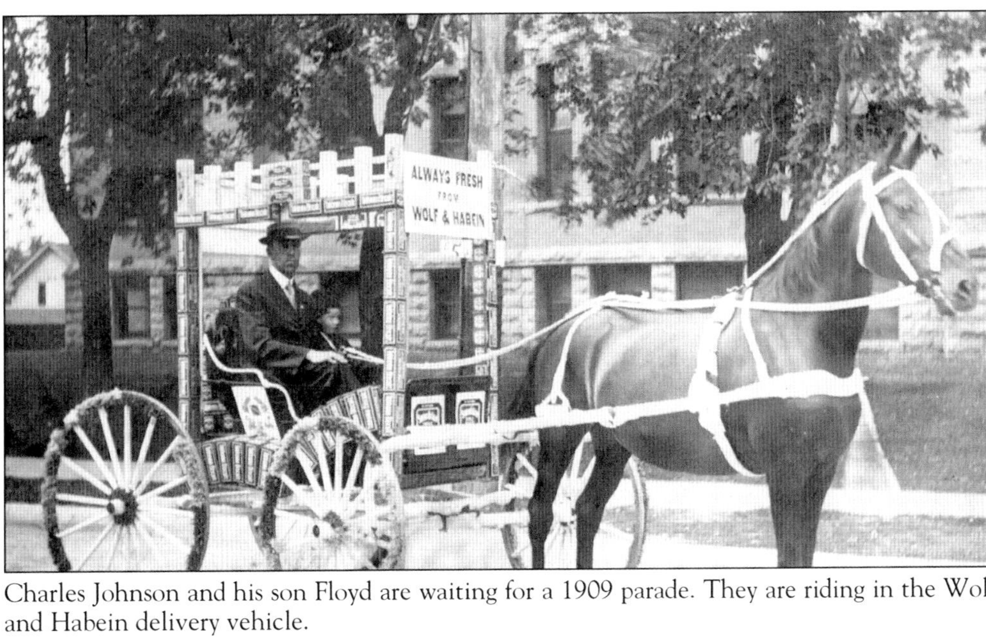

Charles Johnson and his son Floyd are waiting for a 1909 parade. They are riding in the Wolf and Habein delivery vehicle.

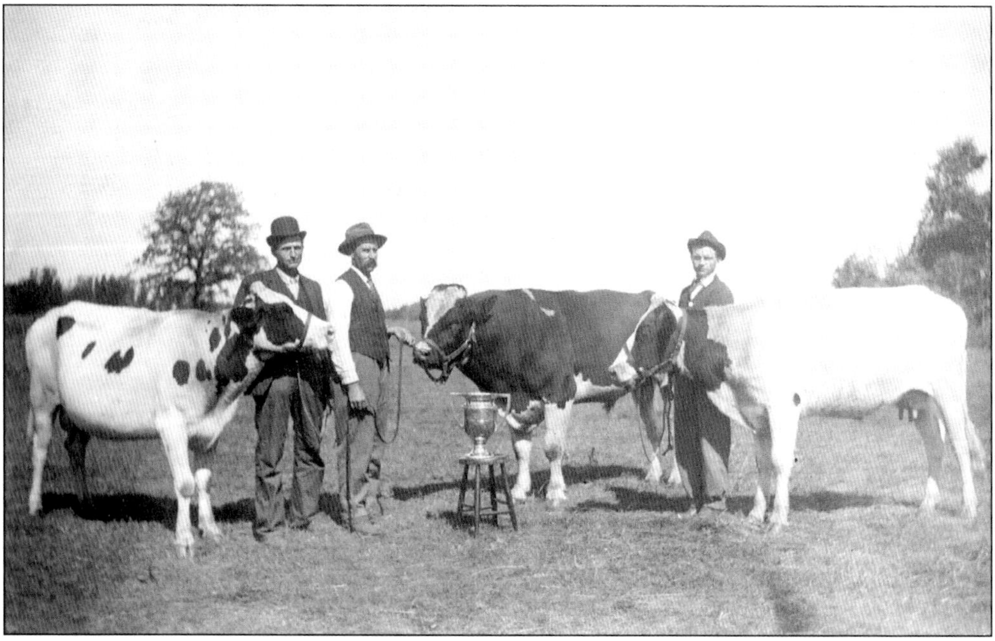

Frank and Seth Winegar took First Premium for their herd of "Jerseys" at the 1911 County Fair.

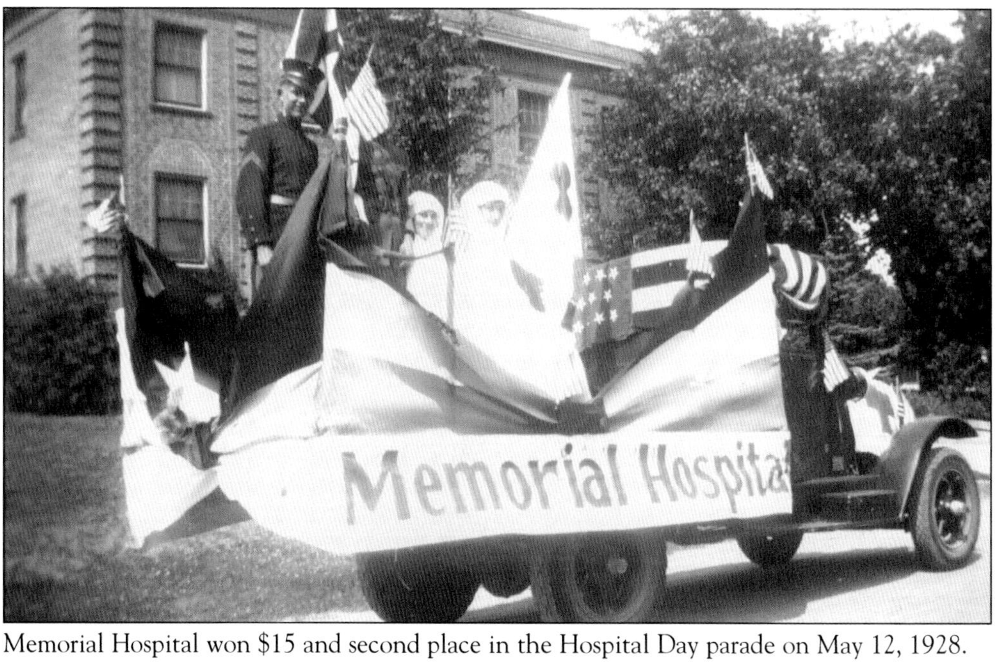

Memorial Hospital won $15 and second place in the Hospital Day parade on May 12, 1928.

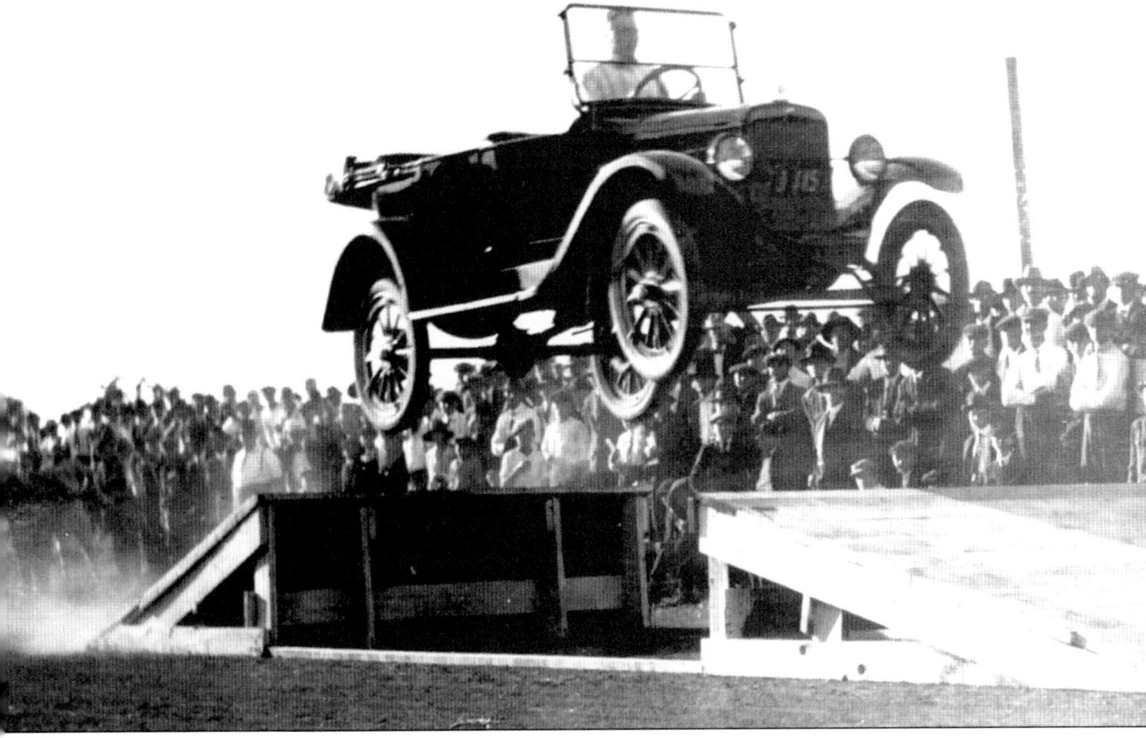

Mr. Lewer is pictured in a 1929 Overland at the 1929 County Fair.

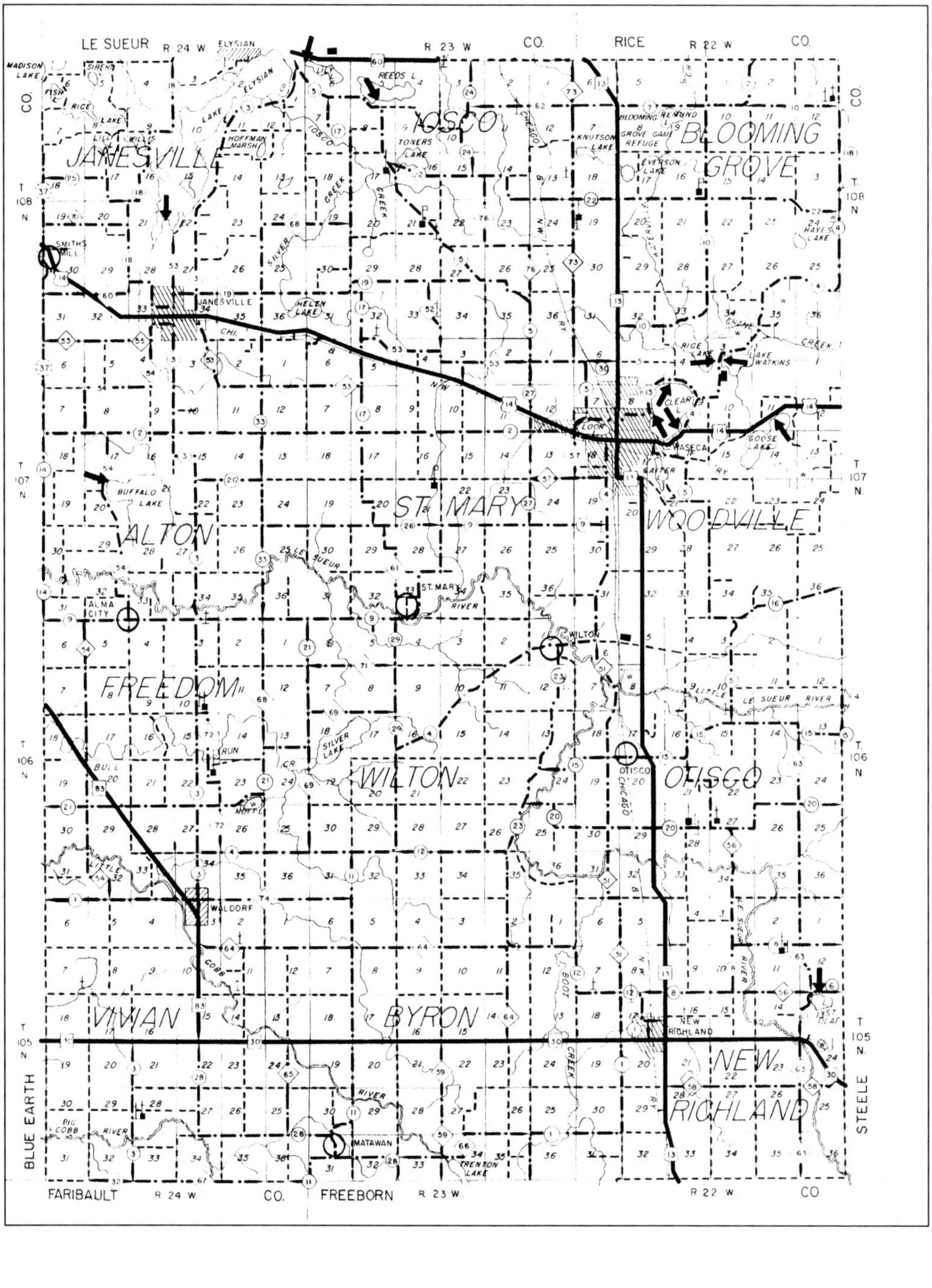

LE SUEUR R. 24 W.
R. 23 W
CO.
RICE
R. 22 W
CO.
JANESVILLE
IOSCO
BLOOMING GROVE
ALTON
ST. MARY
WOODVILLE
FREEDOM
WILTON
OTISCO
VIVIAN
BYRON
NEW RICHLAND
WASECA
JANESVILLE
WALDORF
BLUE EARTH CO.
STEELE CO.
FARIBAULT R. 24 W. CO.
FREEBORN R. 23 W.
R. 22 W CO.
T. 108 N.
T. 107 N.
T. 106 N.
T. 105 N.